# THE CHRISTIAN WATT PAPERS

# THE CHRISTIAN WATT PAPERS

*Edited and with an Introduction by David Fraser*

**Birlinn**

This edition first published in 2004 by
Birlinn Limited
West Newington House
10 Newington Road
Edinburgh EH9 1QS

www.birlinn.co.uk

First published in 1988 by Paul Harris Publishing

ISBN 1 84158 308 1

British Library Cataloguing-in-Publication Data
A catalogue record for this book is available
on request from the British Library

Typeset by Hewer Text Ltd, Edinburgh
Printed and bound by Nørhaven Paperback A/S, Denmark

# Contents

# List of Illustrations

Note: Illustrations 10, 11, 12 and 14 are reproduced by courtesy of the Scottish National Portrait Gallery. Illustrations 5, 6, 7 and 8 reproduced courtesy of Mr Dale of N. Dale & Co., Fraserburgh.

# Editor's Preface

Christian Watt's papers include many letters and documents written by herself or her own forebears, all lovingly preserved and beautifully inscribed. These papers, whether letters in an excellent hand under some of the first Penny Black postage stamps, or testaments, exquisitely written, like the 'Last Will and Testament of James Lascelles, Fisherman', (that venerable, whitebearded figure, who died a few decades before Christian's birth and had lost his own grandson at Culloden) all convey vividly the exact, scrupulous character of her family. Her grandmother's account – 'Granny Lascelles' narrative', – was written in the end papers of a book in the family's possession: *Account of the behaviour of Simon, Lord Lovat*, describing that nobleman's conduct in 1747 between sentence and the block.

The major part of the papers, by far, consists of Christian's own narrative, written in pencil on sheets of foolscap, perfectly preserved and somehow, with its clear yet sometimes impulsive hand, showing the character of its author. All these documents are the property of Christian's granddaughter; I am greatly indebted to her and to her son for their enthusiasm and cooperation, as well as for the confidence with which they have entrusted to me the task of introducing the papers to a wider public. Christian's narrative was compiled in the Institution at Cornhill; in helping the family with information about Cornhill the advice of Dr R.Y. Stewart, Superintendent, has been invaluable.

I am also most grateful to my cousin, Lady Saltoun, for bringing the existence and character of the papers to my attention, and for her support and interest at all times.

Except where the need for clarity seemed to dictate otherwise, I have retained Christian's spelling throughout; and if there are errors of fact in what she wrote, the errors are hers and she has a right to them. But the papers have needed a good deal of editing, in terms of punctuation, of paragraph, and rearrangement of narrative, in order to bring them into a certain, more comprehensible, chronological order. I hope that in no place has this affected the sense or signficance of what she wrote nor diminished the impact of her frankness and spontaneity.

A glossary of some Scots words which Christian or others used is given at the end of the book.

*David Fraser*

Map of the District of Buchan, 1869
(from *Buchan*, Revd John B. Pratt, Aberdeen, 1870)

A
MAP
OF THE DISTRICT OF
BUCHAN,
1869.

Scale of Miles.

# Introduction

In 1880 Christian Watt, a woman of forty-seven who was to be a patient for many years in Cornhill, the Aberdeen Infirmary for those suffering from mental disorders, started to write down recollections of her life. She wrote on foolscap sheets of paper in pencil – pen and ink were forbidden within the institution – with a firm, clear hand. Her memory was encyclopaedic, her gift of narration superb. Before she died in 1923, she had recorded the principal events and impressions of a life of ninety years, describing folk and incident of the mid-nineteenth century in a way which, six decades later, brings both before our eyes.

Christian Watt remembered a life filled with sadness. There was laughter and adventure too: she had the gift of recall with a broad chuckle, and of passing her mood to the page. But the outstanding features in the landscape over which she looked back were tragic. She was born in 1833, of an ancient family of fisherfolk in Broadsea, a village contiguous to and now engulfed by the town of Fraserburgh, in the district called Buchan, on the north-east coast of Aberdeenshire. She started work as a domestic servant at the age of eight and a half, and thenceforth seldom knew rest or peace. At ten, Christian had learned to gut fish. She spent much of her life selling, in the landward parts of the country, fish which she and her family had bought, caught or cured.

For these were people of the sea. They lived beside the sea and the sea brought to them a precarious living, and, very often, a

violent death. Christian lost four out of seven brothers at sea.
Her beloved son Peter, he 'that was always up to some kind of
tricks', died far from home beneath the waters of the Baltic; and
her husband, James Sim, was drowned from the family's own
fishing boat off Fraserburgh:

> It was one of those strange days in August, starting bright
> and sunny, when all of a sudden the sky was black to its
> farthest reaches across the Moray Firth. I had washed all the
> boat's bedding . . . and with the rain threatening I hurried to
> take in the blankets which were dry. The sea had risen
> mountains high. I had a grand sight then. I saw our own
> boat and that of our cousin . . . then a cluster of boats, and
> intuition told me something was wrong, and after nearly an
> hour with the rain lashing down the boats went round
> Kinnaird. The Congregational Minister came to the door.
> I asked him which one of my folk was lost. He said 'It is the
> husband.'

But harsh though the sea might be, salt water ran in the people's
veins, and gave them an innate sense of their own history and
calling. 'Your fathers,' Christian's mother told her, 'are grossly
superior to these tradespeople who look down on you. They can
navigate small boats by oar, and sail to the Hebrides, Shetland
and Greenland, with nothing but the sextant set with the
noonday sun, and the stars to guide them at night.' And
throughout Christian's narrative there was a proper pride –
pride of blood and ancestry, pride in the independence and
sturdy self-reliance of her own Broadsea and Buchan people,
pride of place and race.

Yet if Christian wrote with pride she also wrote with frequent
bitterness. For her life was not only marked by tragedy but
disfigured by poverty and hunger. A woman of beauty, character and high intelligence, thoughtful and avid for learning from
an early age, she passed many of her years in anxiety as to
whence the next day's food would come, for her large family,

dependent, in bereavement, on her alone. She grew up watching her beloved parents work until they dropped from exhaustion – no figure of speech. She herself was to tread the same mill. Pride, and anger at life's inequity, made of Christian a fierce rebel – girning at the injustice of the world, snapping with savagery at any attempts to patronise, quick to remind the haughty that she came of blood as redoubtable as theirs, ever alert to bring down the mighty, contemptuous of pretension. And since she came through suffering to profound religious faith, she was seldom short of a telling phrase with which to rebuke the great of this world from the Psalmist's mouth as well as from her own.

Christian, however, was no bigot, self-righteously warped by her own woes. On the contrary, she delightfully combined tenderness with indignation. 'Mine,' she said complacently of herself as a young woman, 'was not an easy heart to win' – but it was not a difficult heart to touch. And with her looks, her humour, her courage, her sympathy and her high spirit she must have been irresistible. Murray Fraser wished to marry her. Simon Fraser, the Master of Lovat, sought her company and was clearly enchanted by her. She also combined, in a peculiarly Scottish manner, a passionate radicalism with a deep sense of history and tradition. 'You are,' the 'Waterloo' Lord Saltoun told her, 'a Tolpuddle Tory!' She hated the very name of Tory, but she venerated him and he was near the mark. She loved to recall how she had abused members of the aristocracy for their indifference, their callousness, their profligacy and their arrogance. Her descriptions of such encounters, no doubt highly coloured by time, as are all such recollections (and certainly not to be taken as factual evidence for the accusations she levelled!), are among the most lively things she wrote. Yet she heard with sadness of the accidental burning in 1915 of Philorth, Lord Saltoun's house, where she had worked as a laundry-maid, grumbled and laughed and been courted by his uncle, long dead.

In my mind's eye it will remain the same, of how a young
officer of the British India Company and a laundry-maid
experienced the joy of first innocent love, as beautiful as a
clump of snowdrops in the wood. From the garret window
come the strains of 'Annie Laurie' floating over the trees,
sung by Bobby Wilson, the strapper, at the pitch of his voice,
or Mary Ritchie singing the 23rd psalm. One day somebody
may again build there, but I am doubtful if they will capture
the happy ghosts that flit about that place.

Her feelings for the Frasers of Philorth, mixed as they were,
gained poignancy from her blood-relationship with them. For
both Christian's father and mother were descended, through
illegitimate grandchildren, from a daughter of William Fraser of
Philorth, 11th Lord Saltoun.[1]

Christian's days were indeed full of trial and grief, and in the
end it was too much for her stability of mind. She was admitted
to Cornhill, where she wrote and where she died. Her first
admittance was temporary – respite after what would no doubt
today be called a breakdown – but soon thereafter she became a
permanent inmate, when it was clear both to her and to the
authorities that she could no longer cope with the stress and
anxieties of life. Her mind was a good one but frequent con-
finements, physical suffering, hunger, exhaustion and bereavement had tried it overmuch. No facets of her memoir, however,
compel more admiration than the frankness and sensitivity with
which she writes of her own condition, together with the
understanding and gentleness she brings to the description of
those whose minds rather than bodies have been broken by ill-
fortune. Her treatment at Cornhill was enlightened and humane, far from the grim Dickensian image with which such
institutions in the nineteenth century (for she was first admitted
in 1879) have been endowed. She made good friends there. She
travelled from there and worked from there. Cornhill became
her sanctuary and her home.

Christian's turn of phrase when dealing with a miscreant or a humbug is masterly. Her judgements of public personages, of politics, of historic events are pithy but seldom original; but in describing scenes through which she lived her language is very much her own – splendidly evocative and strikingly undated. Her style combines the vigorous, the homely and the dignified. She was, of course, writing as recently as 1923, but by then she was ninety, and her habits of mind and speech had been formed in the early days of Victoria's reign. Yet there is little sense of archaism. The woman who expresses so much of herself in recalling events is entirely contemporary, entirely alive. We feel her in the room as we read. Sometimes we avoid her eye.

Writing of her old age, the role of prophetess became dominant in Christian. She had always hated war; two of her brothers perished in the Black Sea during the Crimean War. The South African War aroused in her feelings of scepticism rather than patriotism. And as for the Great War of 1914–18, whose tragedies overshadowed her last years, 'We passed through Brucklay Station [on the Fraserburgh–Aberdeen train for her first admittance to Cornhill] and as I went up that time to start my life sentence little did I dream that later so many of my grandsons would go up that line to their death sentence.' The losses of that war brought out in Christian the passionate and eccentric visionary, diving into Scripture to show warning of the doom coming upon the world, excoriating with furious impartiality British military or political leaders as well as the German Emperor. But the somewhat demented prophetess was only one aspect. The last page of her memoir at Cornhill is reflective and peaceful, and, as ever, vivid recall breaks in:

I have a steady stream of visitors. Students ask me about subjects to write theses. At 90, I have taken up the teaching job I started at 16. It is most enjoyable and I have happiness and peace. I can ask my guests to stay to lunch if they come in the morning. A lass who used to be a maid in Cairness

House[2] works here, she does my shopping, so I am like a lady of leisure.

I can mind on General Gordon's batman. He was a dark-skinned Armenian who used to come into the Broch[3] on a white horse. He lived at Cairness in a chaumer, he was an imposing figure in a turban and red cloak. Lady Gordon at Cairness was an Armenian. They used to have a clever Greek doctor who practised in Lonmay. It is like yesterday to look back on all these things. At the closing of my days, I have encountered so much kindness. I am blest every time I breathe. My life has been hard, but I would not say it has been a sad waste, for my purpose has been to shed light in a dark place; and I have kept the faith, for which we are told we will be rewarded with a Crown of Life.

Christian Watt was a noble woman. She radiated courage, devotion, conviction and authority. None outfaced her. None who asked her for help or touched her compassion were turned away. 'Had she lived in a later age she would probably have been a member of parliament,' said one who had read her memoir to a relative of Christian who had known her well. 'Not at all – Prime Minister!' was the convinced reply. The times through which she lived were hard, and the folk they produced were not only hard but brave and tender. It is fortunate indeed that they come to meet us through the words of so worthy, witty and fluent a chronicler.

# CHAPTER ONE

## *Origin and Tradition (1833–1843)*

The district of Buchan, one of the ancient earldoms of Scotland, is bounded to the south by the River Ythan, to the west by the River Deveron and to the north and east by the sea. It is not Highland country, of mountain and heather, but good farming land, described in a manuscript of 1680 as 'neither altogether high, nor levell, but rather a mixture of both', and cited by a writer in 1730 as 'called proverbially the granary of Scotland'. Buchan was renowned for corn and cattle, and remains so. It is a land of stone walls and squat stonebuilt farms, of wind-stunted trees and wide skies.

But this is the landward side – what Christian on her selling travels calls 'the Near Country'. In 1721, Alexander Hepburn wrote a description of Buchan which better sets the scene for Christian and her kin. 'Every parish,' he wrote, 'hath one fisher town at least, and many of them have two. The seas abound with fishes, such as killing, lering, codfish small and great; turbet, scate, mackrell, haddocks, whittings, flooks, seadogs[4] and seacatts, herrings, seaths, podlers, gandues, lobsters, partens and several others . . . There is no fishing round the island as we have in our Buthquhan Coast.' Complementing the landward folk were the fisherfolk, living in a string of historic villages around that coast, from Banff to Peterhead. Acting as a centre, a market, and a port for the north-eastern parishes of the district was the substantial town of Fraserburgh: The Broch.

Sir Alexander Fraser, 8th of Philorth, had founded Fraserburgh in the second half of the sixteenth century. Originally called Faithlie, a village lying immediately south of the rocky promontory of Kinnaird Head, it was built as a new town, with harbour, and created a 'burgh of regality' by the name of Fraserburgh, with a free port, in 1592.

The Frasers had at that time been lairds of Philorth for over two centuries. Sir Alexander Fraser of Cowie and Durris – grandson of another Sir Alexander Fraser, Chamberlain of Scotland and brother-in-law of King Robert Bruce – had acquired the lands of Philorth in 1375 by marriage with Johanna, a daughter and co-heiress of the earl of Ross. The great earldom of Ross comprised lands stretching across the breadth of Scotland. Those in Buchan, as well as some parts of Inverness and Galloway, fell to Johanna and her husband, whose style henceforth was Fraser of Philorth – the lordship of Philorth being the Buchan lands of the earldom, and whose principal residence was the castle of Philorth, later renamed Cairnbulg, some two miles east of Fraserburgh.

The 'superior' of a 'burgh of regality' had considerable power of jurisdiction and wide responsibilities. King James Vl's charter, given at the Palace of Holyrood in 1601, confirmed to 'Sir Alexander Fraser of Phillorth and Fraserburgh . . . to be held by the said Alexander and the heirs male procreated of his body and their assignees, whom failing his lawful and nearest heirs male whomsoever bearing the surname and arms of Fraser' power over the 'free barony of Phillorth', which would include, with other named lands, the 'free port and free burgh of barony and free regality' into which the town and burgh of Fraserburgh had been 'erected'. And this gave Sir Alexander and his successors the power and duty 'to hold burgh courts and courts of regality and to punish transgressors even by beheading, hanging, drowning and burning'. These were the rights of 'hereditary jurisdiction' to whose abolition (in 1747) Christian referred, and of which her own forebear, as Constable of Broadsea, had been an instrument.

In 1670, Alexander Fraser, 10th of Philorth, was ratified by Act of Parliament as 10th Lord Saltoun on the death of his cousin Alexander Abernethy, 9th Lord Saltoun. Fraser's mother was Margaret Abernethy, daughter of the 7th Lord Saltoun, and he inherited the peerage on the failure of the Abernethy line.

The original castle of Philorth and lands of Cairnbulg had been sold in 1616 to Alexander Fraser of Durris, a distant relative, by the founder of Fraserburgh. A new castle, Fraserburgh Castle, had been built in 1570 on Kinnaird Head itself, overlooking the Broch.[5] But at about the time of the Restoration of King Charles II in 1660 the laird of Philorth, later to be Lord Saltoun, built a new house some two miles south of Fraserburgh, in a sheltered position inland – no fortified keep but a laird's house appropriate to the age of peace for which all men hoped. He called his house by the old name – Philorth – and this was the Philorth that Christian knew and loved.

The fishing villages of Cairnbulg, Inverallochy and St Combs lay on the coast a few miles east of the Broch. Abutting its western outskirts was the village of Broadsea, Christian's home; in the old Fraserburgh Barony court books, Broadsea is called 'the Seatown'.

The people of Broadsea formed a vigorous and close-knit community, very aware that their efforts and their skill lay at the foundations of Fraserburgh's prosperity, although the 'tradespeople' of the Broch might more greatly profit. There was a story behind each numbered house in Broadsea, and Christian knew them all. She described the old claim of the laird to one quarter of the fishing catches, and the hostility it aroused. It was, in fact, one sixth – a due belonging to the superior. The superior let his rights to a tacksman. The tacksman owned the boats, and employed fishermen as berthed hands, claiming his share of the catch, the fishermen dividing and selling the remainder. Undoubtedly the system led to resentments between the tacksman (who had invested the capital in the form of the boats and expected a return upon it) and the fishermen, who risked their lives and contributed their skill, and who were prevented from building and launching their own boats until the law was changed.

Most folk were related. Their blood, like the placenames among which they moved, was a mixture of Celtic, Pictish, Saxon and Norse. There are some more self-evidently Gaelic names in Christian's narrative – Mackay, McLeman – some long-standing in Fraserburgh, some new. Some, no doubt, were settlers from other parts who had arrived with the fishing boats, or walked from the Highlands to seek berths and ultimately make a home. But, in Christian's time, some were refugees from the Highland Clearances in Sutherland and the west, whence many Highland-men came destitute to seek a living in Buchan, with its still prospering industries and settled population. However, the chief names in Christian's ancestry and story, Noble, Watt, Lascelles, Sim – are the great seafaring names of the Broch and the villages. Of forty-two Broadsea men listed as fit to man boats in 1789 – a year in which, as in most years, the Fraserburgh Barony Court proceedings were full of disputes between tacksman and fisher-man – twenty-nine were Nobles, and five were Watts.

Christian herself had best introduce her immediate forebears and family, as well as her house and home:

> I was second last of eight children, an only daughter among seven brothers, born 1833 and baptized Christian Watt. My two elder brothers were twins. My father James Watt was a twin with my Auntie Nellie, the wife of John McLeman (Black Jock). My father was a hard-working fisherman who braved the terrible weather on the treacherous sea to give us a crust of bread, but my mother, Helen Noble, was the driving force behind him. I was born and lived at 72 Broadsea Village in the County of Aberdeen. The house has been our family home for over two centuries.
>
> My mother was forty-five when I was born and forty-eight when my little brother was born. I fared better than him for

he had always to wear handed-down clothing; as I had nobody above me I sometimes got new, though I often had to do with 'handed-downs' from my cousins. My aunt Annie Watt, wife of Captain Alex Noble of 22 Broadsea, was very good with her needle and made our better clothes for Sundays. Belle Mitchell, wife of my uncle Sandy Watt at 63 Broadsea, had a loom in her chaumer and made homespuns cheaply, though my mother was good with the needle herself. Both my parents were tall. My aunt Elizabeth Noble was so tall folk called her 'Muckle Betty' for a by-name. She had always lived a respectable life, but unfortunately at the age of forty-two she fell with an illegitimate daughter, by her own cousin, a cad who ran away to jeuk his duty. My Aunt Betty and her daughter Annie lived with my granny, Helen Lascelles, widow of Andrew Noble, at 35 Broadsea, a house that had been in the family for centuries. To let my Auntie Betty out to work my mother took my granny and the little quinie down through the day, but there was always a bit of jealousy for my Granny Lascelles always seemed to favour me. She had lost her man when her bairns were all young and had gone through an awful struggle to bring them up. She spoke to us two little girls as adults, as she was busy mending the nets while my father was on the sea and my mother was chaving the country with a heavy creel on her back.

Betty's Annie was a year older than me. At her birth my parents would have taken the quinie as their own, but naturally her mother would not part with her. All her life Annie had a grudge to her illegitimacy, and this was a lot to do with her being jealous of me. From my earliest memory my mother told me to share anything I had with her; this I did and in my heart I always regarded her as my sister.

I never saw my didy Noble.[6] My mother said he was a fine man, 6 feet tall with fair hair; he was the son of Alexander Noble (Noch)[7] and Christian Buchan of St Combs. They lived at 76 Broadsea, a very ancient dwelling. It was as low as you would bob down to enter, and in the but end the fire was in the middle of the floor. The ben had been the byre for their cow, but in my childhood it was occupied by my didy's sister Ellen Anne Noble, my great-aunt. She lived to be nearly 100.

The house at 76 Broadsea had a fair croft attached to it and had been worked as such till the making of the big farms. In 1850 it was taken into Broadsea Mains Farm, known to us as 'Flukie's'. Flukie was the farmer, who wore an old blue coat. He was not a greedy man; after the tattie lifting he allowed the poor to lift and dig out all the little tatties that were left in the ground. The croft housie at 76 was always known as 'Hairy Riddell's', a wifie who had lived there long ago; she was some of my mother's ancestors.

The Noch Nobles were a very clever family and most of the descendants inherited good brains. Through hard work they had gone to College in Aberdeen and took up grand professions as doctors and lawyers and others. All my brothers went to college for learning. My Granny Lascelles[8] was the eldest daughter and heir of William Lascelles, the last official Constable of Broadsea, an office of ancient origin done away with at the abolition of hereditary jurisdiction in Scotland. Wm. Lascelles lived and died at 72 Broadsea. He had a good education and was only about forty-eight at his death. His wife was Jane Gordon (or Crawford) an illegitimate daughter of Jean Crawford, 7 Broadsea, and John Gordon of Kinellar, the son of John Gordon of Kinellar and Henrietta Fraser, daur of Lord Saltoun. The Gordons lived at Fraserburgh Castle on Kinnaird Head: they were last to live there before it was made into the lighthouse. William Lascelles and his wife Jean had about ten children they saw up to adults, but only three survived. They knew terrible sorrow.

I remember Granny's two sisters, both younger than her. Margaret Lascelles, wife of William Noble, 47,[9] and Jean Lascelles, wife of George Crawford, 48. Granny, when she married Andrew Noble, was married into 35 while her own great-didy, the old James Lascelles, was still alive. He lived to well over ninety. My own mother could mind on him as a kind and gentle old man with a long white flowing beard. He was very fond of my mother, who was about five when he died. He must have been sad to live so long: for he saw the death of my mother's father living in the house with him, and that of his only surviving grandson, William Lascelles, and his seven adult children. His other grandson, David Lascelles, was a valet to Charles Fraser of Inverallochy: both were killed in the battle of Culloden Moor.[10]

James Lascelles' wife was Christian Tait of Cairnbulg. My granny said she had a beautiful singing voice and led the psalms in the Broadsea Mission School which her ancestor Andrew Noble, Traveller of Zetland, had founded in 1656. My father was old Kirk and my mother Congregational, but it wasn't a divided household. My mother always felt privileged at having been born in the house with and having known her great-great-grandfather, who willed 35 to my granny who was good to him, and making provisions for my mother as heir. While we sat by her knee my granny would tell Auntie Betty's Annie and me all the tales of long ago.

Christian's description of her grandmother's great-grandfather seems hard to reconcile with historic fact. A man in his nineties in the 1790s could hardly have had a grandson killed at Culloden in 1746, and the first impression is that Christian inadvertently added a generation. Clearly the seeming discrepancy struck others, for she wrote much later in life:

The doctor was asking about my ancestors, and thought I got the generations wrong. I spotted this myself long ago, and asked my mother. James Lascelles was not her great-grandfather but a generation earlier. If you look on his headstone it says,

'James Lascelles who departed this life 1793 in the 98th year of his age.'

He would have been born 1695. He was married either 1715 or 1716: I remember seeing it in my granny's old papers. This my mother explained – he married a Cairnbulg girl called Christian Tait. Their son, James, had to be married at the age of sixteen: that is where the discrepancy seems but the fact is correct enough. Where the error lies is David Lascelles, the grandson who died at Culloden was not sixteen but only fourteen. He probably faked his age to get away with the young Fraser of Inverallochie. It was not unknown in the past for wives and children to follow the drum, and boys of ten have been known to take part in actual battle, just in order to appear as a huge crowd to scare the enemy.

There are two Lascelles brothers, Walter and John. They were brought up at Fedderat Castle, the home of the Crawfords. They are connected in some way with the Saltouns but at the moment it escapes my memory. Walter Lascelles was married to Gissel Noble of the descendants of Maria de Hales. Both lines came down to us and ended in my mother's mother.

Thus, Christian was entirely correct. The beautifully-written 'Last Will and Testament of James Lascelles, Fisherman, in the Seatoun of Broadsea' makes the relationship clear beyond doubt.[11] He left all to Helen Noble, Christian's Granny Lascelles, 'my great-granddaughter'.

Christian was devoted to her grandmother, 'Granny Lascelles', daughter of the last Constable of Broadsea. His 'office of ancient origin' disappeared with the suppression of the Jacobite rising of 1745. Although nearly a century had passed, the shock of those days stayed vivid in the memories of the people. The Constable, William Lascelles – Christian's great-grandfather – left his own account, written shortly after the event. Granny Lascelles, too, inscribed a long and careful paper on her understanding of her ancestry and on the recollections of her youth.[12] Christian's own fierce opinions derived force from written record and verbal tradition. Her proud radicalism grew not only from an innate sense of justice but from origins in which nationalist, Jacobite, and Episcopalian (or, rather, anti-Presbyterian) sentiments were also blended. Surely among the most vivid of the 'tales of long ago' heard at Granny Lascelles' knee was William Lascelles' own narrative of the day in 1746 when 'a garrison of Flemings (mercenaries) has come over the moss to billet in Pitsligo Castle':

A bugler sounded his trumpet and orders were given to search the house. We were ready, for all the lums had been partly blocked, allowing some smoke to escape so as not to arouse suspicion for the deception. Most of the reek going into the body of the house, it disagreeably filled the lungs and smelt the uniforms of the troopers, who spent much time raking through kists and girnals often overturned and the meal spilt. They stripped the dresser of china bowells, ones with Scottish pictures very much in demand. Grandfather and Wagat clocks and brass tallow sticks were all stolen from those who were foolish not to bury them as we had been told to do. The least provocation and the house would be burnt.

Jock Wattie's Belle who was much given to over cleaness through living in a bern chamber to not foul her house, had an impudent and coarse tongue, and gave the encouragement of fooling of children, by constantly hounding them from the playing of eel and ack in her close. She began to abuse and oppose the trooper from stealing her capons. The officer listed in his journal all that was stolen. Belle was whipped for her untoward behaviour, in spite of her vile tongue. She was well up in years. My father volunteered to take the whipping in her stead but the officer would not agree. A trooper cast her on the ground by the Brieve stone and it was considered great entertainment by the bairns as he exposed her buttocks to the Corporal's lash.

It was much regretted the House of Inverallochie was partly burnt and much ancient doors as had carving of the cypher of Marjory, the last Princess of Buchan. Their cattle were driven off to be sold in Aberdeen.

The Lady Pitulie had intervened in a mean theft from the aged. She told them it had been a civil war and they were acting as an army of occupation not as British troops to keep down rebels. She was flung to the ground and indecently assaulted, being a woman in the borders of sixty. In reprisal the officer ordered the firing of the house. Fortunately, a stone gable confined it to the south-eastern section which has never been rebuilt. Sir George Cumming was a participator in the last rising and the house was looted.

Daily going through Bretsie[13] were cartloads of plunder from the Castle of Pitsligo on their way to Fraserburgh, where they were shipped from the harbours if room permitted in Bynge's shipps. So as not to break the setts, cartloads of cheeres would go on one shipping, sureting tables and oil pictures on one other, the high-ranking officers having first pick of the spoils. Posts were all along the Aberdeenshire coast.

A great ransom was put on the head of old Pitsligo who was my wife's near relative through the Gordons of Kinelar. We have all known such places at which he could be found but none there was who would betray him.

Oft he has slept abune the beds in Auntie Babby's house in Pitulie, a most gentle and God fearing man who had long belonged to the Quietists meditating of the Spirit. Now we could see going past all his fine Dutch and Flemish furniture to be disposed of in London. Lady Ogilvie of Auchiries had taken much trouble at the risk of her own head in order to give Pitsligo a comfortable lodging of which she is to be greatly commended . . .

Cobham's dragoons were exceedingly vicious·and had much to answer for in both cruelty and murders, for about forty died around Buchan under terrible circumstances. Few and far between was the kindly one who would carry a bundle of sticks or birn from the Mill Burn to the Seyton and would wish to converse in pleason or who would come in and sit by the fire and be talking civilly and enjoy a cup of hot brose. They were exceeding curious to the peculiarity of our Pictish language and some in time came to talk it.

We found some troopers were young gentlemen listed as private soldiers who were more concerned with the sport of fishing with the boats than with soldiering. Oft they would ask for the hooks and lines to fish from the locks. Mannerly they would ask to enjoin in the dancing at penny bridals. Public opinions were against them and it looked so mean to refuse; none did.

We lived through a rain of terror and Fraserburgh had seen a time as never before, knowing deep in our hearts never in our time would we ever be the same again. The officers would anger folks such as they could not hold it by referring constantly to Buchan as this part of England, and when taken to task were commended for having done a good job. The Episcopal Congregation were permitted to meet only in groups of four, a religion my grandfather led several revolts to uphold.

The justice of the government is as a foul stank. One day this land will yet again be free. Lord Ancrum and his minions could not hold us down. But only so long. This unprincipled blackguard hanged himself at Bath. His wife is suffering from a malady inflicted by kicks through him.

'Old Pitsligo' – Alexander Forbes, 4th Lord of Pitsligo – was probably the most respected and influential of the Buchan Jacobites. Pitsligo Castle stood a few miles west of Fraserburgh. After Culloden Pitsligo was hunted everywhere without success by government troops. His concealments, disguises and escapes became legendary, and each legend increased the reverence in which his name was held. So did the story that when his daughter-in-law's house at Auchiries had been searched (with himself hidden behind the wainscot), Lord Pitsligo told his servant to see that the soldiers got some breakfast and a drink of warm ale, for they were only doing their duty and could bear him no ill will. He was seventy-eight when this incident took place in 1756. There was another side. The officer commanding the government troops in Fraserburgh after Culloden called one morning on a certain Alexander Fraser, an illegitimate son of Lord Saltoun, who had a house in Fraserburgh and a garden of which he was proud and which the officer admired. After a while the officer said to Fraser that he could stay no longer, as he had heard that Lord Pitsligo was at his castle and he had to set out to arrest him. He did not find him at home!

Granny Lascelles, too, had her matching recollections and wrote them down. In her account[14] genealogy predominates; but there are pages, too, where we can see, as Christian must have seen, through the eyes of a child of the eighteenth century:

> I was only a very little girl. I think there was a child wasseling and a child in the cradle.
>
> A heavy snow drift was outside. An old tramp came to the door. A kettle was put on the fire both but and ben, and we all went but to my granny's end, so the tramp had a dock in the wood tub by the fire. My mother gave the mannie a clean shift of under linen, and then we all sat down to brose at my parents humble board. They gave a prayer, for all my people had belonged to the Quietists. They were something like the Quakers, but believed in the new birth through the finished work of Calvary. The old mannie gave a dear and bonnie prayer.
>
> My sister and I slept with my granny. My parents slept in the closet and the old mannie slept in the ben box bed. Again we sat round the table at breakfast. The mannie gave thanks and left very early, still two hours before day broke. The mannie patted my head. I think I had just started to go to school, and as he left in the dark snowie morning my father

said, 'Ellen memorise this day. You met the great Lord Pitsligo.'

It is about five-and-seventy years. I can see the mannie now – poor soul, hunted like an animal for twenty years, but folk were so loyal they were determined the Hanoverian troopers would not get him, to take off his aged head.

Not long after a man came at night to our house to ask my father to the funeral of 'Sanny Brown', who was in fact the Lord Pitsligo, who used that name. My father took me to the funeral. He said, 'You must always mind on this.' As we went up the cassa at Rosehearty thousands had gathered in the park across from the Rathill Kirk. The service was said in the open. As they sang it was very moving to tears. Then they had a little private prayer inside the kirk, and he was laid to rest. The gathering was so dense the military did not interfere, for they marvelled at how they had been outwitted, and how in the midst of poor people none had sought to betray Pitsligo and claim the thousand pounds reward on his head.

'My father,' wrote Granny Lascelles, 'on his death bed said to me, "tell your own children and your grandchildren that you are Scots and never to forget it".' They never did. Nor was Granny Lascelles other than faithful to the traditions of her house. Typical of her was a letter, in her beautiful hand, to the Revd John Cumming, Minister of Fraserburgh, in June 1840. The letter combined historical record, reflecting verbal tradition, with testamentary intention. It conveys the knowledge and pride of ancestry which always coloured Christian's own writings.

Seatown of Broadsea 22 June 1840
Reverend Sir
Broadsea School was built and gifted by my ancestor Andrew Noble Esq., a wealthy Zetland Merchant. He had the mansion near the Brick Lodge on the outskirts of Fraserburgh. He was a son of Anne Stuart, illegitimate daughter of James Marquis of Hamilton and Anne Stewart the widow of the 8th

Lord Saltoun of Abernethy.[15] The school was for long under the patronage of St Paul's in Aberdeen, and was for long directed by my great-grandfather, John Gordon of Kinellar whom I know well as a kindly old man, good and amusing with bairns. He came regular to see my mother, his illegitimate grand-daughter. The Traveller of Zetland was married to Christian Ritchie Noble who was heiress to the House of Noble in her own right, she had been served heir to her grandfather Alex. Noble who was the first harbourmaster at Peterhead. Most records make out Andrew Noble to be heir, but it was his wife. Following the 1745 rebellion, Hanoverian troops were quartered in the school, and every morning lit the fire with books and irreplaceable documents. Broadsea for a time belonged to the Forbes of Pitsligo, folk paid rent to them.

Proceedings of the court case which took place in the great hall of Pitsligo Castle, after the wreck of the *Edward Bonaventure*, the crew of which are buried west of Joseph Mather's croft, many Broadsea folk were listed among those charged, also the Laird of Pitsligo's own sons. All those papers were burned by the soldiers.

The *Edward Bonaventure* was wrecked off Kinnaird Head on 10 November 1556. She was one of a squadron of three vessels sailing in search of a north-east passage to India, of which the other two had been driven ashore on the Lapland coast where their crews froze to death. The 'Edward Bonaventure lay in the White Sea where she was eventually rescued by an expedition from England. Together with three other ships (including the two original vessels, from Lapland) she sailed for home, carrying a very precious cargo and a Russian ambassador to England.

Of the four ships only one reached London. The *Edward Bonaventure* broke up on the Buchan rocks and, although the ambassador was saved, his property found its way into local hands. The assistance of the Scottish Crown was sought and

Mary, Queen of Scots, sent commissioners to Pitsligo to exhort the people and enforce recovery. This was the proceeding to which Christian's grandmother referred. Very little was recovered, and most of the first presents intended by the Russian Emperor for the English court ended up in Buchan.

Granny Lascelles' letter continued, with some torn parts of the manuscript leading to gaps in the first sentence:

> We have always had the right . . . over matters relating to the school, which was taken over by the Parish Kirk . . . had been outlawed by the Govt. When Philorth House was looted by Lord Ancrum, Lord Saltoun never lifted his finger to complain, as he was a peace-loving man and did not want to bring further trouble down on the heads of Fraserburgh people.[16]
>
> My ancestors were the Earls of Forgan in Fife who lost all at the time of Robert Bruce. The last of the Lascelles of Forgan was Walter who was married to a daughter of the 10th Lord of Saltoun of Abernethy. They had been married by John Rowe the Minister at Rosehearty in 1644 during the Covenanting troubles. They had two sons, Walter and John. Both were orphaned before the age of fourteen, and both married in Broadsea. Walter was married to the Traveller of Zetland's daughter, Grissel Noble, who was his heiress. She was extremely beautiful, as her picture clearly shows. I cannot ever recollect seeing a painting of her husband, if it ever did exist.
>
> Episcopalians in Scotland were cruelly and ruthlessly persecuted by the Westminster government, something which will never be forgiven. My parents and my grandfather told me of what they had to endure.
>
> My chief purpose is to inform you I am investing my hereditary right in the School in my daughter Helen Noble wife of James Watt Pyper and of whom failing in time coming to her daughter Christian Watt as in all my other possessions.

The Collegiate charges of Broadsea and Techmuiry were formed after the land apparently held on mandate by the Forbes of Pitsligo reverted back to Philorth. Some say the old Wine Tower at Kinnaird was the dower house of Pitsligo Castle. Fraserburgh Castle was the principal residence of my great grandparents John Gordon and Netta Fraser. All their bairns were educated at Broadsea School.

This document is legal and binding written in my hand the twenty second day of June 1840 and witnessed.

[Signed] Helen Noble or Lascelles

[Sgd] Gilbert Noble.

[Sgd] Alex Watt

The letter was sealed and posted under a Penny Black stamp – an early one, for the penny post was only introduced through- out the United Kingdom on 10th January that year. Thus Christian – seven years old when the letter was written, already avid for learning, and soon to start work which never stopped – was named, and felt herself to be, her family's heir.

With my two young brothers my cousin Annie and I went to Broadsea school to start our education. My cousin Annie was very like her father, William Crawford, Jean Lascelles' son. It was odd, for both Annie's grandmothers were two sisters.

We had to take a bawbee, a lump of coal or peat each day. Bairns who could not produce these things were not put out of school; only Mrs Cox the mistress would go on about it to scare them. She took a keen interest in those willing to learn, and in my first three years I could read, write and spell according to the standard. I left Broadsea school to help mother with the fish. My little brother and I in the dead of winter attended Mr Woodman's school on the Aberdeen road; it cost a penny a day. We were both good at the English and we learned the stops and interrogations in writing. Every odd moment, I could never get enough to read. I read everything I could get my hands on. The school was largely attended by children of would-be gentry from the Broch Mr Woodman fawned on them and they looked down on us because we came from Broadsea which was by far older than Fraserburgh. Our houses were ancient compared to any building in the Broch, yet they regarded them as hovels. My father spent a lot of time with me and my little brother. He was a smart man who believed in learning. We had to work when we were eight years old, but our schooling went on in the winter when fishing was slack.

I hated the small lines, for this meant so much more work for the adults, sheeling the mussels, baiting the lines and wupping on tippings. My parents' day began at three in the morning and often ended at midnight; as my brothers grew up they had to do a lot of the work. I have seen both of my parents fall down with exhaustion at the end of a day, after my father had come in from the sea. Everybody in the village was the same, and for their efforts they got scarcely enough to keep their life in their soul case. But we had a happy childhood in a Christian home, for which I am grateful. My father would take a glass of whisky in somebody's house at Hogmanay, and he had one to give a caller who came to his at the same time, but not through the year. My mother hated drink and all my brothers were totally abstemious when they grew up. Formerly by law the laird claimed a quarter of all the fishers' catches. For well over two centuries, strife and riots had gone on in Broadsea over this. They had been fined and imprisoned for staging strikes, but it did not stop it. My Granny Lascelles had a lot of documents relating to cases up before the sherriff, but after much blood and sweat the tend duties were abolished, and people built their own boats in 1828; formerly the boats belonged to the lairds. With this new freedom a far greater prosperity resulted. Folk were so much better off. When I started work at eight years old I had to take a chair and climb on to the roof of our house, covering all the tiles with gutted and split salted fish to dry in the warm sun. The yellow fish were smoked in our own hanging lum in the house. Apart from my father's catch my mother bought much extra fish at Fraserburgh harbour; these were spread out on the rocks, from Broadsea shore to the Manshaven; the whole beach was white with salt fish. All the little loons and quinies had a lot of fun and daffin as they watched their charges. We were experts at stoning the marauding seagulls who would devour the newly-salted fish. When we saw moisture on the rock it was time to turn the fish over, and threatening rain we gathered the whole cure under a tarpaulin. There were aye folk with tarry fingers who stole other people's fish, but most were honest; and there were the lazy who wanted to scrounge a living off others. If a person was old or sick or a widow with bairns it was your duty to help them out.

In 1841 folk did not pursue the herring so much. My father went to Greenland to the whaling, a very dangerous job costing many young lives. The whalers were a wild rough lot who lived for the day. Never a year passed that some did not return. During the season it was a trying time for those at home, for there was no communication with Greenland.

My mother had her usual round in what we called the 'near country' – Strichen, New Deer or Cuminestown. The 'far country' was the Grampian mountains. When I was nine I took on some of my mother's fish-round in the near country.

My little brother and I would accompany my mother to the near country. We exchanged our fish for butter and eggs and cheese; we carried home a little wooden coggie full of milk with a daud of the loveliest butter floating on top of it. My mother would rebuke my brother for constantly swinging the coggie, for it soured the milk.

Mormond village nestled in a pocket of peat smoke. By the time I was ten we knew nearly everybody in it. We carried on to New Deer and further, less often to Cumineston. I shall always remember Aberdeenshire as it was then, with little parks clustered round the old farmtouns, everywhere the lovely healthy smell of whins and broom and the hum of the bees when the heather was in bloom. Everywhere was yellow broom, for then so little of the country was under the plough. It was still in its wild state. The old Picts must have lived in a beautiful land in the summer. Mr Woodman[17] told us all the history of north-east Scotland, and he said I should go on with my study, but we had no money to do so, but in the winter I went to school as often as I could, right till I was twenty years old.

We always planted our own five drills of tatties at Roadies, and in the season we had to hole them and carry them home in creels, to be put under the ben bed.

In the winter we were always glad when the hungry month of March was out, with ten mouths to feed and often a few others; by then you were well through your tatties and barrel of herring. In a bad year, when winter hung on till May, I have seen us with only a half tattie for dinner with a drop of melted lard poured over it. At Woodman's school the business folks' bairns scorned us for going to school in our bare feet. During childhood some children never wore shoes at all; they were so poor they did not have any, even in winter. My seven brothers slept in the butt, my parents in the ben, and I in the closet with a little window which opened like a door looking on to the sea. When we went barefoot, feet washing was a nightly event, for we were not allowed to go to our beds with dirty feet. We had to give our parents credit for the dignified way they accepted their poverty with great courage. Everybody was the same, yet they worked from morning till night without ceasing and yet you could never somehow get ends to meet.

From an early age my mother taught us table and civil manners, and we were in a position to mix and converse with anybody. When I grumbled about my dress at school, my mother said the fishers were the first chosen of Christ, so: 'Put on your creel in gratitude to His glory,' she said, 'Your fathers are grossly superior to these tradespeople who look down on you. They can navigate small boats by oar and sail to the Hebrides, Shetland and Greenland, with nothing but the sextant set with the noonday sun, and the stars to guide them at night.'

My first job I was eight as skiffie to Mrs Lawson, the banker's wife. It was three months of drudgery and half-starvation. I resented being called all the time by my surname. Everything in the kitchen was done. I had to do the washing, and the scrubbing brush had about three bristles left in it, 'a board to a board will never wash clothes'. The public rooms were beautiful. I slept in a closet under the stairs. I was glad when I left and was given my first fee of three shillings. I had to start raking out the fires at five in the morning, and I always slept sound as I fell into my bed over the bank, at 3 Frithside Street. It had a beautiful view over Fraserburgh Bay: that was the only thing I liked, when I could get a second to admire it.

Granny Lascelles died at seventy-two, she was aged about 80, naming in her testament my mother and me as her heir. When my granny died all hell was let loose. She had by-passed my uncle, for the reason my mother would never wrong my Auntie Betty. Granny's sister Jean was a sanctimonious old hypocrite, quoting scripture and with her tongue ever-ready to tear to pieces some poor mortal. She had demanded the old grandfather clock belonging to her father William Lascelles, and also many other things. My mother gave her the things to keep the peace. Margaret's son Andrew Noble (Dunkie) took nothing. His wife, Rachel Watt, was a real Christian who helped dozens of Highlanders who poured into Fraserburgh after the Sutherland clearances. Rachel had gone on foot to Banff to beg the earl of Fife to allow them to settle on his wasteland. He housed over a hundred families.

Dunkie had a son, Iain Alister, who we called 'Dunkie's Jock', also two daurs, Jane and Maria de Hales Noble, who died young. They were named after one of our remote ancestors connected with the Frasers of Philorth. When I grew older my mother wanted me to marry Dunkie's Jock, who was a dull person I did not fancy pushing through life. If there was to be any choosing I was going to be the one who would do it. The house at 72 Broadsea had stood ten years without a roof. When she married, my mother had roofed her deceased granny's house, which in most cases had come down the long line through females.

My mother had a brother Alister who was press-ganged into the navy and was never heard of again. My didy Watt, my father's father, was Alexander Watt, known as 'Chalky' for a by-name. His mother was a Noble, and his grandmother, Christian Greig from Cairnbulg, was the same folk as the Norwegian music writer. For generations they had lived at 67, my grandparent's home, one of the last old croft houses left with a large plot of land which I can remember well before two grandsons built houses on it. The barn and peat stack stood before the door. My didy was six foot tall: the Watts were folk with foresight and gentle manners, and all were well doing.

My father's mother was Christian Noble (Kirsten Gunner). The Gunners were a wild lawless lot who feared neither laird nor minister or anybody else: my mother aye said I had a good lick of their brush. My granny Gunner had plenty of money: she possessed the chief ingredient for accumulating it – the greed of auld nick. For a tee name they called her 'Siccary' (or 'siccar mittens') she was so tight-fisted, she would hardly have given her grandchildren a piece. She was considerably younger than my didy Watt and he had no easy seat. She was so houseproud he wasn't allowed to smoke inside. When he complained she called him 'grumblie kang', a name that stuck; a nicer man you couldn't meet.

My granny Gunner's father, James Noble, had been brought up as a son by old Gunner, his grandfather. He was in fact the illegitimate son of James Gordon of Kinellar, son of John Gordon and Lord Saltoun's daur. Some said his parents were secretly married in Portsmouth. Old Siccary had an eye to business and was quick to exploit her connection with the peerage. She had shares in the whaling stations at Greenland, and at her will placed her sons where she wanted them to be. She put her eldest son, my Uncle Sandy, into her father's house, No. 63. After my grandparents' deaths his two sons built houses on the croft at 67. Siccary was a grafter for work and permitted no idle scat at any time. Regardless of age she would aye find a job for you, though only to gather horse dung from the street for her riggs. By my constant refusals I was never on the list of her favourites. On the road to the Broch she was attacked by a purse snatcher. She blacked both his eyes, though a little wifie. She died first, aged about 84, and my Aunty Kirsty, wife of Andrew McLeman, No. 54, took my old didy up to live with them. Kirsty was the youngest of the family, a greedy raking brute like her mother. Her man, Andrew McLeman, was a jewel, always in a pleasant humour. Like my didy they did not have a great life.

Kirsty had two sons Alex and John, and she sent both of them to University. Her daur Nellie was a slave, and a nice lass. When didy Watt died he left everything to Kirsty, to the outrage of the remaining seven sisters and brothers. My mother wouldn't allow my father to ask for anything from didy's house. My Auntie Nellie who lived at 49, wife of Black Jock, had been very good nursing her mother in her last illness, they were at each other's throats. My Aunt Annie said, 'If they take your coat let them take your cloak also.' Many years passed till Nellie spoke to Kirsty. My didy Watt was ninety-four when he died leaving to his daur 67, 54 and 27 Broadsea, also a fine house at 13 North Street, Fraserburgh, and 137 sovereigns. My mother did not envy her. If we got the day and way alike we were thankful. My Uncle Wulla had died at 7 Broadsea. His widow Anne Pirie was left to bring up a big family. Her youngest daur Mary was one of my best friends and remained so until her early death. Anne Pirie could well have done with some of didy's money but none came her way. My Aunt Annie paid for Mary's schooling from five to eight years old.

# CHAPTER TWO

## Fishing Sales and
## Highland Clearances (1843–1849)

Alexander, 15th Lord Saltoun, married Marjorie, daughter and heiress of Simon Fraser of Ness Castle, a West Indies merchant, an Inverness-shire Fraser. Saltoun died in 1793, and his widow long survived him, dying in 1851 at the age of ninety-seven. She was Christian's first employer at Philorth – 'Ness Madgie'. Her son, Alexander, became 16th Lord Saltoun, succeeding at the age of eight. This, the 'Waterloo' Lord Saltoun, first received a commission in 1802 at the age of seventeen, and exchanged from the 42nd Highlanders (Black Watch) into the 1st Guards[18] in 1804. This was the Saltoun that Christian first knew; her acquaintance spanned five generations of his family.

Lord Saltoun distinguished himself in the Peninsular War, and very particularly at the Battle of Waterloo, where he commanded the light companies of the 1st Guards in recapturing and defending the orchard of Hougoumont. He was promoted to the rank of Major-General in 1837, and in 1841 was sent to China with some reinforcements from India for the army, which was then engaged against the Chinese and Manchur Tartars. When operations had been successfully concluded, Saltoun was placed in command of the army of occupation, with headquarters in Hong Kong. He left Hong Kong for home in January 1844.

On his return home there were great festivities in Fraserburgh. The Broadsea men were as loyal as any. They addressed a letter to the returning Saltoun on 10 October 1844:

> My Lord,
> The fishermen on your Lordship's estate here, being anxouse to pay all the esteem in their power to your Honour, came to the Resolution, if your Lordship should accept of it, to draw you and your friends from your seat at Philorth to the entry of the Town of Fraserburgh, on the day of the dinner to Your Lordship from the Farmers, in a Boat mounted on four wheels, and acquiped for the purpose; Your Lordship may depend that the utmost decorum will be observed, and a slow peass kept, in order to prevent the least chance of accident.
> I have the honour to be, My Lord,
> Your Lordship's most obedient servant
> James Noble (Preses)

The splendidly decorated boat/car did its duty, drawn by sixty fishermen, with Saltoun at the tiller, escorted by some three thousand cheering people.

Saltoun returned to a Scotland in religious turmoil. Although profoundly religious Christian often had some tart things to say about the Kirk. The Church of Scotland – the 'Auld Kirk' – did not have in Fraserburgh and the north-east the sort of popular folk-tradition which it enjoyed in the south and west of Scotland. Indeed, when Presbyterianism was established by law in place of Episcopacy in 1689 after the accession of William of Orange, Fraserburgh was strongly Episcopalian, and remained so. The first Presbyterian Minister was installed in the Broch in 1707 only after considerable rioting and resistance. Some four fifths of the people, including Lord Saltoun and his family, were Episcopalian. The Episcopalians thereafter became something of a persecuted sect, a status exacerbated by the fact that Fraserburgh was probably Jacobite in majority sentiment in the first half of the eighteenth century, and Jacobitism was linked to Episcopacy. In 1746 Lord Ancrum's soldiers burned the Episcopalian church in Fraserburgh. The Episcopalians were restricted to meetings in which no more than four people could congregate in one room – a sanction to some extent circumvented by having a cleric in a central hall and members of his congregation, limited to the statutory four, gathered in the doorway of each room around it; some local farmhouses are constructed on that principle and for that reason. Meanwhile, the Kirk increasingly represented the respectable and the victorious. It was certainly not seen as the champion of the poor and oppressed.

However, although her folk had been staunch Episcopalians, Christian did not look at the matter from an Episcopalian standpoint, and her attitudes reflect another strain in Kirk history – that of dissent. The fisherfolk of the Buchan coast have been described as apt to embrace every new form of religion on offer. Whether or not that is fair, Christian certainly always aspired to direct religious experience, and invariably regarded with suspicion the established and the institutional. Her strictures on the Kirk were part of her radicalism. But in her note on the Disruption of 1843 – the year when the 'Free Church' of Scotland, the 'Wee Frees', left their established brethren and formed a separate community – Christian does not do justice to the causes. These had to do with the rights of congregations to resist ministers appointed without their consent, with patronage and with the relationship between ecclesiastic and civil discipline. They certainly were not directly related to social questions like eviction. But Christian's animus against the established church made her see the matter so.

My father was on the *Brilliant*, and shot a polar bear. He gave the skin to Lady Saltoun, who folk called 'Old Ness Madgie'. She lived mostly in London. She was a nice old wifie, well over ninety, and not a dottled hair in her head. I went as her maid in the fall of 1843.[19] She was pleased with my work and wanted me to come south with her, but I had no intention of accepting this life at everbody's beck and call. She offered me a dress length as a gift; I said I would rather have a dictionary. She thought it a strange request, but gave me one from the library. It opened up new realms in my life, for my nose was never out of it. Her son, Lord Saltoun, had been a widower for many years. Some said he took up with a wifie from Rathen; in my time I saw no evidence of this, for he was abroad soldiering most of the time. The wifie was a fly schemer, with an eye on his money and title, but it did not work. Lord Saltoun's wife had been an illegitimate daur of Lord Chancellor Thurlow; her mother had been a chorus dancer. Lord Saltoun fell in love with the lass, and against the wishes of his folk he had married the girl.[20] At home he was thought a lot of for it. She made him a good wife and unfortunately she died childless and very young. I don't mind on her.

On the west side of Philorth stood Cottarfalls, and between two burns on the south side stood Thiefsee, both farmtouns of old black houses occupied by folk who worked in the house and home farm. When the nephew took over both were completely demolished and beautiful policies laid out. In my granny's time Philorth House consisted of two double fronted houses and a half house joined upon end, but so constructed with connecting doors to serve as one dwelling. In the first lived her grandfather, John Gordon,[21] the Saltouns in the middle; the half-house was kept for the lady dowager. I can remember it facing the green, three storeys high with small twelve-pane windows, the top ones half set in the wall. When they built the bit facing the wilderness, the ceilings were raised and big windows put in, completely ruining the appearance. Inside all the open fireplaces were replaced with fancy grates. I had a shilling a week as wages. My mother had told me to respect aristocracy only if they were prepared to respect you, for 'Titles are man-made with no degree of permanency: in God's sight all human beings are the same, only those who are blessed with more have the greater account to give of their earthly stewardship.'

My mother told me never to depend on a living from landed proprietors, for it took away one's independence, in much the same way as a caged wild bird. It was preferable to be a poor fisher compared to being a well-fed lady's-maid: though a Lord or a servant, money will never make you if you are not right yourself.

I liked old Madgie. She told me all the history of the Earls of Ross, and how the joint heiress, Johanna, had married the first Fraser of Philorth, and how Donald the Lord of the Isles had tried to take it. She came often to tea in our house when she came into the Broch in her gig. My mother went regularly to Philorth with fish, Creeshie's Meg was washerwoman, her daur Christian Crawford also took on the job. The factor's wife was a fool who tried to speak proper English. She was the laughing stock of the whole area, the mention of her name set folk off in howls of merry laughter.

In 1844 Lord Saltoun returned from China, amid great demonstrations from his tenants, to find himself in the middle of a conflict with the kirk. It split Scotland down the middle, and the government were worried in case it would stir up the old 'Prince Charlie' spirit. The kirk had become an organisation to suppress the working class. Several folk had been evicted from crofts on the side of Benachie. The Aberdeenshire folk banded together right away – it must stop forthwith. Ministers preached it was God's will to go if told so, but folk had had enough. If you had no profession you were of no consequence to a minister, save only to fill the kirk on Sundays. As bairns we went to the Congregational Sunday School[22] and to the auld kirk bible class. Lord Saltoun asked my mother and father their opinion. My mother said, 'Do not oppose the dissenters in any way, but give them a bit of ground to build a kirk on.' He did, at the back of Manse

Street. They preached on Broadsea boat shore, the whole natural arena of the braes black with people. As youngsters we had a lot of fun, for the unread said a lot of silly things, but it gave a shock to a lot who thought they were infallible. It was an awful smack in the face to the would-be's who were left with nobody to look down on.

Domestic service, however hard, gave Christian opportunities of which she took full advantage. She went to London, and later to America, and she sharpened her mind with many an encounter and many an argument. But her life would for the most part be dominated, as was that of her parents, by the fishing.

The fishwives sold the fish in the landward parts, and their daughters helped them. They also looked after the men on distant voyages, for the herring fleets fished waters all round the coast, and brought Christian to the West Highlands just as her marketing journeys with her mother took her to the central Highlands of Aberdeenshire – the 'Far Country' of Deeside – as well as all over her own Buchan.

Christian makes clear how different from her own kind were the Highlanders, but there were degrees of that difference. The west-coast people she clearly found attractive but supine. They tolerated, she reckoned, treatment which east-coast folk would have vigorously rebuffed in any age, whatever the balance of power. But the Highlanders of the Upper Dee she found more akin. They spoke the Gaelic but 'the young ones could all speak Doric' as well, on Deeside. The bracing eastern air was not entirely remote. She found the people had 'Aberdeenshire characteristics', although 'very, very far from the sea'. These were the days before Queen Victoria bought the estate of Balmoral, and before Deeside acquired its reputation for fashion and its attraction for visitors.

Christian's generous and indignant nature was revolted by the Highland Clearances. These involved the eviction of great numbers of Highlanders from their homes in order to make large-scale sheep farms or, later, deer forests. The clearances had their defenders; and it is probably true that in many cases, ultimately, those 'cleared' won for themselves a better and more prosperous life than could ever have been their lot among the diminishing resources of a Highland glen. But Christian saw only greed, cruelty and indifference on the one side, and on the other the displacement of a suffering and ancient people from their tribal homes. She saw the destruction of a culture – in many cases by those whose tradition was or should have been to protect rather than to evict. She could react in no other way.

The most essential part of a fishwife's equipment was her plaid. In Inverallochy and Cairnbulg they wore a red and black dice of a different check, St Combs was blue and black, Broadsea black and white, Pitulie grey and white, Rosehearty natural and brown. Often you were glad to dry your plaid at a tinkie's fire. We always had a friendly relationship towards the tinkies, who lived in hoop tents on Strichen and New Deer moss. My mother aye smoked a pail of whitings to give to these folk, and they also got our old clothes. As solitary women on the road we had a certain amount of protection from the tinkies. I have been glad on a dark night to walk from New Deer to Strichen in the company of old Foly Stewart, who told me much of the misery of their hard life. His great-grandfather had fought with Stewart of Appin, and fled to Buchan from Culloden; they had no wish to settle in houses. My mother also gave a fishie to several mannies who lived in slab-built shelters, with a fire between a circle of stones on the side of the road. They broke stones into road metal. They were glad of any titbit – 'He that giveth to the poor lendeth to the Lord.' Fishwives were often attacked both for money and carnal knowledge. All carried sharp gutting knives. I would not have hesitated to plunge it into anybody who attempted to molest me. The fisherwomen met at Strichen and came home in a bunch. An old iron pot and kettle lay in a sheltered corner above the Ugie. Here the group would often brew tea and boil an egg. I have seen Maggie Lonnie from Cairnbulg, and Kirsty Taitie from Inverallochy and half a dozen more. We sat down in a circle round a fire, and one of the number gave thanks before we ate. Old Mal from St Combs would ask the Almighty to bless our feet on our way home.

Many folk were scared to pass Catchie's brig on the Broch side of the Witchill Road. Here it was said a headless horseman rode; some said they heard the hoofs. In the past witches had been burnt at Witchill. If folk had any sense they would have known if the witch possessed extraordinary powers she could have destroyed them long before they got at her. I discredited all these old fraits as a lot of dirt. The feeing markets at the Broch and Strichen were hilarious affairs, where bairns bartered themselves into slavery. After the making of the big farms when lots of strange men came into the area, it was considered bad taste for a woman to be seen at feeing markets. Before there were stalls with candy and more like a fair, and wifies and bairns.

I have walked with other folk from Broadsea to Port Erroll, and often to Peterhead. I mind on the old wifie Ritchie at Brucklay Castle; she owned the Techmuiry Estate. I also knew the first Brucklay MP, who did not live long after the wifie. We supplied them with fish for generations. Some of the folk on that round lived to long ages. A nice soul was Mrs Dalgarno, an aged wifie in Auchreedie. Jeems Forrest in Bonnykelly was about 100; so was Eppie Milne and Jean Ogston in Drum. Our old customers were like part of our family. They came down to Broadsea to see us: the Johnstones in Old Mill of Strichen, the Thirds in Dencallie. Old Elspeth Noble in Fridayhill was about 100: she was connected with Bredsie. Mrs Ross in Adziel was as old. We went as friends to the Campbells in Bransfarm on Mormond. Auld Jeems Findlay in the Greens (his wife was a Taylor from

Bredsie); we were great friends with the Keiths of Bogenjon, also the Cruickshanks of Burnshangie. Old Kirsty Walker in the toll was a nice wifie. My, how those folk had to work, even in their old age, they chaved from first light and earlier to beyond darkness. We went right over the crown of Mormond to no-mans land, and Bettysyard, which had belonged to my noble ancestors, and where Halkett the Jacobite had hidden from the redcoats; a fast flowing burn came down from the hillside to Wauchtonhill. The old houses in farmtowns were furnished and similar to the ones at the coast, with box beds, two ends and closet, two long stools both sides of the table, the deece and open dresser, often a grandfather clock. My mother said they had been like that for centuries.

I had learned to gut when I was ten: curing had started in a big way. In 1844 during the summer, most Broadsea fishers went to the west coast and the Hebrides. We as lassies went to cook for the men. We lived in sod-built bothies on the shore, I shared one with Annie Rogie and Suffie Noble, at Loch Eishort in Skye.

The work was hard for children, but we had a lot of fun. I enjoyed the long sail round the north of Scotland hugging the coast. I was with my father, and had faith in his skeelie seamanship. The scenery was really bonnie. For some reason the Highland folk didn't trust us. You could not make friends with them easily, but I did, with a few who could speak a little English. Kate McLeod, a quinie who brought the milk from Susnish, gave us all the clake. We gutted the herring, packed them in barrels and ships from Glasgow took them away.

Lord Macdonald of Slaet was a greedy character. He charged a fortune for the bothy; the factor collected it every week. He lived in a place with trees called Ostaig. One day I noticed the factor and his groom lift a barrel of herring onto their gig. I asked what they were doing. They said, 'Just taking a barrel of herring,' I told them to put it down; if I stole vegetables from his garden he would have had me up before the court. He said, 'Didn't I know he was the factor?' I told him I did not care though he was Prince Albert: if he did not put it down I would go up to Broadford and get the police. Lord Macdonald was a handsome batchelor who lived in style at Armadale Castle. Folk told us his mother was an illegitimate daughter of His Royal Highness the Duke of Gloucester. He was a first cousin to the Queen. Later he married but local folk said he was a 'droll hare' who took up with men, and was marrying only to get an heir.

Some of the tenants were very poor. An old wifie of over eighty we visited regularly in a hovel. She kept goats and hens, Annie Rogie gave her her mother's old kwite and I gave her a sark. Suffie gave her two pairs of worsted hose, this old creature was banished to Canada along with the whole of Sleat Peninsula when Lord Macdonald started the Clearances with unbelievable cruelty. He drove the people out; when we returned in later years not a soul was to be seen for miles and miles. I met his Lordship on the pier at Kyleakin. He had a party of toffs with him. I was not going to lose the chance. I said to him before this audience, 'You are lower than the outscourings of any pigsty, causing all that human suffering to innocent people.' Had he been on the east coast his fine castle would have been burned down; though I was a herring gutter I was as much a descendant of the Lord of the Isles as he was.[23] We went to Lewis and Barra and Strathy in Sutherland. I liked travelling the fishing, for it gave a true picture of the Highland way of life, and the Clearances which the Government turned a blind eye to.

We went again and again to Skye. The coastline was dotted with the bothies of girls; it was hard work to bake, wash and cook to twenty-seven men. The catches were not big; at this time the fishermen did most of the gutting; it had not yet become wholly a female job. We were several times to Steen. The Laird of Macleod was a better landowner all round, and his wife was one of the most beautiful women I have ever seen. She was sweirt, bone-idle and took him out of the door, for she fired away money as you would do foul water. She had a grand barge anchored in the loch, and huge tea parties took place every day. It was a show, with all the ladies' satin tea gowns.

One of the young Dougals from Pitullie had a big row on the boat with his father, and went ashore to get a job as kitchen steward in Dunvegan Castle. The Skye folk called the Macleod's wife Lady John, she had gone off in a huff to London, and he had gone after her. It was Sunday, our only free day. The whole staff of Dunvegan had gone to the kirk for two hours. Young Dougal had the skowth to show Annie, Suffie and me over the Castle. It was beautiful inside; a fortune was spent on rebuilding. Lady John had a room full of dresses and coats, and I insisted on trying on a sable one and admiring myself in the looking glass.

Two years following each other the summer was scorching hot followed by constant wet. All over the north of Scotland the tatties had been devoured by weevils. The harvest was also nothing. All over folk were starving. Macleod was good to them, and to his credit he carried out no cruel evictions. I tried to fathom what was wrong with the whole set-up. I questioned why one man should be in a position to subsidise thousands of folk; we were equally hard hit at home, yet I could never imagine Lord Saltoun dishing out meal, any more than I could imagine the least one of his tenants accepting it. Highland women worked hard, and often their men were prepared to stand by and watch them do it. Many were extremely good-looking and intelligent, and what I saw wrong was they should have printed school books in the Gaelic, for I could always think much quicker in Buchan Doric[24] rather than English, a language I had to always learn. If they had taught them in their own tongue they would be more self-reliant and have a greater pride in their heritage. In forcing them to learn English, education was suppressing their self-respect. It was said the Sleat folk were Picts, the same as us. I had visited Dunscath Castle which was linked with the cove 'Kataritchie' at home, where Scathack the Queen who dwelt in the east of Alba was said to reside with her two sea-monsters, Gropus and Pilgaupige. But the awful Macdonald had banished everybody: the folk were fools to go, for if somebody attempted to burn my house, I would have lifted their skull with the sharpest stone I could lay hands on, and organised the others to do the same. Kate Macleod, the quinie from Susnish, wrote to me for a lifetime; she had married later an evicted crofter from Mull and they settled in Wallaceburgh in Canada. Macdonald brought in English shepherds with their children which could have but a tragic effect on the Gaelic language and on the whole Scottish nation.

I liked August best. Then the whole coast of fishwives went into the Grampian Mountains to dispose of their summer cure of dried fish, barns were cleared out and wifies and their bairns moved in. My mother, my two youngest brothers and I always went to the barn at Corrybeg: young Charlie Forbes's wife was connected with us in some way. We paid a small rent for the barn where we slept, and our food was cooked on a fire outside. We had a lot of orders to deliver on our way out. Mistress Gordon at Cortes always gave us an order to deliver at Craigevar Castle. The change was so health giving, for the Highland air and the sun built you up to face the winter. We stayed two weeks till all our cure was sold. McGrigor, the horse-hirer at Strichen, took about ten tons of fish inland for us: I shall aye regard this as the happiest days of my life.

The folks on the upper reaches of the Dee spoke the Gaelic. They lived to awful long ages. Old Granny Betty who lived with the Stewarts in Linmuie was well over 100, she could remember the Hanoverian troops occupying Mar Castle and all the cruel things they did. Nellie Hunter in Lynohaun was an awful age; she spoke the Doric and Gaelic. Lamont, the gamekeeper's father in Corndavan Lodge, had a great memory. His father was a weaver in Auchendryne; and Meg Macgregor in the old Castletown of Mar, Mrs Clark in Aberarder, must have been a century old also. An interesting wifie was Jean Macdougal in Crathy. She lived to be 105, and Betty Macdonald who lived near her was almost as old; and very nice they all were.

The smell of the hills and the air was so wonderful, at night the whole valley was filled with the sound of the bagpipes. This was long before the Queen came. I have joined in the dancing at Mar Castle on the green at night. I think I may have danced with John Brown, the gillie who the papers made so much speak of in later years. My mother and I had a creel on our backs, my brothers a clean pillowslip of dried fish. Along with folk from Cairnbulg, Rosehearty and everywhere we scoured the mountains to all our regular customers. Lady Janet Farquharson at Invercauld always took an order. We went to the McGilvies and Macallaspicks, and an old wifie Cattanach in Glen Quioch. The Duchess of Leeds in Dalmohr House always bought a big order. We had customers on both sides of the burn at Inverey. There were a family McArdie, and Ranaltoch, in Glen Eye, but the land was very poor. The folk in Altander ha' House always took fish and a few crofts in Glen Derrie; here we reached Ben Macdui. In Glen Gedie and Glen Binyack there was Lord Fife's ha' House and very old black houses where the folk spoke mostly the Gaelic. They did not look like west of Scotland folk, with high cheekbones, but were dark and tall with inbred good looks and Aberdeenshire characteristics, for the young ones could all speak Doric apart from Gaelic, but few understood English. They had the dry humour of that folk, and were very hospitable and would detain you for hours. They were always eager for news of the outside world, but we couldn't spare the time. We were very, very far from the sea.

Inside houses were more comfortable than west of Scotland houses, with panelled breasting on the box beds, a deece, stools and usually an open dresser often with a lot of bonny dishes on it. Most were Catholics but very poor. Children were very mannerable and would come with us to outlying places, for if the mist came down they knew the rocks and boulders like the back of their hand. My mother aye took a bag of our outgrown clothes to give to the bairns. Hanging lums in houses were often made of reindeer skins, stretched over a wooden frame, the fur still on the outer side. Deer and golden eagles abounded around Lochnagar and Cairngorm. Here we met the Buckie folk who came up the Spey to work from Calumbrig. In Glen Binyack we met Maggie Dovan, Isie Deedle and Jessie Dottie, wifies from Portgordon and the Sloch. The old Castletown of Mar was shifted a lot nearer to Auchendryne. Near the Clunie Briggie was an ancient ruin. All the entrances were blocked by fallen masonry. Local folk said it had been Malcolm Canmore's hunting castle; there was much more of it when we went first, but they cleared it away to build dykes when they made big parks. We got an order from the factor at Aldourie. We went right up Glen Gairn to Strathdon.

After Royalty came Deeside was ruined. The rich came and built huge palaces to try to outshine Easter Balmoral. Some of the ha' houses were very grand. In our fisher dress a group of us stood by the roadside near Crathie. The Queen came by; she looked so sour you could have hung a jug on her mouth. The carriage stopped and Prince Albert came down and spoke to us. He was very pleasant. The Prince of Wales was a bonny loon then; nobody would have thought he would turn out the foul bawdy man he did. The whole area was now invaded by the curious. Our hill-trade was ruined, for we were no longer permitted to traverse the mountains after they made the deer forests. During stalking you might disturb the quarrie or get a bullet in your head. After the sport was properly organised we were officially banned. For all that hard work, after your expenses were paid, you had a few pounds to help educate your sons and see you through the winter. (I was always furious that girls were not allowed to be educated. It was assumed a man must work for a wife and needed learning. A lot of men I would not have seen in my way – I would have worked any of them blind.)

Years later a chap tapped me on the shoulder in Aberdeen. He said, 'You are Kirsty, the lassie who came with the fish wifies.' It was Andrew Coutts and his friend Alex Ruanach, now both granite masons. I had known them when we were all bairns. They told me Lord Fife had cleared the whole glen to make a deer forest. All had to go on three months' notice. Lord Fife's uncle was an honourable man who would never have evicted anybody, but now they were building vast palaces in relentless pursuit of pleasure, at the expense of a race who had probably been there since the end of the ice age. Both boys vowed vengeance, and said the day would come when the Skene Duffs[25] would call on the mountains to fall upon them.

# CHAPTER THREE

## Philorth and First Love (1849–1851)

The year before Christian was born there was a severe outbreak of cholera at Fraserburgh. In 1849 there was a second epidemic. It broke out at Cairnbulg, brought thither by the crew of a boat, but this second outbreak did not affect Fraserburgh itself, where strict precautions were taken to avert it.

There was another very serious outbreak in 1866, and this time Fraserburgh was hard hit. Christian wrote of the cholera epidemic, but it is obscure to which year she is referring. The first outbreak in her lifetime was in 1849 – but that did not affect Fraserburgh, although there were some deaths in Broadsea. The second – very severe – was in 1866, but by then Christian's mother, to whose part she vividly refers, was dead. It is likely that she was describing her mother's own recollections of 1832, probably reinforced and mingled with her own experiences of both 1849 and 1866.

> Following the famine we were all so hard up for food. Folk were so run down, and an epidemic of cholera broke out. About thirty died in Broadsea. There were about 200 in the Broch. My mother boiled all the water, the house was scrubbed from top to bottom, and folk spread quicklime round the outside so that the hen's dirt would not carry the disease. We spread chloride of lime under our beds: your breath was taken away with it. Many people were very brave, including my mother who helped to kist many of the dead.

She wore gloves and muslin over her face and boiled the clothing outside whenever she took it off. She stripped on the brae in a tent made of old sheets. Nobody near to us died, but many orphans were left. The Broadsea folk called a meeting to resolve what was to be done. An old spinster, Creeshies Luck, would occupy 31 Broadsea, her brother's house: both he and his wife, his brother and his wife died, leaving a lot of bairns. Luck would look after them, and also about four other orphans. She had about twelve in all. At the Saturday night prayer meeting, everybody would contribute a bowl of meal, and when the tatties were holed each family would give a share and the bairns would be kept in Broadsea with a real home life. Old Luck was kind to them all, and they adored her. She could keep discipline, which was necessary, and when her funeral went up the road several grown men wept bitterly for the only mother they had known. She was an unrewarded Christian on this side of time.

When our whole family was at home, my brothers were all scholarly, and what a din round the table at diet hours! They would argue about their superior knowledge, and your lugs were deaved. My father would bring his hand down with a thump, and often he would bring it down on their lug, if they did not stop. I had made up my mind to be an old maid. There were several in Broadsea, sitting in blissful solitude and the polished brightness of their hoosies, and I amid the noise of my seven brothers. My father stood no nonsense. Once I called him a fool in front of fishermen on Skye, and what a clout he gave me! I saw millions of stars. My mother was a grand knitter and did all the stockings. She was good at ganseys also, the rope, barleycorn and links of love and all the fancy patterns she could do, long before books came out to copy.

In describing her visits to 'the Far Country' of Deeside, Christian refers to her customer, the Duchess of Leeds, at Dalmohr House.

This was a house (on the site of the present Mar Lodge, built in 1898) upon the estate of Inverey. The Duchess was an American from Baltimore, and a Roman Catholic. She was several years older than her husband, who does not appear in Christian's narrative.

The last time we went to Inverey the Duchess of Leeds fixed myself and Kate Mason up with a job in London. Kate had been an orphan from Inverallochy. In the month of September 1849 we sailed from Aberdeen on the *Holyrood Palace*, calling at Leith and Hull on the way. My mother was sad at the parting, but I wanted to see around a bit. She had dinned into us the folly of getting in the family way, and always to mix with respectable company. I was not going to lose this chance. What an eye opener was the London dockland! Nothing can describe the sights we saw. I wondered that anybody could possibly observe human decencies in such atmosphere – aged folk in tatters, children almost naked. I had to harden myself to the sight of such suffering to prevent me giving away the little money I had. Her Grace had a beautiful house in St James', we had plenty to eat and a comfortable bed in the basement, but we had to work long and sore hours. After luncheon on Sunday we were free to sightsee. The Duchess was a Catholic, and a well-intentioned woman.

Kate and I went regularly to the Kirk of Scotland, and we danced late on Saturday night where all the Aberdeen folk gathered in a close off the Strand. There Kate met a nice young man who, after we came home, courted her for eight years. He came to Fraserburgh for two weeks every summer: he was a tradesman with his own business. He married Kate and they had a beautiful house at Putney. She kept up with me for a lifetime. We both explored all the famous places – Westminster Abbey and the Houses of Parliament. I saw the tomb of Mary Stewart. Another maid, Cathie, took us to her

home in the Borough. We made friends with her parents who
gave us a welcome open door. The man was a slater and the
wife a grand baker, who went out early in the morning to
bake for a pie shop to get a bit extra money to make ends
meet. They were very nice folk, and Cathie's nephew came to
the Broch and liked it so much he married a Pittulie girl and
stayed there. The west end of London was fascinating, and
the houses so grand. Her Grace was sorry when Kate and I
left in April. My brother's ship was in the river at Wapping,
so we got a run home. I had seen Buckingham House, St
Paul's and even Billingsgate, where Kate and I showed how to
split a haddock without sparking your clothes. The mannie
wanted to give us a job. He gave us the two haddocks which
we gave to Cathie's mother. When we returned we felt we
had scored over our friends. I often think of the terrible
poverty in London, and wonder how it came about to start
with, and what would put an end to it. We were off to
Castlebay in Barra to cook for the men. It was like pottage
and old clothes after London. Her Grace had in fact looked
after us well and on leaving she gave us two gold sovereigns
for our pay, the most I ever possessed in my life. I handed
them over to my mother on my arrival home. Next year we
went back to Skye.

The following year, along with a party from Rosehearty,
Cairnbulg and Inverlochie, my parents went to London to
the great exhibition. As the Queen's Consort, Prince Albert
had stepped down from his carriage to recognise a group of
fishwives, which was a gentlemanly act on his part, he
wanted them represented at the Crystal Palace, so the party
went to spell each other for the duration of the exhibition.
They mended and made nets and sheeled mussel shells stuck
together with glue, inside was a sweetie joo-joob which was
baited on the lines. It was a success. My father had been to
London before, but not my mother who was not impressed.
Like me she wanted to see London Bridge where Sir William

Wallace had died heroically. In 1822 before her marriage my mother had gone to Edinburgh as lady's-maid to Lady Saltoun at King George's Ball. The King was a big fat man who had worn silk bloomers under his kilt, they came down over his knees and they said you never saw such a ticket!

The 'Waterloo' Lord Saltoun had no legitimate children. His wife produced no heir, and the Master was his heir, Alexander ('Big Zander' to Christian), son of Saltoun's younger brother, William Fraser – 'Slave Willie'.

House at Philorth was thus kept, in the days when Christian worked there after the Dowager's death, by the Waterloo Saltoun's sister, Mrs Macdowall Grant of Arndilly. There was a cross-relationship, since William Fraser's wife was Elizabeth Macdowall Grant, his brother-in-law's sister.

Unlike his elder brother, William Fraser had a large family, 'swamping the house', Christian observed sharply, 'like the Ugie Water full in spate'. One of his sons, younger brother of the Master, was Murray Fraser.

Saltoun did not spend a great deal of time at Philorth, even after his active soldiering had finished. He took a lodge and a moor near Rothes, together with a stretch of salmon fishing on the Spey, where he spent August and September. He lived during the hunting season at the house of Lees, near Coldstream, on the Scottish border, which he rented and where he hunted with Lord Elcho's and the Duke of Buccleuch's hounds; and as a Scottish Representative Peer he spent the parliamentary session in London. He passed October at Philorth and the domestic economy felt the presence of his sister, his nephews and nieces more than his. Yet, while not ever present, the Waterloo Saltoun was much admired and deeply respected. He was devoted to music and to the opera, and he sang and played the violin. Indeed, he had picked as his Brigade-Major for China an officer who played the cello – very far-sightedly: the cellist became a general in due course. 'A quick, abrupt man,' said Christian of Saltoun, 'but he would listen to you.' He was clearly fond of her parents. 'A man's man,' Christian called him; and, after he died, 'This humble man, who was a Lieutenant-General.'

Several times I had gone to work at Philorth House during the shooting. In August September and that, they would take on a few extra young folk. Lord Saltoun would employ only single and literate people. Macdowall, his sister[26] acted as hostess, and a real tyrant she could be. She would only employ those who came from what she termed a good home. I can remember twenty-nine of a staff at one time. I worked in the laundry at different times. The head laundry-maid was Mary Smith, whose brother was gamekeeper. He lived in the old Longhouse on the bents, where the animals and humans had once gone in at the same door. Now the byre end was a shoppie where Mrs Smith sold sweeties and penny, wabble ale and groceries, she had a good trade, for all the over the water folk passed that way and (something to do with the parish boundary) marriages took place there. The other washerwoman was Mary Lunan, from the cottar town at Bungie's, next door to Kinglesser. Mrs Lunan was a comic who swore like a trooper and sometimes she was so funny I would double up laughing. I learned the facts of life from her. She had a large brood of barefooted and scantily clad bairns who went to Rathen School spotless clean. Her man was at Bungie's and both worked hard to give the bairns a bite. Annie Trail, who lived over the stripe briggie not far into Cairnbulg, did the ironing; she was about twelve years old. Her Aunt Maggie Milne was dairymaid. The head housemaid was Mary Ritchie, a spinster who still had her deceased parents' hoosie in Inverallochy; she slept in the loft with a London quine, Betty Sheperd the tablemaid. Ben the house, in the loft, Jimmy Robinson, a cockney footman, shared a bed with Bobby Wilson, the strapper, who drove the carriage. Both were young loons full of fun. The rooms at both ends of the loft were the only ones lined, the others were just the open roofing beams. One lined attic was occupied by Jean Anderson the cook, the other by the wifie Drysdale, the housekeeper, who tried hard to get Lord Saltoun to put a ring on her finger. She was only a young deem and many wondered why she got the job so young. Macdowall and Drysdale did not hit it off well. Macdowall knew she was young enough and capable enough to marry Saltoun and have children by somebody else and pass them off as his. Drysdale was always sitting with a candle poring over her books. Money saved went into her own pocket.

Jock Jye's daur was scullery maid. She was about eleven years old. (The bathbrick she used to scour the copper pans took the quinie's hands all out in holes; she lived in the middle row in Cairnbulg.) Mary Smith and Maggie Milne shared a chaumer at Thiefsee, like the rest of the buildings falling down. Annie Trail, Jock Jye's daughter, Nellie Massie the under-housemaid and I slept four in a bed in another chaumer at Thiefsee. The roof was thatched with divots, with a hanging lum and a small four-pane window. We put on lace screenies and a valance on the box bed. On the south side of the barn stood Meston the gardener's house, a good stone and lime but and ben with a large garden. His eldest daur was a pupil teacher. He had a lot of bairns who walked into the broch to Woodman's school every day. The bairns had no truck with us and Mrs Meston was very bigsy and ambitious; she educated her family by making jam for shops and selling berries and produce in the garden at Aberdeen. She worked hard but would not pass a remark of the day to anybody but the housekeeper or cook. Meston must have had only a few shilling a week, but his children did not work. He had them all trained: if they saw a fallen leaf they would pick it up and tuck it under a hedge; they were mannerable bairns. Meston was the only married man on the estate, apart from the gamie. In a third chaumer at Thiefsee, slept three a bed, were Billy Dennis, Jim Milne and Dod Addams, all young loons who worked in the garden. They were all quiet, for Meston was a hard taskmaster who kept them at it from 5.30 in the morning till the light failed. Lairds did not encourage hordes of scratching bairns on estates, for with the chums they brought about the place, they would raid the gardens and eat the produce. It cut two ways, for it was also an embarrassment before their guests, with paying their fathers a shilling a week, the bairns could not be but ragged, and constantly placed before their eyes a question the Tory Government wanted to sweep under the bed. Lord Aberdeen had done a lot for the working man, and for his friend Gunterstone, the social reformer. Four young loons were taken on in the fall to work in the stables and kennels – Alex Shand, Jim Leel, Willie Jaffra, and Sandy Will. They were about ten or twelve years old. They groomed the guests' horses and dogs. They slept two in a bed in the loft above the stable, and were always up to some devilment. Sometimes it got out of hand and came to blows and they had to be separated.

In the thatched lodgie at the gate lived Polly Burnett, a kindly old creature on the borders of 80. Twice a week she scraped the brook from the iron pots and kettles in the kitchen. She also did the washing up at meals. The staff carried her a lot. My parents had always told me to be kind to the aged and I aye brought her a fishie. Her folk had been cottars at Broadsea Mains. She remembered well and spoke highly of my great-great-grandfather James Lascelles in 35 Broadsea. Old Polly always prayed she would die in her sleep, for she had not a soul belonging to her; she had 9d a week and the lodgie. If she lost her roof she was faced with the dreaded poorhouse. She almost got her wish, for she died after two days' illness. Mary Ritchie and Mrs Lunan sat up all night and saw her out. She had pre-arranged with the undertaker that he would accept her grandfather clock in exchange for a decent burial beside her man in Rathen Kirkyard; he was as good as his word. She had also arranged with Mary Ritchie to give all the staff a keepsake of her very scant belongings. I had a little lustred milk stoupie which I kept until I lost my home. The staff all contributed tuppence to pay the doctor's bill, so Polly left this scene with no debt.

Lord Saltoun was a soldier, not a farmer, and had not gone in for elaborate farm buildings as at Strichen house.[27] The steadings were the same as they had been about two centuries earlier. The but and ben at the home farm were occupied by the grieve, Jock Craigheid, and the Baillie, Jake Tyler. Both were single and shared a bed in the butt end – the ben was part of the dairy. Maggie Milne kept it spotless, all the brass pails were gleaming. Her day often started at three o'clock in the morning, for a shilling a week.

At Cottarfaals was an old black-house. The dividing wall between the byre had been demolished to make a long room. A hanging lum was on the gable next the Aberdeen road. Two windows about a foot square let in the light, with a glass tile set in the turf roof; the long length of the back wall was bulging and falling outwards. Like all the other chaumers it got a lick of limewash in the spring when the stables and byres were done. In one bed slept Willie Leask and Willie Clubb, two older men, and in the other bed was Billy Penny and Jock Ironside, two halflin loons always up to some tricks. Bits of harness and all kinds of things hung about the walls. I have seen many a more comfortable hen-house.

On Saturday nights you would hear the fiddles going and all the staff would gather in the chaumer. It was a grand night's entertainment. Some of the ballads were hundreds of years old. Though we had not a penny to spare, we would walk into the Broch Links after 10 o'clock on Saturday night just to see the revelry. They were a jolly crew and I was happy to be free from the close outlook of my parents, for only a few weeks. In spite of our dire poverty we made the best of it, for if you cannot laugh when you are eighteen when can you?

There was a high standard of discipline and morality at Philorth. We started in the laundry at 5.30 at 4.30 the farm bell would toll and all the staff would be about. All dined in the large kitchen at Philorth, with staggered diet hours, for it was a lot of folk to make brose for. This was ever staple diet, apart from broth. Some of the lovely things Jean Anderson made made my mouth water but none ever came our way. It was the same in every similar establishment. What a washing up old Polly and the Cairnbulg quinie had! We had an hour to meals, but what a laughing and joking went on in the kitchen when different crews were seated.

The laundry was down beside the home farm on the edge of the wood overlooking the Cairnbulg road. The clothes on the tows got a good wapping from the fresh sea breezes blowing over the bents. I always took this job, so my mother could lay by an extra bag of flour for the winter from the shilling I earned. (Laundry is so personal and reveals so many secrets. Mrs Lunan was constantly commenting on Mrs Drysdale's sheets and her various admirers; some of the stuff she said is quite unprintable!)

The cook and housekeeper had nice beds, but the others had only chaff sacks. We brought our own blanket, so as we were four to a bed we were not cold with four blankets. We also had our own pillow slips and towels. At the fire where the irons were heated, we made a pot of tea under cover, for Drysdale would kick up dust if she found out. We had to keep the two boilers going for bath water for the house. It was carried up in brass roozers which had to be kept polished like the sun. We were not allowed to walk on the avenue from Polly's lodge at the gate to the front of the house, but had to go through the wood to a separate back door with no contact with the main entrance. A separate stair led up to the garrets where the staff lived.

When the nephew[28] inherited it, he built a lot of alterations beyond all recognition of what it had been. He added a lot of little turrets and fancy lums, apart from a big wing and huge hothouses. Old Philorth was beautiful inside, with all the silver in the huge dining-room and oil paintings on the walls. There were dozens of oil pictures stacked into the lie of the roof in the staff attics, also dozens of locked boxes. Sitting on one, the footman Jimmy Robinson went through the lid. It was full of wabbs of gorgeous chinese silk materials; they had to borrow a hammer to mend the lid. There was a kist with a whole eastern dinner set in it. Once a year Drysdale checked all the contents. She was like a jailer on her rounds with many bunches of keys. Philorth had an atmosphere all its own: the fragrant smell of dried roses in china bowls, combined with the stink of a seldom-fired clay building.

The Saltouns were not there often, but at Easter and all through the summer till October members of the family came for a month or so at a time. The Laird's younger brother was not liked in the Broch. He was known as 'slave Willie'. Along with a blackguard called Neilson from Liverpool he had taken part in the vile traffic of selling human beings in America and buying them in Africa. Willie did the books and Neilson did the dirty work, and after this awful trade was abolished, both landed in the gutter where they belonged. I can mind on Willie; he died after I worked at Philorth first. The mannie Neilson had several sons, all in the Army, where a smart officer's uniform can make an erraster look like a gentleman till he opens his mouth. They used to shoot at Philorth, a lewd foul-mouthed lot. The staff breathed a sigh of relief when slave Willie died first. He was Lord Saltoun's heir, and they had visions of his occupying Philorth with his vast brood. Saltoun could not suffer them, he took himself off to a lodge at Keith whenever they appeared.

Willie's wife and Macdowall's man were sister and brother; he had died in the big cholera epidemic of 1849. I think
there were twelve or thirteen of a family. They swamped and
flooded the house like the Ugie Water full in spate, sisters
and sweethearts, brothers and brother officers, horses and
flechie deerhounds. The Saltouns had two overflows, the
haunted Brick Lodge in the Broch and the big house on the
knap at Kinglasser. Old Lady Saltoun told me the latter was
older than Philorth, it had been built for a factor's house
while they still had Cairnbulg Castle. At Kinglasser all
the young men staved for the shooting. They had that
artificial polish of their class and often a sarcastic biting
wit, which I was always on the ready to cap. Margaret
was the nicest of the lot. She married the young Lady Saltoun's brother, a Captain Evans. There were a lot of daughters, and what a useless bunch of articles. Not one that could
wash a dish; they kept ringing bells asking for things they
could have got up and got themselves. After their mother
died I don't know what kept them, but something of their
genteel shabbiness always aroused pity in me. It never
seemed to strike them to go and take a job. They couldn't
go down to the sands but a wifie had to escort them, she
was like a shadow behind them walking into the Broch. I
would have told the wifie where to go! Those girls did not
pass a remark of the day to us; a great gulf lay between them
and us. I would look at the avenue which we were not
allowed to use. It was like a mighty river of power, but
petered out at the gate on the Aberdeen road, the public
highway which laird and tinkie man shared, the only thing
they had in common.

The Fraser sons were different. They would try and take on
the girls, but we were well prepared. One morning, while
giving a hand to make the beds at Kinglasser, a Captain Leslie
Melville put his arms round me and embraced me. I dug my
claws in his face and with all the force I could I tore for all I

was worth; his journey into flirtation land cost him the skin of his nose.

Fishing villages are so bad for nicknames. My father was known as Piper[29] – why I never knew. He was a grand fiddler, in the long weary hours at the whaling in the Arctic, he would play in the hours of off-duty; he was good at bagpipe music on the fiddle, so that may account for his byname. I was known as 'Piper's Kitta' when I was a wee lassie. As an only daur among seven brothers, I was always very well buckled, and, through jealousy, somebody said I looked like a fairy. The name stuck and they called me Fairy Kitta. I detest this, and would rap anybody who said it openly to me. One day I heard David Fraser, the Master's second brother, say to somebody, 'Ask Fairy Kitta to collect the laundry'. I went for him, I said: 'Look Slavie Davie, you are lucky I did not make your lugs dirl. When I worked in London effeminate footmen were called fairies.'

The next morning David Fraser was all toffed up to go out shooting, I had a pile of sheets in my hand. Hidden among them was a decanter of scent I took from Drysdale's dressing chest. I pretended to stumble and sent the whole contents over him, in front of all his brother officers. I said, 'Now you are Fairy Fraser.'

He stank the whole day, and they all ragged him. The name went back to his regiment! He married a beautiful Irish girl with a spicy temper. She could sort him. I liked her, she was straight and not put on.

Another brother Murray was in the Bengal regiment. I had seen him weigh me up in the past. He made excuses to come to the laundry with handkies and trifles, until Mrs Lunan said to him, 'I will give you a job as an assistant.' I would be nineteen on the 26th Feb. This was the previous August I met him on the Broch links late on Saturday night. I said, 'I am going home to Broadsea to see my parents.' He said, 'Can I come with you?' I replied, he would not be eaten, but would get a cup of tea. Going up the Fish Cross, I nearly fell through the ground when he asked me to marry him in two years' time. He said, 'I am going to see your father and ask his consent to become engaged.'

I was horrified. Not that I thought these people better than myself – save my Lord and Saviour I can see none better but plenty of people worse. My father said no consent to marriage would be given till I was twenty-one and outside his jurisdiction – but in any case I had no intention of getting married to Murray, for his life must be spent in India. His brother Jamie had told me of the terrible poverty, of the beggars with only sockets for eyes, and how the dead are placed like an effigy on a Hallowe'en bonfire, or given to the vultures to eat. We kept all our meetings secret and not one of the staff knew – only my parents, who were against it. My mother pointed out that by her and my father's connections and Murray's, our children would be eight times great-grandchildren from one couple, which was not too healthy.'[30] Murray said he had loved me for two years. He said he liked my way of thinking.

Murray had a large mouthful of flashing teeth, bigger looking than Blair's horse. They tended to make his mouth look too big. He did not have the small bun face of his father, but the thin good looks of his mother's folk, the Grants. He had a way of inclining his head in a half thoughtful smile. It gave him a most attractive face. He said, 'I am as hard up as you. I would have to start a fish round in Calcutta,' he said, 'an excellent idea; our children would end up millionaires.' He told me Lord Saltoun, his uncle, had paid for all his family's schooling, their commissions and uniforms. If Murray had stayed in Scotland, as a farmer, may be I might have married him, but his life was the Army and Empire. He tried to talk my parents into going out to India. He said, 'We will keep 72 Broadsea, the old Constable's house, for coming on furlough. It is a part of Philorth history, and without damaging the original to put another storey on top.'

I told him I had no intention of going to India, that I wanted to be buried beside my kin at Kirkton of Philorth, not thrown to the skurries like a plate of mouldy loaf. Mine was not an easy heart to win. In any case I would have been so unhappy in that artificial environment. When Lord Saltoun died slave Willie's family were upgraded to 'honourables', the worst thing a society woman can be saddled with; it is regarded as a kind of booby prize, and when they can get no higher they are nothing but a bunch of evil spitting cats left on the lower rung of the ladder.

Murray was a chaste and clean-minded young man. Tragically when on manoeuvres he and others drank infected water and he died from fever at the age of forty. When my two younger brothers were killed he sent my parents a beautiful letter.

The Master married Charlotte Evans, an Englishwoman, the best thing he ever did. One Saturday night in Dunkie's house she accepted Christ as her Lord and Saviour and never looked back. Murray pleaded to be engaged. His brother the Master and his wife were in favour of such a match, also his sister Margaret and his brother Jamie who married an Edinburgh girl, a child's nanny in India. The poor soul contracted consumption and died, leaving him with several young bairns; he married again, and the second wife ill-treated the bairns. Old Ness Madgie, Lady Saltoun, died, she was about 100.[31] I don't think they knew her real age, nobody was living who minded on her being born. She had a big public funeral. Two of my brothers helped carry her in the road, she was widow of the chief of clan Fraser. Three pipers stepped forward at Derby Ha' cottar houses and played her into the Broch.

After the funeral, along with old friends, my parents were invited by Saltoun to have a cup of tea in the Saltoun Inn. In the space of two years Macdowall died, then Murray's mother, and Lord Saltoun, who was a quick abrupt man, often openly nasty to the Master, but he had a nice side to his nature. He would listen to you and consider your point of view. Often I would sharpen my wits with him in heated argument. Though his mother was old she was there to keep on the fire. She had not been able to come north for the last year or two. After her death he was a lonely man, riddled with rheumatism. He liked walking to the Broch to keep him swack, and would come regularly to the Saturday night prayer meeting in Broadsea school. Afterwards he came down to our house for a bowl of gruel and tea. Because my parents were honourable poor fishers they did not consider themselves better than Lord Saltoun, but he knew they accepted him on their valuation of him. Respect cannot be bought – it must be earned, that is why they were friends so long. He was keen for me to marry his nephew. He always said, 'You have a mind of your own and you are an unusual thinker.' He said, 'If I had been forty years younger I might have asked you myself.'

I cannot understand why any young woman could ever marry an old man for money, I think the idea is so repulsive, what with their ruptures and prostate glands. I told Lord Saltoun I would look out a wife for him, but it must be on a commission standing on his total possessions. He said I was a Tolpudlian Tory. When he died the papers were full of his military glory; but none told the real story of this humble man who was a Lieutenant-General. For some reason he preferred to be known as Fraser of Philorth rather than Saltoun of Abernethie. In the Broch many would-be tripe tried hard to cultivate his acquaintance – bankers and lawyers and their snotty wives. He was so much of a man's man accustomed to living in tents and any kind of makeshift accommodation in the Army, he would not have noticed if their drawing-room was hung with blue silk or red velvet.

Anyway, who would have wanted to waste their time with such cheap snobs.

I had tolerated his sister Macdowall for years addressing me as 'Watt', my surname. When I was older the worm turned. I replied to her question, 'Yes, Macdowall.' Saltoun always called his staff by their christian names. I always referred to her as 'Macdowall' and all the others did the same. They might as well call you Fido or Whiskers. I think it the height of impudence and degradation to treat a human being as a dog or a cat. Bobby Wilson, who was aye at loggerheads with her, he had a south of Scotland accent and in a temper would say, 'If she narks me again I will ca her into the grun like a tacket.' From time to time I would meet her with relations in shops, and she was furious when I would say, 'That is a bonny day, Macdowall.' She said, 'Society rules cannot be changed to suit you.'

Neither could I be changed to suit society rules. That is why I rejected her nephew's offer of marriage. He was a sincere fellow, without the completely double façade men of his class have. To their own ladies they are polished gentlemen, to the maids like a spider enticing a fly. How many have fallen for this charm, only to find they are saddled with an illegitimate child to bring up! Half the folk in Aberdeenshire must be, and they are none the worse for this, for only the ignorant would put a stigma on any innocent child. I certainly have plenty such folk belonging to myself and all are decent respectable citizens.

Macdowall knew I would never take her seriously, I regarded her as a comic cutt. She interfered with the staff so much all threatened to leave. We had a powerful weapon in our hands for she could not have it both ways. She had a grand hard-working crew, very efficient, but no intelligent person will tolerate impudence for long. You may hold them down if they are illiterate, but in the middle of the shooting she knew she was sunk if the staff walked out. It had happened before: Saltoun took them all back when he came in October. Macdowall would say, 'You have been paid for your work.'

I replied, 'My father pays Lord Saltoun a guinea a year so you have it all back.' She would say, 'We look after you.' To which I replied, 'The road to the guillotine was paved with good intentions.' Her tongue added a bit of colour to a dull day!

We laughed and sang and I enjoyed my stay in spite of all the hard work. I had no ill feelings to anybody, in fact I had a kind of affection for Macdowall. She had an old-fashioned shape, her bust and belly seemed to be all one piece. She would ask me and another girl to fasten her stays. I would say 'I would call Miss Annie' (I always called the maids 'Miss', for she addressed them by their surname). I called the strapper 'the honourable Robert Wilson'. If she interfered I told her I had not been speaking to her. Annie Trail and I would tug at the busking of her stays, and then when you thought you were getting somewhere, and had her all tucked in, suddenly a huge pap would shoot out and hit you in the face! Who was going to work for nothing and put up with her impudence? Nobody with any guts would; it was criminal enough to underpay without reducing you to the level of a dog or a cat. The first time I had seen maids bow to their mistress was in London – I thought they were going to do a 'strip the willow'. The Duchess of Leeds was an American and did not ask us to bow. I would not have done so in any case; it is like bowing to graven images. Nowhere in north-east Scotland have I seen this; it is totally against the Buchan character to do such a thing. The Earl of Erroll tried to get folk at Cruden Bay to bow to him, but he was feeble minded. One wifie took his walking stick and gave him a hiding.

# CHAPTER FOUR

# Mormond Tam (1852)

Christian described vividly the agricultural revolution, which struck north-east Scotland, 'sudden like lightning', in the early decades of Victoria's reign. The reclamation of moss, moorland and bents[32] for productive agriculture was clearly beneficial, but more controversial in their effects were the means.

The cottars of Aberdeenshire had been independent small-holders, holding their land as tenants-at-will or feuars, with virtually complete security of tenure, and able to bequeath the same rights. It was essential, if the benefits of a new agricultural system were to be economically obtained, to make large hold-ings – the equivalent of the earlier enclosure of smallholdings and common land in England: and this involved buying out the tenants, and thereafter employing them as labourers. The farms prospered and more food was produced, but Christian was not alone in her bitter reflections upon the human cost, which she called 'the making of the big farms'.

The tenants of Philorth rented both farms and crofts – small holdings – right up to 1925 when the estate was sold, and the croft enabled the farm servant who saved to get his foot on the farming ladder. The most frequent problem of the crofter was insufficient capital, and the Philorth rule – a merciful rule by preventing tenants over-reaching themselves – was that to lease a croft a man must show capital amounting to £10 per acre. Christian, as often, over-simplified the issue and looked at it as a matter of oppression, of the unjust overturning of an old order.

But under the old order, the small-holder was, as often as not, heading for trouble through lack of capital funds, and something had to change.

When we came home the hairst time had come, when folk came round the fishing villages looking for shearers. I always enjoyed work in the harvest field. In my mother's day the girls used to go as far south as Glasgow and Edinburgh to big harvests but this had stopped some time ago. In the spring, when much tangle came ashore we burned it to make kelp to put on the land; it was wet mucky work and brought in very little return.

And then the whole world changed. It was not gradual but sudden like lightning. Whole gangs of men came in to reclaim the land. They ploughed bogs and stanks. Everywhere was the smell of burning whins. Suddenly huge big parks were marching up the side of Mormond hill, so greedy did they become for land. Around Cairnbulg and St Combs what had been large tracts of bents suddenly became farmland. You could make a good bit of money at drystane dyking if you had the skill, for all the parks were enclosed. New steadings and farmhouses were going up everywhere. In ten years they would put another storey on top of the new house, and in some cases they would abandon it altogether and build a huge rambling farmhouse beside it, while the cottar remained in the same hovel. The Greigs at Middlethird were my father's relations: they made their new house part of the steading and built a huge mansion. Bankie's, next door, took in half a dozen crofts. In the new order the cottar was hardest hit. Formerly he was a tenant at will with the same rights as a free man, for he could sell his little holding or leave it to his son. Now he was a slave, with a shilling or two to break the bond. Every Laird's place was covered in scaffolding. Brucklay Castle seemed to be for years; it was changed beyond all recognition. Every place was the same. What a lot of back-breaking labour went into clearing the land of stones. The very big ones they would make a fire round it and break it while still hot. After this prosperity farmers started to marry out of their own class and often took professional mens' daughters as wives who were not brought up in the country and did not know the land. They looked down on their employees and aped the gentry, they looked down on us as fishwives. We were no longer welcome and part of the family as before. But cottars and croft wives remained the same. Some farmers' wives were very nice, but a young prosperous farmer tended to marry for money. I often wonder what brought it all to a head, so that so radical a change could take place. A lot of money was coming in at the expense of the feedman and cottar, who were being paid with sweeties in return for their slave labour.

The Frasers of Lovat were descendants of Sir Simon Fraser, younger brother of Sir Alexander Fraser, the Chamberlain of Scotland and the grandfather of the first Fraser of Philorth. The brothers were killed in battle within a year of each other – Sir Alexander at Dupplin in 1332, Sir Simon, with two younger brothers, at Halidon Hill in 1333. Sir Simon's grandson, Hugh Fraser, was first Fraser of Lovat; and thus second cousin to Alexander Fraser, first of Philorth.

Thereafter, the family of Lovat had a very different history from that of Philorth. Having acquired by marriage considerable lands in Inverness-shire, their followers became a Highland clan on the old Gaelic pattern, a warrior tribe, pastoral rather than agricultural, patriarchal rather than feudal. Lovat – the fifth Fraser of Lovat was created Lord Lovat – was not only a substantial landowner in the fertile districts of the Moray and Beauly firths, but a powerful Highland chief, commanding a fighting strength of many broadswords, with numerous cadet branches, chieftains and lesser gentlemen of the Fraser name, and with the Gaelic patronymic 'MacShimi' – son of Simon.

But because the Frasers of Lovat had come from outside the ancient Highland system, with the habits and ancestry of the Norman–Scots nobility rather than the Celtic warriors of the West (as had many others, such as the Stewarts or the Grants), and because their principal seat was at Castle Dounie, near Beauly, and their most prosperous lands were near the port of Inverness and the more feudal and agricultural society of the north-east, they had a foot both within and beyond the mountains. They were familiars of Edinburgh and London as well as of their own glens. They married into the families of Wemyss, Leslie and Gordon, as well as among the mountain tribes of Campbell, Mackenzie and McLeod.

These were the people who were condemned by their Chief, Simon Fraser, 11th Lord Lovat, after the Jacobite Rising and Simon was the last peer to die by the axe on Tower Hill in 1747. His title was then attainted – removed – for high treason, and his own line failed in 1815 when his youngest son died.

Thereafter representation of the house of Lovat passed to a distant cousin, for though the great majority of branches of the name of Fraser sprang from Lovat rather than Philorth, they stemmed from very early Lovats. The Chief had no near relatives. Most Frasers were very remote cousins indeed, not only to Philorth but to Lovat as well.

Thomas Fraser, a younger son of the 4th Lord Lovat, married in about 1580 Isobel Forbes – confusingly, the widow of another Thomas Fraser, of Strichen, younger son of the 7th laird of Philorth. Isobel's first Thomas was murdered by Gordon of Gight in 1576 and her second Thomas acquired, with her, the lands of Strichen. The Frasers of Strichen, which lies beneath the hill of Mormond some seven miles inland from Fraserburgh, were, therefore, cadets of the family of Lovat. Like the Frasers of Philorth they married, predominantly, into Aberdeenshire families – Forbes, Irvine, Leslie. Though cadets of a Highland chief they lived for two centuries the lives of Aberdeenshire lairds. Alexander Fraser, 6th of Strichen, was a noted lawyer and Lord of Session – Lord Strichen – who entertained Dr Johnson and James Boswell on their famous journey to the Highlands.

Lord Strichen's great-grandson, Thomas Fraser, 9th of Strichen, showed his descent as the nearest Fraser relative to Lovat when the chief's line failed in 1815. He was fifth cousin, three times removed, to Archibald Fraser, the beheaded Jacobite's youngest son. He was created Baron Lovat, as a new peerage, in 1837: but in 1857 there was a reversal, in his favour, of the attainder of the original Scots title. He thus became 14th Lord Lovat: laird not only of the lands of Strichen but of the now restored, and extensive, Lovat estates in Inverness-shire, 'Mormond Tam'.

I was hairsting at Strichen House in 1852. It was a time of great hilarity. My team was a quinie Elspet Oliphant from the cottar town at Banks. She was bandster. Our shearers were George Grant the young forester, and a feed loon Peter Sinclair from Rashierieve. Peter was comical and made us all laugh by mimicking Miss King, the overseer's daughter, a sour spinster of thirty whom no man had asked to share his bed; she wore an artificial hair-piece. Peter said it looked like the stuffing of an old horsehair couch. King himself was furious at our laughter; he let out a volley of oaths at Elspet and the quinie was greeting, I flung down the winceyette apron and said, 'I am going over to Brucklay to get a job.' King said Elspet was not tying properly. I firmly told him she could tie with him any day. I threatened to leave. Miss King said, 'What did my dad say?' I told her, 'Your dad has muckle need to wash out his filthy mouth.' This was not the only brush I had with this impudent brute.

There was not a large staff at Strichen house, for Lord Lovat lived most of the time at Beauly. There was only Mrs Bremmer the housekeeper and a servant quine. For the duration of the hairst we lived in the loft above the stable block which in masonry was as grand as the nearby mansion. The girls were segregated here, all the men were in the steading further down mains road. We had to take our own bedding to put on top of a chaff sack. We were allowed no naked lights so we had to do with the failing light of day. They were a cheery band, all sorts – students, fishers, tinkies and anybody; we were paid the princely sum of 31s 2d a day; that was from first light to darkness, and we had brose three times a day. I was so fed up with the stuff, you had to take powder of jalap, eating so much meal. Spalding, the gardener's wife and Mrs Bremmer the housekeeper were sisters. Their aged mother lived in the gardener's house, but she used to have a croft at Peathill. (Annie Bremmer the housekeeper was in fact a Miss, Mrs was a courtesy title. All housekeepers were addressed as Mrs!)

I had gone to Strichen House with my mother on her fish-round since I could walk. We were very friendly with Mrs Bremmer whose nephew built the sawmill at Broadsea. Strichen was one of the most beautiful mansions in Scotland. Big houses and titles never impressed me, but from the point of history, as I grew older, it was interesting to see over these places. Fraser of Strichen, the laird, was known as Mormond Tam. He was very wealthy. It was one of the finest estates in Scotland. For long they had been leading in organised farming, and on a system of short leases they got crofting tenants to break in land from the heather and then they took it over.

Tam was very smart to offer all his tenant-at-will cottars what seemed a reasonable sum to vacate their holdings; they were the heritors of the rented land and now they became scab wage-earners in a tied house. Strichen House had a magnificent double staircase, fifteen feet wide. There were oil paintings of the Dukes of Argyll in full Highland regalia, lining the stair, and also all the Frasers of Strichen in red kilts; many of the old pictures were by Jamieson of Aberdeen. The house was enormous, and full of old and valuable stuff. Tam had been brought up a Catholic, and he married an English wifie, Jerningham, a daur of Baron Stafford, who constantly complained of the Buchan climate. At the height of the scorching summer she always wore two pairs of flannel drawers, and she was always known as Lady Cauldock. Tam came in from the side and claimed the Lovat title, as he was separated from it for over 300 years.[33] Most people thought the Frasers of Forrest nearest and liefeler to it, but they were working-folk in farms and crofts and unlikely to bother. Old Lady Saltoun's father, Simon Fraser, was nearer; he had made a vast fortune in the slave trade. His only son had been a blackguard and waster and left one of the Frasers of Forrest with a boy child, and she had gone with her son to Canada. Mormond Tam started calling himself Chief of Clan Fraser, it gave umbrage to Lord Saltoun, who in fact had he pressed the claim could probably have got the Lovat title also.[31]

Tam was a very ambitious man who habbered when he spoke. He had aye his eye on the chance to make money. The woods at Strichen were like an oasis in the desert. Lady Cauldock disliked the Buchan people who are so blunt and say what they think and mean what they say. None or few would be mealy-mouthed and buttery to her, so she preferred to live at the Lovat estate at Beauly which was a milder climate. They came to Strichen for the shooting, all the big wigs like the Duke of Norfolk and well-moneyed Catholics from France. In the harvest field we would see them come out about ten in the morning. The kitchie quine came to the park with the brose or broth or whatever, and sometimes with slices of cut loaf wrapped in old newspaper. These I would gather and read later; my shearer Peter Sinclair was literate and read them also. Papers were so dear the poor could not afford to buy them.

Peter said, 'In a year or two you and I could be married, my bachelor uncle who I am called after has plenty of silver and would put us into a croft.'

I said, 'Peter, I will be taken up for kidnapping', (he was a year younger than me), 'also if you have any sense you will wait until you have enough silver to set yourself up'.

He was really only joking, but it is stupid to marry young and have bairns strung round your neck like tinkies' pails and be bogged down for the rest of your life. For as hard as all the county folk work the crofter is the hardest; it is one slave and traughle from the marriage-bed to the grave. Peter came down to Broadsea to see us. He was a likeable boy. I never went with him as a lad, but I met his mother, a fine wife. Not many years later I met her in the Longate Peterhead, she embraced me warmly and I was shocked to learn not long after that Peter had been killed in a lumber camp in America. It was a moving thing to hear a whole park of reapers sing 'The Lord is my Shepherd' with everybody joining in, or maybe 'The old Rugged Cross' and all the old hymns. The melody and tune carried for miles in the hot sun. We were as brown as a berry by the time we finished hairsting, it was so healthy. There were eight Broadsea girls in the hayloft with me, and there must have been the best part of a hundred folk hairsting.

I would rather have starved than knuckle down to King the overseer, who was always out to impress the laird who he ran the home farm for. Hurriedly eating our brose, Peter and I face down read a newspaper; King shouted, 'You two slackers', (a thing nobody could ever accuse me of in my whole life). Passing he gave a flick of his riding crop, which stung my bare leg, I flew at him, attacking him like a ferocious wounded animal, I kicked his shins and with a resounding smack sent the fire flying from his face, first one side then the other. He fled in fear. A deafening cheer went up from the park in front of the gardener's house. Suddenly there appeared a polished young man in whipcord breeches and tweed coat. He said, 'Calm down and carry on with your work. I will talk to the overseer. When your day's work is over come to the house tonight after ten o'clock.' The others thought I was to be sacked.

After the light failed I washed my face at the horse trough and dressed myself in a clean pinafore. It was tiring after a seventeen-hour day at 31s 2d for all those hours. It was about twice what one got for skiffieing. The English butler from Beauly announced me in the drawing-room, well lit and gorgeously furnished. The young man was the Master of Lovat – darkish, with features reminding me of pictures I had seen of Ghengis Khan in a school book. He was alone, and beckoned me to sit on a gilded chair; his family called him Shemmy.

The maid brought tea and scones, and as we ate he fired me all sorts of questions, about my life, my family, my past employment, my home – and I added the scab pay that the poor earn for long hours!

He said, 'Are you not happy about it?' I replied, 'Would you be?'

He said it amazed him, how we could educate ourselves and preserve all the decencies in a but and ben. I said, 'That is a very specialised education you have never learned. If you suddenly lost all this how would you go about it?' (He said the thought had never crossed his mind.) 'Firstly we are taught above all things cleanliness which entails godliness, purity in one's life and thoughts, and the things that really count like how one treats one's fellow man.'

While I said these things he was silent. Then he said, 'You are far more interesting than any girl I have ever met, certainly you have a greater knowledge and superior education.' He asked me to meet him the following night after hairsting. We set tryst at the roadie behind the doctor's house in Mormond Village, leading up the hill towards the hunting lodge. The heather had that lovely dewy smell bathed in the light of a brilliant harvest moon. I said, 'Is not the creation of the world really so wonderful? Just fancy the mountains and all the billions of tons of water in the oceans hanging in space.' Shemmy was not interested in science.

As the lights of the village below flickered, we discussed everything from politics to religion. I am staunchly radical, labouring, and hotly defended my views. When we were children we would raid hen-houses during an election, and go to the hustings and batter the Tories, for, scarce as food was, we thought it was not wasted on these despots who kept the working class in bondage. I always found, in male aristocrats, their Eton and public-school education set their minds like treacle candy. Nothing but a good hammering can break it. I could never convince him the world is full of injustice. I can appreciate there can be no actual equality as such except under force, but there will be one day equality of opportunity, when the hereditary system is abolished, and when men become honest and just – a fairer distribution of wealth. Shemmy could never see a labourer being equally entitled to the same privileges as a peer; he actually believed they were ordained by God. He spent whole days wading in the Ugie, since he was a keen angler. He had not as strong a character as his father, he had none of Tam's ruthlessness. He did not think the hundred people in his harvest field were being exploited by being paid 31s 2d for a seventeen-hour day, while the oats and barley they reaped sold for a ransom on the Continent. He could never see the workers being entitled to a share of the profit. I asked his opinion on restoring the Government of Scotland. He was absolutely loyalist, and when he wrote to me from Beauly his address was always given as 'North Britain'. It infuriated me to hear people refer to Scotland as England.

For a fortnight our walks became nightly. He came to my home at Broadsea. My parents liked the young man, and he had a great deal of respect for them, but they did not approve of us becoming too close. My mother said, 'You are heading for disaster.' My parents said you must tolerate everybody's religion. We had many Catholic friends on upper Deeside. There was never the least animosity but they would willingly have helped you if they could; everybody is entitled to believe what they like. Shemmy was a Catholic. I had learned something of it in the Duchess of Leeds' service. She was a very good and generous Catholic woman. Out of curiousity I had gone to mass in London. It struck me as a religion that may lend itself to a warm Mediterranean climate, where it began, but not to cold northern climes. Cold and hunger sharpen one's desire for explanations; never under any circumstances would I have been converted to Catholicism. Shemmy came at Easter. He said, 'One day I shall have to take a wife. I shall speak to my parents.'

I was not clear as to what he meant. He had never asked me to marry him. He was leaving for London, but his parents wanted to see me at Strichen two days hence.

I had hardly ever seen Lovat. Long ago two mannies came to Strichen house to stay. They claimed to be Prince Charlie's grandsons; my Grannie Lascelles had met them. They came down the coast to look for all the old scraps of tartan. Since the poor cannot afford to throw anything away many had old patchwork quilts hidden after the tartan was banned by the Westminster government. The two men were interested in every scrap, and made copies of what they found. My mother or granny would never hear they were fakes. They said they were who they made themselves out to be, but not in the way they said it. Prince Charles Edward had taken ill at Elgin, and his kist and personal belongings had been sent to Pitsligo Castle for safe keeping. After the tragedy of Culloden, a niece of Lord Pitsligo's second wife had been given the task of conveying to the Continent the personal papers of the ill fated Prince; it was said she bore him a son. Anne Pirie, my uncle's wife, firmly maintained that this was true. She came from Peathill. Generations of the Piries were quietists, and very close to the Forbes family; all in the Pitsligo district in old age verified that the two brothers were genuine. Mormond Tam was kind to them.

I met the Lovats in their drawingroom, it was after their evening dinner, about 9 p.m. Lord Lovat said, 'I hear you have been keeping company with our son. It is causing a great deal of concern to his mother and I.' He spoke of the seriousness of marriage, and how it could not be entered upon lightly. Then Lady Lovat said, 'You know we are of the Roman Catholic faith.' She asked if I was old Kirk or Free Kirk. I replied, ' I am a Jew; all who believe in and worship Christ are Jews, for he was born and brought up a Jew, baptised a Jew, practised the rites of the Jewish faith, died and rose triumphantly from the grave a Jew, the one and only mediator between God and man.'

I told them I respect their beliefs in the same way as I would those of a Hindu or Muslim, but personally I did not believe the Virgin Mary had divine power any more than Mary Stuart or Mary Tudor. I also do not believe the Pope is infallible. Tam said, 'A good point, which more than demonstrates how unsuitable you are to each other.' (I believe Mary was chosen as a very pure source, though she came of the line of David the murderer who put a man to death in the front line of battle because he coveted his wife, a fact Christians seldom care to admit.) Lady Lovat went on, 'Our son has been very well brought up.' I pounced on her: 'So have I.'

Mormond Tam now spoke of his son's noble birth and background. I told him there is only one kind of birth, natural or ceasarean, and a pretty painful business it is. The tinkie wife on Strichen moss and Mrs Fraser in her fine bedroom went through the same process: twice I acted as necessary girl to Benffs Kitta the howdie wife and saw at first hand the agony women endure. He spoke of the trouble we were loading on both our families. Lady Cauldock kept glancing at me, then said, 'I hope you have not got yourself into trouble.'

'I am a virgin woman,' I replied, 'and your son tells me he is a virgin man and I believe him.' Tam said to think sensibly of what might only be a passing fancy. The best of all this, was that Shemmy had never asked me to marry or even actually suggested it. I do not know what he had said to them but obviously they were determined to end our friendship. Tam said one should think well from every angle, and it might end in marriage. I knew what he meant, but the wifie took him up wrong and in an unguarded moment of weakness, showed her true colours. 'Tam, how could you say such a thing, it is unthinkable for Simon to marry the fishwife's daughter.'

She was beautifully attired in cream silk; the heavy piping and large buttons of her gown were covered in a fine check Fraser tartan. I decided 'Now I shall let you have it, I will take the wind out of your sails.' I asked what she thought she was. He replied one must maintain standards, I told them they would be in a bonny mess if the poor disappeared overnight, and 'it will be a bad day for you when they decide to maintain standards'. He said, 'This is a democracy, with reasonable opportunity for all,' I said, 'That is the biggest load of dirt since the dung cart went round the Broch gathering the dry closets yesterday.' He was excited and started to habber: 'Please do not talk such vulgarity in presence of my wife.' I said, 'Your wife, she may dress and put on an act and travel to the Continent in season for the fact is she has never known what it is to have to work for it.'

He gave an awful glower. I said to him, 'You founded the village of New Leeds, hoping to rival the town of that name. What a piece of conceit! You had Capability Brown to lay out the beautiful park surrounding this house, but you did not get him to lay out New Leeds; some of the first inhabitants are living in shacks of divot and tattie boxes. You had dreams of huge spinning factories rising in Buchan, not, as you say, to give work to the poor, but to further your own wealth and interest; and you took good care that a mountain lies between your fine house and such ugliness. You despise, but you also fear the poor, and you have every reason to do so. This massive mansion was built at a cost of £70,000 from the fruits of a slave plantation belonging to your grandfather, Menzies of Culdares. Your fine art collection has come from the sweat of thousands of human beings, both in Buchan and Jamaica; and you have the nerve to look down on any fishwife's daughter. You may say we have reasonable opportunity, £70,000 for a house, discounting that one must eat, live and clothe oneself, you are paying us 31s 2d for a seventen-hour day. It would take between 16,000 and 17,000 years to cover the price of this house. You are making pretty sure we never get up alongside you. Sixteen millenniums indeed! I am doubtful if your dynasty will last sixty years, but a thousand years after this, if the Lord tarry, you will still be judged for your inhumanity.'

Lord Lovat was a man of set ideas, he thought privilege God-given and leadership entirely hereditary, belonging to the aristocracy; but foolishly he thought intellectual power natural to wealth and class. He had only to look to his own daughters, grown women who could not go out without a chaperone. They looked awful stupid, all that type of girls. They spoke awful trifling dirt for conversation, and in character as thin and artificial as the skin of walnut veneer they put on chests of drawers, and with heads as thick as the whitewood they were covering up. I told him all this: 'My class were directed to the hire house to earn our own living at eight years old, I have seen boys of that age clean lums in London.' I went on, 'How any of the wealthy whether they be Protestant or Catholic or anything else, have the sheer hard neck to enter any church and call themselves Christians! God will spew them out of his mouth.'

The maid brought tea but it was never touched. Lord Lovat was silent. He was so angry his stutter prevented him from speaking. Cauldock herself broke the silence, 'My son has a duty to his ancient name and heritage.' I told her, her 'ancient name' was but of fifteen years' standing and there was a lot of bridging to do in the 300-year gap. I said, 'I am also proud of my heritage,' when for centuries the fishers of Broadsea had fought to abolish the cruel teind duties, whereby the laird could claim a quarter of all fish landed and grain grown. They had lain down on the beach and let the sheriff officers ride over them. One lad was struck with an iron hoof and died later of meningitis. I said, 'Is that not something to be proud of, in an age when for very little you could be sentenced to death by hanging or burning?' Tam said, 'If people have no inclination to work you will never force them.' I said to him, 'As a small spark can ignite a huge conflagration the example of their courage will one day sweep the whole universe.'

The gilt clock on the mantlepiece struck eleven. I said to the wifie, 'As for you, madam, your heart is as cold as your backside is reputed to be.' Tam rang for the butler. He said, 'N-n-n-never has anybody sp-sp-sp-spoken to her ladyship in such a manner.' He said to the butler, 'Show Miss Watt to the door.' The butler was an Englishman from Beauly. I have never seen any locals in that or footmens' jobs: probably they lack the polish and would only poke fun at the clientele. The butler and maid had been listening to every word, and next day all I said bounced like a kickball, from Fraserburgh to New Deer.

It was a beautiful starry night with a touch of frost. As I gathered my plaid around me my head was as calm and clear as a bell. Under no circumstances were they prepared to listen to my opinion for I had no right to have one, but the sheer arrogance lay in the fact that you must accept your lot, and you must never notice the difference in their standard of living and yours. The Lovats had no truck with anybody on the estate. They were impersonal to all employees, even the factor and his uppish wife who thought they were the axle the whole up revolved on. If I had asked Lord Lovat a question about forestry or farming, I would have had the uttermost respect for his answer, for I appreciated he was an expert on these things, but he and his wife were asking me questions about the working classes and answering themselves; it was taking away one's natural integrity.

I came home at one in the morning, and made my parents a cup of tea. My mother said, 'I hope you were not impudent to the folk.' I said, 'If you insult people you ask for it.' My father said, 'That is the price of you, you should bide among cats of your own kind and your kittlings will be like you.'

My mother said, 'I can't go to Strichen house with fish again.' I said, it is a poor beggar who cannot pass one door; but Mrs Bremmer watched for her and told her to make no difference. So did Shemmy, the Master of Lovat. He was an honourable young man of the highest category. He wrote me saying he was not ready for marriage and that he would keep in touch and did not care who knew; he wrote, 'Kirsty, you would not look out of place in a ducal coronet.' I still saw him for the next two years, until he went out to be valet to his brother in the Crimean War.

Like most up-to-date lassies, I had also two strings to my bow. Murray Fraser of Philorth wrote me from India friendly informative letters. If Dame Fortune smiles in her benefactions on the favoured, she certainly must have a warped sense of humour, for here was two fellows interested in me. I did not really want either, while not one soul of my own class had asked the price of my hand. They probably thought me far too proud and haughty.

# CHAPTER FIVE

## A Voyage to America (1854–1857)

I had gone to Shetland and Lewis to cook at the greatline fishing. I liked the bit of life at Stornoway. The Shetland people had no love for the Scots, though it had been overrun by the Vikings. Before that King Brude of the Picts had sent St Ninian to christianise his domains beyond the Pentland Firth.

Then tragedy struck our lives. Early in the spring the emigrant ship *Powhattan* foundered off the coast of New Jersey. The crew and 250 passengers perished; not a soul was saved. My brothers, Sandy and Wattie were lost. My brother James died in August of the whiteblood in Australia. Then, in November, Jock and my little brother Billy were killed in the Black Sea. A screw steamer was sabotaged and blew up after hitting a reef with almost 100 aboard and half a million pounds worth of ammunition. They had joined the Navy at the outbreak of war,[35] thinking they were going off on some wonderful adventure. Sandy was twenty-nine, Billy eighteen. Only three of us now remained. 'They had been lovely and beautiful in their lives' – nothing can describe the sore heart. The bottom of our world fell out.

Tragedy comes to all eventually. Now it was our turn.

I saw my parents wither and grow old overnight. My mother was about thirty-four when she married, my father thirty-six, much too old to have so large a family. They had been married two years and thought they would not have any, then started with twins.

It is amazing how kind folk are. Sympathy came from the most unexpected places. How short is man's life, and brings home how much nicer we should be to each other. Life had to carry on in spite of two vacant beds in the but end. It stood for a whole year untouched. I could not bring myself to go in and move anything. Then one day I put on the fire and laid away all the books and personal things. My brothers' clothes I took to the mission in Aberdeen, for I did not want my mother to see them again. I put their brass flutes in a box and put them in the loft. All my brothers had played in the Broadsea flute band which led the walk on New Year's day: this was an ancient tribal custom in north-east Scotland – when the temperance started up they battened onto the older custom, but nobody can mind how old it is. The Broadsea folk walked to Pitullie and Rosehearty, and Rosehearty came over to Bredsie.

I have always found a great healing of the mind in the harvest field. As the war progressed, girls took on men's jobs. We cast the peats, saved the grain and set the tatties and holed them, determined for victory. A woman would be seen driving the plough while her man was at the front with the Gordon Highlanders. A very high number of Buchan loons were in the thin red line at Balaclava. But there is no glory in war. Lord Aberdeen got the blame but he was not the guilty party, but his cabinet which agitated for it. Half a million lives were laid down for nothing. I have always been bitter towards warmongers.

My two remaining brothers were abroad, so I had to carry the whole burden of a sad and broken world. I did not think I would ever smile again. My father never spoke of his sons, even years after, but it brought a lump to his throat.

There was a drive to increase the food supply, Jenkins the curer wanted girls to go to the south of Ireland to gut. We went by coach to Perth and Stirling, and climbed up the brae to the castle, to see it, then to Glasgow. What a terrible place!

It was worse than London docks with naked bow-legged bairns apparently starving, in some of the most awful places. The Church of Scotland appeal for funds to send missionaries to darkest Africa: they should send them to Glasgow, for charity begins at home. We took ship to the Isle of Man, a pleasant isle with very nice folk, then to Waterford and a little place called Dunmor East. I liked the Irish. They were very friendly towards us, but very poor folk, with a much poorer standard of living than the Hebrides of Scotland. We stayed in a housie with an old wifie, Mrs Ryan. Her home was on the same plan as the west of Scotland houses with the byre in one end. She was a kindly old person and a devout Catholic. I felt the good of the trip: it helped me to take an interest in life again. When you have had a multiple tragedy in your life sometimes you wonder what you are rising for in the morning. The lovely air of Ireland with its traditional forty shades of green was as a healing balm to my reasoning.

Of my brothers Wattie had left a young widow and two infant sons in New York, James a young widow and infant son in Melbourne; Sandy, the elder twin, left a will with a bank in Aberdeen, leaving all his possessions to me. With his marine insurance it came to nearly £300, a fortune to us. Fully two years passed and not a penny came our way: it was deposited in a banking house in New York. I was prepared to let it go, for I felt it was tainted, but the banker in Aberdeen said that is a foolish attitude. He told me the only way was to go out to America and never let on I was going, and collect what belonged to me, or it would disappear into somebody's pocket. In 1856, after the terrible war ended, Captain Peter Noble, my cousin (his father Captain Alex Noble, Fraserburgh harbourmaster, and his mother, Janet Carle, a Cairnbulg woman, lived at 25 Broadsea. The harbourmaster was the eldest son of my Aunt Annie Watt, 22 Broadsea).

Peter offered me a run to New York. He commanded the sailing ship *Albatross* of Liverpool which I joined at Cardiff.

I enjoyed going from London to Wales and the Welsh language. Peter Noble was five years older than me. He had asked me to marry him which meant living in Liverpool, a dreadful place with almost as much poverty as Glasgow. Both my parents would have liked me to marry Peter. My father was his uncle. But what put me off was, out of the eight sisters and brothers only he and his sister Jessie could speak: all the others were deaf mutes. Jessie was a Mrs Clare. She was married to a London druggist and had a beautiful home called Fraserburgh House in North Woolwich. I had stayed there two nights prior to going over to Wales to sail. I would never have hurt Peter's feelings by saying it was not a nice thought to bring a family of deaf and dumb children into the world, for there is a history of dumbness. It has not appeared often, but exists among the Watts, and we both came from them. Peter's family were all very clever deaf mutes. His father died in 1862, and much later his mother and sisters built the house at 91 Charlotte Street and sold 25 Broadsea to Dookie. Peter was a Christian young man who never smoked or drank. I never went with him as a boyfriend, but I liked him as a person. He was tall, fair and of handsome countenance, but one has to be honest – we are what our ancestors dictated we would be; nothing can change us, no person can say a Persian cat should become a Collie dog; we are what God made us and provided us with sources to live accordingly if we do His will.

We sailed in fine weather, but what a voyage! It was like an eternity. There were twenty-two passengers. I made a pal of a lassie from Liverpool, a mariner's daughter. Anne Everett was her name, and she had relations in New York. We helped the galley-boy make the tea and wash up, but we were quite fed up of salt beef and fish for weeks. Water was greatly stinted. On that watery waste one is aware that man will never beat nature, as we tossed and heaved and lay in our bunks listening to the rats scraping – what they lived on was a puzzle for you never saw them. Our hearts were uplifted as the coast of Canada hove into sight.

I loved Nova Scotia, docking at St Johns in Newfoundland, then Cape Breton. I felt very homesick, for everybody was talking the Gaelic. I spoke to two boys born in Canada. They were shodding horse and spoke Gaelic fluently, I asked if there were any Skye folk near at hand, and met a Donald Macdonald from Sleat. In his heart he spoke for all the evicted. Their one desire was eventually to return home and avenge the wrongs and cruelty inflicted on them, but I thought sadly it will never happen in our time, for Scotland is now one vast playground for the wealthy.

I could have stayed with the Highlander but we carried on to New York. I was impressed with the delta of the Hudson River, but not with the city itself, it was so frighteningly bustling with life. Captain Noble would collect me again in eight months. I went to a hire house in New York to get a domestic job to earn my living. My sister-in-law rented a small farmhouse at Manhattan. She was very good to me for two weeks till I settled in. She privately taught bairns who where slow on the uptake and made a good living to support her two boys.

My reference and friendly letters from the Duchess of Leeds were accepted. The Duchess herself, both daughter and widow of American millionaires before marriage to the Duke, was well known in New York. I got a job as a tablemaid with a Mrs Jerome[36] who had a beautiful mansion near the Eyrie waterway at Palmyra. She had two charming sons. Her sister was married to her husband's brother over in Brooklyn. Often we would go over on the ferryboat on loan to wait at huge dinner parties, where we met the Vanderbilts and many other well-known folk who gave us generous tips. Both houses had huge staffs, French, Scots and free Negroes. They treated us with the greatest of respect and paid us well. I had a dollar a day, four times the pay at home.

Both New York and Brooklyn were fascinating, with all the street cars and wonderful stores. I made friends with Mary Goldie, a housemaid from Ayr. We haked everywhere together. Sailors from the ships along the front would whistle and wheep at us going past, but we paid no heed. We would go to the druggist's, where you could get a cup of tea, or buy roasted sausages at the end of the boardwalk out by Potters field at Madison Avenue. Mary would say, 'Look, that fellow keeps winking at us.' I said, 'Poor chiel must have something wrong with his ee.'

Mr Jerome was a heavy built jovial man. He got my legacy for me in a week. He went to Wall Street every day.

I met many home folk, Ritchies from Rosehearty, Duthies from Inverallochie, and Shands from New Pitsligo; we were more Scottish than we had been at home. I had a weekend off and went to the Gordon gathering at Barre Vermont, what a sight – every accent was Aberdeenshire! I would have loved to stay, but intended to keep my promise to return. My parents needed me and I felt I owed them that duty.

In London I had met Negroes when out shopping one day for the Duchess. I passed the charity school at Charing Cross: a few little black faces cowered in a corner, I went into the yard and hounded a bully who threatened to hit them – and then thought what a pity we are not all one colour, but 'All souls are mine saith the Lord'. In America I had come face to face with reality, and the bitterness that burns in coloured folks' hearts towards those who brought them there; the African chiefs who sold their own people for gold are as guilty as the purchasers. As a subjugated Scot I could sympathise, for a handful of greedy blockhead peers should never have had the power to vote to sell an independent-minded nation for English gold.[37] Underneath I had the intelligence to see the situation was really serious. A black footman told me, 'One day we will rise and overpower the white man completely.' I said, 'I and millions of others have done you no wrong. Surely there is enough room in the world for every-body to live at peace with each other.'

We were living under the same roof in perfect harmony. We had the same pay and conditions and our employers were extremely kind and considerate to us. This was the first time the race question was brought home to me. Years later, when the American Civil War came, my sister-in-law sent me all the papers, and what awful things went on, of murder and rioting, looting and burning of houses. It must have been terrible to live through, but then I thought, 'That was only the start. One day the whole world will run with blood.'

The Jeromes were good employers, and as my eight months were going in I felt unhappy at the thought of leaving. My parents' letters were always longing for me back. My mother was going to the country with her creel; what a different scene from New York, and what a pity my two little nephews were not nearer, for it would have done my parents a lot of good to have known their grandchildren. My mother had knitted fairisle jumpers for them and tammies to match. I could have imagined my mother on Broadrow with all the theatre shows and dancing girls; she would have thought it all so sinful, but I considered it a privilege to see New York and to be so lucky in my employers. I loved my two little nephews and would have been prepared to work my fingers to the bone to bring them up. I could have made that my life's work. Their mother married again but had no family, to a nice fellow, who was good to the boys. I gave twenty-five pounds to each nephew, and also my nephew in Australia whose mother also married again, rather putting us out of touch. Here were thousands of folks of every creed and race with one common factor and aim – poverty had brought them. Anybody with eyes could see the rising of a great democratic nation, that will one day be as a lamp to the western world. It is true that many worked for poor wages, and conditions in some places were bad, but you could scout about to find something better. There was a kind of snobbery based on money, but it degraded nobody as in class-ridden Great Britain.

With a heavy heart my stay was drawing to a close. We got a week's holiday – something I had never heard of before. I went to Boston to meet my sister-in-law's parents, very kind, gentle folk. It was very English in appearance, but I loved every moment. I toyed with the idea of talking my parents into coming out, but they were too old and sad, so I kept my promise and sailed for home on the *Albatross*, back to scab wages and the awful grind. My mother was quite ill and I was glad to be back to look after her. We docked at Liverpool; then I shipped to Glasgow and then by road.

Christian left a little of her heart in America. Clearly, the sense of freedom and opportunity she found there inspired her, as thousands of other Scots had been inspired. At the worst crisis of her life some twenty years later she tried to seek health and renewal in the New World – and when she failed it was not the least of her disasters: the end of a dream.

I promised my parents I would stay only eight months in America, which I did. With the legacy I intended to start a dressmaker's business in Aberdeen, for there I could refuse tick, while fishing villages are notorious for defaulters who will never pay anybody – not by any means all, but certain families are black-listed from one generation to the next, and they craftily swick folk from anything from groceries to fishing gear, so that it was 'out' to start at home. My Aunt Annie Watt went to her grave being owed hundreds of pounds for dressmaking; to be a good ticker one must have a mealy mouth and a sad story. We had been brought up to pay cash or do without, for if you cannot get something you covet you have lost nothing . . . I made all my own clothes and watched the papers for the fashions.

My mother would not accept a penny of my brother's

money. It made me feel a kind of guilt to use it myself, so I never touched it. The presents I brought from the USA I bought with my own earnings, I had changed my dollars to sterling and now was a comparatively well-off woman.

There was a certain sadness and emptiness about our house which had always been so full of noise and laughter. I slept in the butt; the closet bed and narrow spare bed in the trance were made up but never used. It was strange to set the table for only my parents and myself, but one has to keep going though the sky has fallen about your lugs.

A fisher's life, male or female, consists of being always on the move, one is hardly ever at home. For the last time I went to Bayble in the Isle of Lewis to cook at the greatline fishing in the winter of 1857. I was about twenty-five. With my companions we had walked for miles to see the druids' circle of standing stones at Callernish. It had an eerie feeling about the place. How they quarried or moved such large rocks will always be a mystery.

The Lewis islanders are very 'free Kirk'. Matheson, the laird, had been very generous to them during the tattie famine; but then, like the laird of Macleod at Dunvegan, if you and your forebears have taken a quarter of all the grain grown for centuries, you owe the people a bit more than something! But most lairds didn't look on it that way and were always on the lookout for more. I like the Lewis folk and have always got on with them, long before the droves of Highland girls came to gut the herring.

It was good to be back home. There was something about 72 that spoke to me. I am as much a part of it as the rumble stones of its clay walls. I often wondered what former occupants had thought within these walls; if they had been happy thoughts they clung to the stones and passed them on to me. There has been a great deal of sadness there, but I am sure there must have been a lot of happiness also. Human beings are as leaves on a tree, flourishing in beauty, then lying on the ground, and with the sunshine of a new spring comes a fresh lot equally as beautiful as those that have gone before. There were many old antiquities in 72 which several people coveted. Unfortunately human antiques lose value quickest! Every winter my mother was killed with bronchial trouble, and it seemed to be getting worse. Fisherwomen of her generation had been born to a terrible life of drudgery, with their skirts kilted above the knees they waded into the sea summer and winter with their men on their backs to ensure the man would go to sea dry. Between that and the rigours of the winters in the country, it filled their bodies with illness.

After Charlotte Evans became Lady Saltoun she raised a minneer about folk going through Philorth Wood from the Aberdeen to the Cairnbulg road. They never used the avenue but the roadie through the trees which had been a right of way since no man knows when. Lady Charlotte got the wrong side of the Broch folk by this. There is no law of trespassing in Scotland, and the bold ones never heeded her but just carried on as before. I went to work at Philorth.

Charlotte Evans, the new Lady Saltoun, was a nice person. She told me all her little worries and secrets. She said, 'These Fraserburgh and Broadsea folk frighten me.'

I told her not to go to old folk with a few cold tatties and a spoonful of mince in a bowl, for they would feel nothing but ingratitude. It only showed up so sharply the contrast between her standard of living and theirs. I have seen her deliver such a dish, and before her gig was out of earshot the old recipient would feed it to their neighbour's dog or cat; a bag of sweeties would have been more appreciated. She called on Annie Catheid at 75 Broadsea, a wifie over 80 who wore a white mutch and her face and hands were yirded as black as the back of the lum. Knowing Annie as well as I did it was not surprising when she said to Lady Saltoun, 'Put your arse on a stool your leddyship.' Lady Charlotte was a 'born again' Christian and was absolutely sincere in all her doings. I had ceased writing to her brother-in-law, Murray Fraser, also the Master of Lovat, whose parents disapproved of our association. Had I wanted him I would have gone a different way about it, with his parents never coming into the picture until after we were married. I did not want to marry, for I had enjoyed my freedom, but fate had something else in store for me.

# CHAPTER SIX

## *Christian Marries (1858–1861)*

Both my parents constantly urged me to marry. I was tall and good looking, for many told me so. I dreaded being landed with a fisherman for (I will tell no lies) I hated the chave from morning to beyond night, and I dreaded marriage like the plague, but unfortunately I fell head over heels in love, and knew it was the right one whenever I set eyes on him, so all my own plans for the future came to nought.

Since my brothers' deaths I had not set foot on a dance-floor, neither had I looked at any man, apart from Murray Fraser who had been several years in India. We wrote only as friends. He had asked to marry, but the Master of Lovat never did. The other person who asked me was Peter Noble, who was now recently married to a charming English lass. He brought her over to see us. His deaf and dumb sisters were grand needlewomen, their granny Annie Watt had taught them dressmaking and embroidery. My parents insisted I go to the Broadsea walk on New Year's Day of 1858. They did not want me to sit like a wallflower at home, but to mix with young folk.

Passing through Pitullie my eyes met those of a handsome tall young man standing at the gable of a house. He joined the walk, and as we proceeded towards Rosehearty he asked me, 'What, is a pretty girl like you walking alone?', for it was the custom for lads and lassies to go arm-in-arm. He asked if he could take my arm. I said, 'Please don't, as I don't really know you.' He was two years older than me and had gone to Woodman's school at the same time, also to the Congregational Kirk, but I had never spoken to him. He asked if he could come back to Broadsea that night, for he had arranged to have his New Year's dinner with his own folk.

My mother liked the young man: my father did not. I knew this was the person destined for me, and was not surprised when he asked me to marry, which against my better judgement I consented to do. He was James Sim – called 'Jimmy Brave' for a tee name, and a name he mortally hated. At the age of eighteen, in a raging sea off the west coast of Scotland, he had swam in terrible conditions and attached a running line to a Norwegian ship which was foundering. All the crew were saved; the shipping company presented him with a beautiful gold watch which he never wore. His father had been Peter Sim (Breeme). He had died suddenly of abdominal pain. His mother was Janet Sim, or 'Jinna Carlie', of the Gibb Sims of Pitullie; she was lucky and unusual in having had only two bairns while everybody else had ten. He lived at 13 Pitullie with his mother and sister, Jean. She doted on her son, and later I was to learn she had somewhat spoilt him.

He was a chiel of high principles and intelligent and read a lot. In a special enlistment for the duration of the war[38] he had joined the Royal Navy, and would have stayed in but there was absolutely no hope of getting from the lower to the upper deck so he came out when the war was ended, having served at the Crimea. We had so much in common.

I entered into a marriage contract at the end of January. It was a bond of handfast, drawn up by the lawyer. Within a year and a day we could produce evidence of a forthcoming child; or failing, by mutual consent, we could end the contract with no liability. If we married and I died the following week, my legacy, and (under my granny's will) both 35 and 72 Broadsea became the absolute property of my mother and father jointly. If my husband died, 13 Pitullie, which was his, also his grandparents' house, 50 Pitullie, became the property of his mother; without such a contract, in the event of a death, the property passed to the remaining spouse. My father insisted on it, for he had a business streak of his deceased mother, old Siccary. I felt perfectly happy and my mother was glad for me.

In April my mother was quite ill with chest trouble. She had been sheeling and baiting to my father who was at the small lines. She was admitted to Aberdeen Royal Infirmary. My father went through to stay with the Nobles at 4 South Square, Footdee; they were distant relations. I was alone in the house and thought many thoughts as I poked the fire to kindle the peats into a blaze, as generations before me had done the same. The white reek went up the lum where the steam of a million broth pots had gone before it. I thought how short is man's life. Should I bother to marry? I had been to Aberdeen, my mother was getting on fine and would soon be home. I had the house shining for her return. My mother was aye fond of nice things and had a lot of bonnie linen and bedding and bonnie china which she told me, if I married, to take the lot with me apart from my own bottom drawer providing.

It was a Saturday night, the boats did not go out the next day, I had no fish to split and smoke. James Sim came over to see me. It turned out a terrible night of wind and rain. I suggested he stay and sleep in the closet, but eventually he ended up in my bed in the butt end. Rain was lashing on the window. He was six foot three in his stocking soles. My brothers had been as tall and when they grew up the butt box bed had been extended, which made the wardrobe at the end shorter. Life had given me its last and final hidden secret, a moment poets have all written about. I was under contract, but still felt a sense of guilt having taken advantage of my parents' absence. The rain ceased to pelt down. At four in the morning I told him to draw the back window and leave that way. I had left the ben lamp still burning and I intended leaving it till daylight came in; the reason was for prying eyes across the road. Our neighbour, Annie Gatt, in 71 (she was Onty's second wife and a born clake, gossip to her was like sun and water to a flower) – from the darkness of her butt window I noticed a shaft of light from the other end and her face on the glass. She had seen my lad arrive but did not see him go. My parents were away, the light was still on, so she would have the teem errand of sitting up all night seeing nothing! I laughed to myself.

Two weeks later James Sim left for the whaling at Greenland. He had pleaded to be married right away, but I wanted more time to think. When I went to hack mussels from our scaup west of Mawcraig, the lovely ozone on my face awakened desires in me as the fresh sea breeze quickened my nostrils. I was once again heaving and tossing on the Atlantic, and I could feel the wind filling the topsails and I knew part of my heart would always be in America. My sweetheart had been there at the sailing but had no love for it. The cold grey German Ocean did not hold the same romance. Lying in my bed when the rummel root was singing in the auld butt lum, I could hear the roar of the Atlantic in my ears, but now my consideration was for the child that was with me. I had let the father away and should there be delay with ice at the Arctic, my child would be born illegitimate in January, which meant I would have to go before that bunch of hypocrites, the Kirk Session. If so I would very quickly clean all their dirty neuks. During the conflict between Episcopalians and Presbyterians several times my ancestors had wrecked the church; now I would wreck the session. I would ask to appear in the body of the kirk, not the vestry, and I would start on one elder, a Fraserburgh business man who had in the past been known to frequent bawdy houses in Aberdeen. In fact I toyed with the idea of turning down the father and keeping the child; today I wish I had made that decision.

It was characteristic of Christian to look with not unpleasant anticipation at confronting the Kirk session. Since the Reformation the Kirk had had a very authoritative oversight of both public and private morals, and the power to make and to enforce regulations governing behaviour. The Kirk session was an instrument of discipline, as well as a means of local government and charitable relief.

But Christian was not greatly exaggerating when she said that 'several times my ancestors had wrecked the Church'. The people of Fraserburgh, led by Fraser of Philorth, their Superior, had greatly welcomed the restoration of Charles II and the consequent reestablishment of the Episcopal Church in 1660 – and the end for a while of what had been a thoroughly unpopular Presbyterianism. The subsequent change back to Presbyterianism after the accession of William of Orange caused anger in Fraserburgh and took time to become accepted by the Episcopalian majority. Opposition was often violent. A presbyterian minister only got possession of the Parish Church of Fraserburgh in 1707, displacing a popular Episcopalian seventeen years after the Episcopal Church was disestablished. The Presbytery Minutes at Deer (the Presbytery then responsible for Fraserburgh) referred to how the new Minister, Farquhar, and an escorting laird, Forbes of Boyndlie '. . . suffered a most fierce rabble by throwing of stones and other indignities that were done to them – that they got open the church doors, and Mr Farquhar did pray in the pulpit, and declared the church vacant, but was forced out again and could not get opportunity to preach.'

When Farquhar tried to preach the congregation rushed the pulpit and threw him out of it. In the following year a new Presbyterian minister, named Auchinleck, was appointed to Fraserburgh and duly arrived. The presbytery ministers again reported a disorderly reception: 'The Master of Saltoun being in the Town Counsell House with the Magistrates and several other inhabitants about the tyme that the Ministers came into the town the said day, sent a letter subscribed by many hands to the said brethren . . . showing that they desired the Presbytery not to settle Mr Auchinleck among them because he was not acceptable to them . . .'

And when they went to the church 'they were assaulted on the high street with a rabble of people who threw stones and dirt or mire upon them, pursuing them into the church with the same weapons, so that they were forced to retire to a corner under a loft.'

Then, 'The Master and Magistrates turning impatient for an answer to their letter . . . came into the church with a great rable at their back, and the said Master [of Saltoun] being in a passion called furiously for an answer in write . . . that if he got not a satisfactory answer in write he would not undertake to keep off the rable, but let them loose on the Presbyterie . . .'[39]

According to Christian's grandmother, her own grand-mother, Anne Noble, led the Broadsea women:[40] and it is likely that she had many ancestors or connections among the 'Magis-trates and several other inhabitants' with the Master of Saltoun on this deplorable occasion! Her robust reference to her ances-tors wrecking the church, which was undoubtedly passed down as one of those 'tales of long ago' which Granny Lascelles recounted to her, was tradition based on established fact. The Broadsea folk had, anyway, a reputation for being thorns in the flesh of the Kirk session.

Christian's accounts of the herring fishing industry are central to her story. Much of her life was spent dependent upon it. It would be easy, but inaccurate, to get the impression from this and subsequent chapters that the fish curers were a new tier in the historic chain between the primary producer – the fisherman – and the customer. In fact, the fish-curing business expanded throughout the eighteenth century, encouraged by government in the form of a bounty per barrel of gutted and cured herring.

But the industry had periods of recession, and at such times, the fisherfolk, having least to fall back on, were hardest hit. One such came in the 1830s about the time of Christian's birth, and must have greatly affected the impressions of her early childhood. The abolition of slavery in the British West Indian possessions in 1833 greatly reduced the market, for herring had been the major part of the slaves' diet. Another period of recession was now – in the 1850s. Catches in 1857 were unusually small and prices correspondingly high. In 1858, the year of Christian's engagement to work for the fish-curer, Bruce, there was a general complaint that prices had been increased by the previous year's shortage, that the fishermen were continuing to receive a high price for the catch, and that a heavy catch was depressing the market price and thus attacking the profit margins of the curer. The curers had a bad year, and Christian's strictures on the greed of her employers should be set against the fact that times were difficult – and that the company of Bruce, for which she worked, was still the only fish-curing firm, out of about thirty, to be in business fifty years later. They were big people, with over sixty boats fishing for them alone. Christian referred to them as 'the new system of fishing by engagement to a curer whereby he bought his entire catches at his price' – but it had, of course, to be an agreed price, and it produced a certain stability. Furthermore, the fishermen often did better than the curers by the bargain, a fact hard to guess from Christian's partisanship.

I took arles from Bruce. He was now a big curer. Some Cairnbulg quine had the first Bruce. The family were very greedy masters; huge gutting stations were going up at the links and Bruce had built on Commerce Street. Sometimes the crans of herring were so overpowering the farlands would not hold it all, so were tipped on a sail in the yard and we would go down on our knees and gut them. The Bruces were so mean they would not have parted with a bawbee extra. It was very hard work, especially if you were expecting, but the fishing wore to a close. I had a lot of barrels for my fishing. We were paid a penny halfpenny for every barrel. A crew of three gutted and packed.

During the weeks of waiting, I read nothing but my Bible, and to my own joy and astonishment I found the Lord Jesus as my own personal saviour. Only in my own personal experience did I discover how man was alienated from God, and how we were reconciled by his death on Calvary's cross. In my own room that night I knew I had passed from death unto life. 'Oh joyous hour when God to me a vision gave of Calvary, my bonds were loosed my soul unbound, I sang upon redemption ground.'

My duty lay in carrying out my betrothal contract, for whatever happened nothing could separate me from the love of Christ, whose very purity can see through the false, swicks, liars and cheats. His very majesty can make the greedy, envious and covetous hang their heads in shame.

Once again tragedy came to our family. The *Albatross* of Liverpool was lost with all hands on a voyage to Singapore. My cousin, Captain Peter Noble and his 20-year-old English bride of only a few months both perished. My Aunt Annie Watt had also another grandson on the ship, young Watt Taylor, a son of her daur Jean and Neister's Wulla. I was sorry for old Annie: she had seen most of her family away before her. Our next-door-neighbour, Robert Taylor (Bouff's Sanny's son at 73 Broadsea) had written a letter to his mother saying he had met a flitting of rats coming off the ship at their departure. Also there was Alex Noble, from Leith, a young cadet. His father was mother's first cousin, and had gone from 76 Broadsea to Leith. His nephew became surgeon-in-chief to the king of Siam. My first cousin Harold Watt was also lost. He had married the only daur of a Chinese merchant. I have seen pictures of his family, and they have all oriental faces. Harold was a son of my uncle Wulla and Anne Pirie 7 Broadsea. They had been off their course in a hurricane.

Much wreckage and many lifebelts came ashore on the coast of Borneo. So at my marriage I was having no fuss of any kind, but in spite of this sad bereavement all Anne Pirie's family jointly contributed half a crown each and gave me a beautiful dinner-set for twelve folk. They all knew I had plenty of small stuff. I had the full of the butt of bonnie things.

My sweetheart returned from the whaling the last week of November and we were married in the middle of the floor in the ben at 72 on 2nd December, 1858. We stayed in the butt until my son was born in January. I wanted to call him after my brother, but my father said, 'Please don't', as it would only start my mother off again after she had been so well. My husband said to my father, 'Is it all right to call him after you?' – so James it was.

My husband's Aunty Betty in 23 Pittullie had gone to Leith for six months. She gave us one end of her house to mend nets in her absence, just after we married. When I think of all the hard work that was put in for nothing!

We set up house at 50 Pitullie. It had been my husband's paternal grandparent's home: the other end was occupied by his spinster aunt, Jean Breenie, I liked her very much, she had life-rent of the house and had given us the big end until we could get a place. I did not want to live with my parents or my good-mother,[41] for it is best to start on your own. Jean Breenie kept a little shoppie in the butt: sometimes I would serve in it and got to know the Pitullie folk quite quickly – they were a friendly lot. I was very happy. I was really no stranger because my father had both a brother and sister married in 17 and 27 Pitullie. Both produced a crop of doctors and professional folk. They had all the pride and big mindedness of the Watts.

As a child, every fine Sunday, my father would walk with me and my two youngest brothers over to Pitullie. Sandhaven was nothing at all, Bremner of Wick built the harbour, I can mind on it starting. Before that there was only the Pittendrum Meal Mill, and a good distance west was a short wooden pier called the port of Pittendrum. It was so old it was rotting and falling down. Behind the pier was a stone-built corn store occupied by orra gangrel folk, who called it 'the Puzzles'. In the past from here the old Cumine lairds had shipped their grain to the Continent. There was nothing else but a stone well in the corner of a park. You had to climb up the steep brae to Pitullie; the road meandered along the edge of the sea from Broadsea to Rosehearty.

The very first thing I did was to order a new fishing boat so my husband was self-employed. I wanted to call it 'The Watts', but I knew it would not go down well with my parents. It came from America and I called it the 'Ocean Foam'. I wanted a house of my own, but could not afford both it and a boat, so I would have to wait and work hard to put a house on the stocks. I would have liked to live in Broadsea, not because I belonged there but for its nearness to Fraserburgh harbour. My husband insisted on Pitullie; he eventually saw his mistake when it was much too late. I would have even gone to live in the town of Fraserburgh.

My mother-in-law was cold and distant. Try as hard as I may I did not get through to her. On New Year's walk day, I gave a grand dinner. My good mother and my own parents, Aunty Jean and her son and daughter and their spouses, and my sister-in-law Jean Sim all came and enjoyed themselves. They admired all my bonnie dishes and cutlery. I heard my mother-in-law whisper to her daughter, 'She surely thinks she is still working at Philorth house.' I hid my hurt and never let on. Also my Aunt Betty and her daur Annie were at my Hogmanay dinner. I had borrowed a long table from Pitullie schoolie.

My son James had his will crossed from the first hour of his life. My husband had been in the Navy and was a strict disciplinarian. He had seen public floggings and tolerated no disobedience. I found he expected me to do the things his mother had aye done for him, and when he presented me with boots to polish, he was aye particular of their appearance. I said, 'I will brush them through the week but you are going to do all the Sunday shoes on Saturday night.' He did not like it, but I was starting as I intended to end.

The running of the house was solely my domain. He gave me every penny he earned. We paid his mother's taxes and ground rent, also the same for my parents. I would not have got a bag of tatties for my mother without giving one to my good-mother. For some reason she never liked me, possibly because I had taken her breadwinner. My father never really liked my man, who had argued about our marriage settlement. He thought he had married me for my money. We had the room at 50 Pitullie only until we got somewhere else. Rooms were so scarce we could find nowhere. I felt awful at putting Auntie Jean out of her way. It was a short housie and the two box beds were both together with no closet.

I told my mother I thought I was in a certain way again. She told me to speak low as my father did not know about such things. I thought it mighty funny to father eight children and not know! My son Peter was born just a month before we left No. 50. He was called after his grandfather.

My children brought a new lease of life to my parents. My mother was aye knitting for them, and James was the apple of their eye. She allowed him to play with all the polished brass stuff around the fireside, something no other child had got to do. In Scots law the second son is usually the mother's heir, assuming the first is the father's heir. When Peter arrived my mother said, 'I am glad I have seen my heir.' My father made a little wooden paling to go round the fireplace to keep James away from boiling kettles when we came in to see them. I told my husband how worried I was about hampering his aunt in her home. He said, 'The house is mine anyway.' I replied, 'Not till her decease; it belongs to her at the moment.' As it happened she lived nearly 20 years beyond him.

His sister was under contract of betrothal to William Pirie from Portknockie. He was at the sailing and she was expecting. I ran in my bedgown, with my plaid thrown over me, all the way to Rosehearty for the howdie wife. I hauled the wifie out of bed. They married two days after a lassie, Jeannie Pirie, was born to my sister-in-law at 13 Pitullie. (Peter was born two months later). Pirie was a nice, sensible chap and she got a good man.

My husband announced we were to move in with his mother once his sister and brother-in-law had gone back to Portknockie.

I was not happy about our forthcoming shift. My mother-in-law gave us the larger ben bed, which was better for sheeling and baiting. The earth floor had always to be sanded, and sprinkled with dry quicklime for the smell of bait. I had a little sheddie built and did the lines in it. I smoked my fish in a barrel. My man wanted to build a proper half-house with what remained of my brother's money. It was the worst site in Pitullie. No. 13 stuck further out onto the road than any other house in the village. It was shortsome, in as far as the front window looked right ben the street, but now very noisy, as the mail coach to Rosehearty (now become a busy herring port), and cartloads of herring barrels from the Broch going past dirled all the things on the chumley-piece. I saw in the future, as Rosehearty grew, they would demolish this house to widen the road. I argued it was nonsense to put money out on it. My husband could not see my point of view.

His mother was an impossible person. I never once raised my voice to her; I will admit I often ignored her when she would start with her nasty ways. What misery I knew in that house and never told a soul! To start with I offered her a cup of tea – she was always 'just finished'. Nothing I did was right. I washed and varnished the breasting in the trance. I heard her say to her sister, old Mullart's wife in No. 14 at the back of us, 'You would think the place belonged to her.' A tinkie wifie I knew came to the door. I gave her tea and was in fact glad to speak to the wifie. I was not setting off time wantonly. The wifie came again next week; my mother-in-law was not pleased. I said folk who came in peace 'I can't take by the shoulders and push out' – yet my mother-in-law convinced herself she was a devout Christian. How many more of her kind abound in this world! Then you could have got an old hoosie for twenty or thirty pounds. I would not have cared how tumbledown or orra, if it was my own, but nothing at all came on the market. Often I felt like packing up and going home. I don't know what the cold attitude was all about.

Old Jean Breenie was a nice person. Once she said, 'I know by your een you have been crying.' I confided my troubles. She told me my mother-in-law had caused trouble among them ever since she married Peter Breenie. She told me not to say a word to anybody for it would only bounce back on me, but to take my bairns for a walk along the Rosehearty road and to tell my troubles to the wind and I would never hear them repeated. She said, 'A few years over your head and the boys will be at school and you will have much more to interest you.'

Sometimes I played the fiddle to amuse the bairns. The noise annoyed Jinna in the butt-hoose. Both my husband and his sister would not have crossed her for anything. She ordered their lives, but was not going to order mine.

For a big part of the year there was a lot of swell in the sea at Pitullie and the boats could not get out. It was a done thing for fishermen to take a day's work in the country. They were paid 41s 2d a day. The last time I worked in Philorth wages had risen to 1s 3d a week. Half a million had to die in the Crimea to get this rise. All over the country employers were shouting it was scandalous that workers should want a 25 per cent rise in their wages.

There was not the same supply of fish at Pitullie as at the

Broch. I could not go into the Broch and buy extra and cart them on my back to Pitullie to split and smoke, so naturally our standard of living fell. With two bairns I could not go far into the country. In 1855 my cousin, Mary Watt, married our neighbour, Johnnie Crawford, in 69 Broadsea. I was glad she was next door to my parents, for they were very friendly. Mary was like something of a daughter to my mother. She had never been a strong lassie; she was the youngest of Anne Pirie's family. After my older bairns were at school, I would take the little ones in to Mary at Broadsea and leave them for the day to let me get to the country for food. I had asked my good-mother if she would look after them but she made some excuse; on a second excuse I never asked her again.

Working folk all mended their own shoes and made most of their own clothing. We wanted to teach ours independence, but a new set of rules applied. We had never had any need for wiles or underhand business in my youth. Now curers employed casters who very cunningly had small spikes attached to a kind of signet ring. They would jostle their hands through a herring sample and many torn bellies appeared; hence the curer got the entire catch for almost nothing, for a torn belly is a spent herring. Life had changed for the worse, for the new system of fishing by engagement to a curer, whereby he bought his entire catches at his price, led to a lack of confidence and loss of trust. Naturally he wanted the herring as cheap as possible. The farmwife to fishwife goodwill had also gone, but there were still many fine folk in the country at poorer places. Big farms now aped the gentry in every way. Some had very grand houses. Real aristocracy grew so grand it was unbelievable. They competed in houses, and appointing. We were still on speaking terms with the older ones, but lairds' bairns no longer wanted to know working folk. One of the daughters from Boyndlie House was an Anglican nun. She did a lot during the fishing time, dressing poisoned fingers and distributing old clothes to poor bairns in the Broch. She dedicated herself as a young lassie; several times she had tea in our house.

In studying the scriptures I could clearly see this was the thing which preceded the time of the coming of the sorrows, when the Empire was at its greatest glory, but woe betide the poor cooper and labourer bairns. Also, the worst tragedy of all, the bairns of the unemployed had to go through the hard winter hungry and barefooted. Fortunately the soup kitchen gave them a bowl of soup at least once a day.

# CHAPTER SEVEN

## *Return to Broadsea (1860–1869)*

I had seen my mother on the Sunday. She had a dry cough and herse voice: two days later my cousin Mary came over to Pitullie to tell me my mother was quite ill with bronchitis. It was just before Christmas, and she had been to Philorth wood and got a lot of evergreens to decorate her house, on my bairns' behalf. She had them beautifully garlanded round the chumbley piece, holly and laurels. I went in every day. The doctor, Alex Grieve, told me to push the dresser further up the wall in the ben and put my mother in the narrow trance bed set up by the gable window in the neuk. I set an old kettle on the bink containing menthol oil. In the stroop I put a bairn's pea-shooter which sent the soothing steam into the room. What a cruel thing is acute chronic bronchitis! My mother's breathing became of a wheezing sound and quickly worsened.

The following Sunday my husband had gone to the kirk, (we slept the weekend in the butt). I was making ready the dinner. My mother said, 'We shall take the sacrament', and pointed to a text hanging on the lum, 'Where two or three are gathered together in my name there am I in the midst.' The minister's wife had given her a bottle of port wine for invalids. She said, 'Kirsty will drink first of the wine', my father second and her last. She had washed her hands in a basin, and broke a portion of bread, giving each a bit, and said, 'The Lord's body broken for you.' Then she said, ' I will take in the New Year in the Glory.'

Christmas[42] passed and a severe and continual cough took over. I had now to come in to look after her with the two bairns. She kept asking to see them and I was afraid of infection in so young children. I believe in fresh air and had the window up a little through the day. On the morning of the 30th December a shaft of sunlight came in the front window, lighting up the room. I noticed a strange blueness round my mother's lips. She kept asking the time. Then she said, 'Give me your hand.' As I held hers she said, 'Jesus, my only refuge, Jesus who died for me, safe in the rock of ages ever my trust will be.'

She asked the time again, at ten past ten. She spoke to my father, something about my brothers, then passed away at twenty-five minutes to eleven that morning. I took down the evergreens and tied them in a bunch with a tie-on label, 'With love to Granny from Peter and James'.

Before my mother died on the Friday night I worked into the Saturday morning to finish a pair of socks she was knitting. It was so close to the New Year, and it was not considered lucky to have anything unfinished in the house if New Year comes in. Nothing must be on the weens after Hogmanay night.

It was a sad Hogmanay for us. At midnight we heard the kirk bells ring in the New Year of 1861. My mother was lying on the table, her plaid neatly folded, as was the custom, and laid across the foot of her box. Folk sat all night with the dead. Often they were robbed, and this custom, I think, arose from that. Several of my aunts took turns to watch vigil. My father was in the closet, Jimmy Brave and me and the bairns, in the butt. Through the night my father was fumbling about in the dark. I thought, 'Whatever is he doing?' He had preened a little sock of James and Peter to the mantelpiece, and unknown to me had gone to the Broch and bought a sugar piggie and an apple and orange and some little gifts to put in the socks. He said my mother wanted it.

Mary Duthie's Jimmy came to me and asked if they would put back the walk to the 3rd January till after the funeral. I said 'No' – so much work had gone into arranging it, so let it be as usual on New Year's Day. I thanked him for his kind respect. Their drums were muted as they went past.

We had our silent New Year's dinner, only the three of us and two bairns. As is the custom of putting funeral cards in shop windows, I sent one up to Strichen so folk would know that my mother would never return there. She was buried on 2nd January, in the grave with her father, Andrew Noble, and mother, Helen Lascelles, in the second row immediately in front of the door of the old kirk of Philorth in Kirkton Kirkyard. A fine dusting of snow lay on the road, at the end of the funeral procession. Several farm folk came down on horseback. Among them were Lord Saltoun and the Master, a boy of about 10; they spent Christmas in London but came to Philorth for Hogmanay. Dingwall Fordyce from Brucklay also came down: my mother had gone there for over sixty years. She was seventy-two. As they led their mounts by the bridle the horses' hoofs had a hard metallic ring on the icy road. It was a bright winter day, and as I watched the funeral go up the brae I noticed a group of tinkies in the walking cortège. They had come from Strichen moss. My husband took them back for a bowl of hot soup – no greater tribute could they have paid my mother.

The house at 72 was now my own but I wanted my father to have the life-rent of it. Shortly after my mother died my good-mother said, 'Your father can't come here, because the way I am placed folk will speak.' I said, 'What is not true is not true, and what is God knows.' My father cried when I told him he could not visit me. Then Providence opened up the way. There was a three-storey house next the Ark Inn in Sandhaven: nice folk had it, and a tenant was moving out. I would have taken it for ourselves but the landlady didn't want bairns. I asked if she would let the house to my father.

When she saw his beautifully clean home she let the end next the Ark on the ground floor. He was there for seven years, and got on well. I put a tenant in the butt end at 72, and we mended our nets and kept them in the ben. My father would come and go as he liked.

I signed over 35 to my Auntie Betty; my husband was not too happy about it. It was an old rickle so much in need of repair. So often some sleekit sneakie member of a family had come in and ousted a single member of a family and taken their housie over their head, I wanted my cousin to have a home when her mother was done with it. My tenant, Andrew Noble, an uncle of Macauley the Canadian millionaire, went to live at 53 Broadsea, so my Auntie Betty asked if she could occupy 72, which was far superior to 35. I let them – it's the worst thing I ever did.

My father was happy in Sandhaven, for I could look after him. I felt that I had to remain in his debt for he worked so hard to help us on our feet. Living was so much harder than at the Broch for there was so little fish to spare; Broadsea folk scored, being so near a buyer's and seller's market. I thought, when I lost my mother, that I could make a friend of my good-mother. If there were faults on my side it lay with my independence of nature, for I had been brought up to be beholden to nobody. It may have been a vice or virtue on my part. I was to find out. I went to Strichen once a week, and had my dinner as usual in the cellar of Mormond Inn by the brig. My good-mother was furious when she knew, and went on about 'frequenting a public house'. I have never been in such a place. I went in the kitchen door of a hostelry where I could wash my face and tidy myself at my leisure and on cold winter days I sat down at a lovely peat fire.

Lord Lovat had sold the estate to the Bairds of Gartsherrie. They were good customers and fine folk. They had made their money in scrap iron. They used Strichen chiefly as a shooting lodge and in the season I sold a lot of fish. Lovat had parted with the best estate. Strichen estate was roughly seven square miles of the best land in Scotland. I wrote to Dingwall Fordyce and several MPs that it would be a good thing if the government would set up a fund where working folk could borrow money to buy or build houses, and if it was not paid in one generation it could carry on to the next; now over-crowding was in a terrible state. They all gave the same answer – 'They had noted my suggestion'. That is all right if you are living in a 30-room mansion with as many staff!

My husband had an Aunt Betty at 23 Pitullie, the last house at the far end face on to the street. It had been his mother's parents' house, Betty was not married. There lived with her a nephew, Sanny Gibb, and his wife, Jessie Lobban, a very fine woman who always made me welcome; her mother was Maggie Taylor, Benff's Kitta's twin sister. My own Aunt Mag in 17 Pitullie was very ambitious; she was always so pointed and formal. She was married to a man called Trail. Their sons were shipmasters, and the young one a doctor of medicine. No. 17 had been raised with the whole height of another storey and was very grand inside. However you train very young children they will persist in touching things when you least expect it. For that reason I did not go often to my aunt's – she was nice enough, but I am sensitive to atmospheres and I know when folk are genuinely warm and when they are cold. The Trail sons who did not go abroad built mansions in Victoria Street in the Broch. My Watt cousins in Pitullie were the same kind of folk, but I hope folk didn't think me the same. How I prayed that somewhere would turn up. I asked the Lord to go before me and make the crooked places straight.

I do not know how I endured No. 13 for nearly seven years. In the little garden next the park I had the centre full of tatties and honeysuckle, roses, columbines and other beauti-ful cuttings I brought from the country; my mother had a little yardie at Broadsea which she loved looking after. On my 'country day' my good-mother gave my man his dinner when he came home from the sea. He would sit in her end for hours and I was pleased, for it put her in a good cut.

The time came where I told her where to get off.

I had just about as much as I could thole, and we became something like casual acquaintances. She was spotless clean and a good baker and knitter. I admired her and gave her credit for this, but she never failed to get a mean dig at me. One thing I have learned in this world, 60 per cent of folk who call themselves Christians are fakes, especially round north-east Scotland and the Moray Firth seaboard. Their Christianity is a form of Godliness and respectability, but it is absolutely necessary it be applied to prosperity! Poor Christians are not the thing, for who wants to be seen with folk with barefoot bairns. I have beheld the saints on a Sunday night forming little groups in parting at their kirk doors, with that 'holier-than-thou' kind of tone of voice. They are either discussing herring or harvests or houses, but not the Lord Jesus who had not a place to lay his head. My mother-in-law was a typical example. She thought that heaven might be as far as Finechtie. Man cannot envisage the height or breadth of God's domain. We do not know, but there may be seven suns, ten million light years away from the Earth, and one day man may go there, God willing, for the power of the Almighty goes beyond the highest heaven and transcends the lowest hell. The same power that lifted Christ from the grave can send the planets hurtling through space. How many go into the highways and byways to help the poor? I always did give a tenth of my week's takings, by giving some widow with bairns a half dozen eggs or maybe an old widower living alone a quarter of tasty butter. I found it paid me dividends in the future, yet I have never let my right hand know what my left is doing. Many of my cousins were prosperous Christians, but I find when working men climb the paling into another class they do not knock down the paling to let their friends through but build it higher to keep them out. For that reason I did not see them often.

I took the bull by the horns. From time to time the Congregational minister came to have tea with my good-mother. I always knew when he was coming, for a lovely baking of gingerbread and fine pieces would take place that morning. I went right into the middle of their tea party and told all I had gone through. Jinna was dumbstruck, his Reverence flummoxed. Then she let out the truth. She told him she had advised her son not to have anything to do with me, I was grossly mismatched, I did not share his interests: but her chief objection was that a history of insanity and consumption was in my family, and that our marriage could never be a success.

She had certainly done her best to achieve that aim, but I felt so much better at having it out. I told my Auntie Betty. She said I should have given her a rap on the jaws. I do not know why I did not, only matchless grace kept my hands off her. I knew who would win if I declared open war. Being humiliated before the minister had a devastating effect and for a long time I got a kind of peace which gave me fresh courage to try hard and find a house or rooms for ourselves. I asked myself – 'Was there something wrong with me?' All my life I had got on well with folk, especially my fellow workers in a team. I had travelled the world and had enjoyed it, I did not particularly socialise with complete strangers and I hated clake and sma' talk, speaking nonsense. My home was neat and tidy, for it had to be, in so small a space. I was very well groomed. I had a temper under pressure, but by the grace of God I could control it. I tried to be completely honest with myself. My good mother would never warm up to me through her possessive hold on her children, and my husband thought I exaggerated the thing a million times worse than it was, but only those who experience something similar know just what it is. I realised I had gone into a bond of handfast in an undecided state of mind. I felt the loss of my brothers, that may have helped it on, but I loved my husband and children and wanted so much to make a success of marriage. Now my mother was gone I really had no genuine friend but my cousin Mary Watt, one I could tell my tale to, so I had to be thankful I had her. Of insanity and consumption, I always thought my Granny Gunner a bit mad; she was often high but not insane. Her folk, the Gordons of Kinellar, had a spinster daur who lived at Philorth, who in her old age was liable to set things on fire (my Auntie Betty told me this). Of all my granny's offspring of thirty-seven grandchildren, five were tainted with mental illness; unfortunately I had to be one of the five, a very small per centage. I do believe many of William Lascelles' children died of consumption, for it is a very smitting disease, but nobody near to me had died of it in my lifetime.

I took my troubles to the Throne of Grace to be resolved. There were two years between my son Peter and George and three years between George and Joseph, so that long space gave us a breather to save a bit of cash towards the house. My father helped me all he could and put in an awful effort. He would split my fish and smoke them in my absence; he broke all the firewood and went in a ripper boat at Sandhaven; he mended all our nets and in the season redd a line for us or sheeled a bucket of mussels. He would bring all my errands from the Broch and he was a great help. At the back of my mind I always had a fear his landlady would want her room, so the quicker I got a house the better. I would have liked to build in Pitullie but no stances were available. It took years for Clinton to get permission to develop the front of the wall green, as it was communal owned land. I would have been happy to go there but it was years after it was opened up.

Charles Trefusis, 20th Lord Clinton, owned land in Buchan by right of his wife, Williamina Forbes. She was descended from the only sister of the 4th Lord Forbes of Pitsligo, the noted

Jacobite. Pitsligo and Pitullie castles, both ruins for many years, stood next to each other on the Buchan coast, west of Fraserburgh, just as Cairnbulg and Inverallochy castles were built within sight of each other to the east – sentinels of the shore against the sea raiders who once harried Buchan. Pitsligo had been taken into the family of Forbes by the marriage in 1423 of Sir William Forbes with Agnes Fraser, daughter of Sir William Fraser, 2nd of Philorth.

Lady Clinton's ancestress, sister of the last – and attainted Pitsligo, married John Forbes, younger of Monymusk – and, subsequently, Lord Forbes. Lord Clinton added the surname 'Forbes' to his own after marriage and succession.

There were a lot of fine folk in Pitullie. The estate factor was a hard customer who thought himself infallible though in fact only a glorified message boy. He said we must go over to Sandhaven and build, as this port would eventually rival the Broch in fishing. I pleaded with my man to go to the Broch. Stances were still available in North Street. My Auntie Kirsty owned No. 13. It was a bonnie Street and near the Broch harbour. At the back of my mind I intended some day to return to 72 and take my place in history.

At Queen Victoria's Silver Jubilee[43] there was a big bonfire on the Broch links. We took the bairns in that night, besides a big parade with Neptune sitting on a cart of herring barrels, and many other novelties. I approached Lord Clinton himself and he was very nice, but no stance was available in the village of Pitullie. The factor poked his nose into our conversation. Clinton turned to him and said, 'Have you arranged, as I told you, a coach for her ladyship?' the glorified message boy!

Then a terrible epidemic of cholera[44] broke out – not as bad as the previous one, but still many died. Pitullie school was closed and turned into a hospital. I took all the care necessary, and we took spells to nurse the dying in the

schoolie. What a sight! Folk were screaming with pain, some
were writhing in agony. Three nights Annie Tam and me sat
up all night. It was our turn to help; how glad I was to see it
over, my mother-in-law's brother, Sandy Gibb, and his wife,
both died at 3 Pitullie. Their boxes were taken out at the ben
window and the service was said in the street. I made the tea
in my house after the funeral, for we were not encouraged to
enter the infected house. I have never been afraid of illness. I
boiled all the dishes and tableclothes and everything that had
come into contact with the mourners. I had baked the bread
for the occasion. That time everybody baked with a large clay
flowerpot upside down. You built tiers of plates inside,
separated with equal sizes of pebbles between them. Round
the flowerpot you built a peat fire. It fired the cakes beautifully and was done outside. We were thankful to see the end
of the cholera. All the wifies of the place set to and scrubbed
the school from head to foot and the bairns took over again.

I had four boys, George, my third son, was a dull child. His
father and I spent a lot of time teaching him to read and spell,
but he was a poor scholar. We finally, with my father's
efforts, managed to get the first site at the corner of the west
shore at Sandhaven. Clinton would only give us a tenant-at-
will; I wanted a proper lease and better still a perpetual feu,
but he would not hear of it. Also I wanted a single-storey butt
and ben of my own, but my husband would not hear of this.
His sister Jean and her husband, William Pirie, wanted to
come down from Portknockie; her mother Jinna would not
let her alone; half the time she was in Pitullie anyway. So a
two-storeyed house went up, costing £120 paid on the nail. I
wanted the whole ground floor to take in my father, but my
husband said no, the way his mother was placed it would not
look bonny. I argued, and he threatened to go over to him
and explain why he could not live with us. I knew if he did it
would break my father's heart. Most of it was my brother's
money, and my father should have got the good of it. Besides,

*Christian Watt with her mother, Helen Noble,
and her cousin Mary Watt*

*Christian Watt in her old age. 'For my 90th birthday I had my portrait painted.'*

*Outside a Broadsea house in Christian Watt's time*

*Main Street, Broadsea, in the nineteenth century*

*Fraserburgh harbour in the days of sail*

The Foreshore

'We were paid a penny half-penny for every barrel, a crew of three gutted and packed'

*At the harbour*

*Philorth as Christian first knew it — 'I am doubtful if they will capture the happy ghosts that flit about that place'*

*Alexander Fraser, 16th Lord Saltoun, 'The Waterloo Saltoun'*

*Alexander Fraser, 17th Lord Saltoun, 'Big Zander'*

*Charlotte Evans, Lady Saltoun*

*Marjory Fraser, widow of 15th Lord Saltoun, 'Ness Madgie'*

*The Hon. David Fraser, 'Slavie Davie'*

he had helped us so much in raking together the last of the cash. Then women foolishly believed they must obey their husbands. I tried to explain in as kindly a way as possible. Fortunately for the last four years he was easily forgetful of present issues but had a good memory for the past.

The Piries were first into the house, three months before us. They had two rooms on the ground floor and we had two on the other side of the lobby. It had a lovely big garden, which I liked. There was a young Portessie couple up the stair, and also a man called Ross and his wife. He was gardener at Pitsligo Manse.

Jean Sim and William Pirie were very fine to live with. She was not in the least like her mother.

I felt like the Israelites in crossing the Red Sea away from Jinna, who was not long in being hot on our heels. I had only been in a week when I had twins – a boy and girl I could well have done without. I wanted the girl called Janet, after my mother-in-law, to please her. Instead she would not hear of it, and said to her son, 'Don't under any circumstances call that child after me.' She was called after Mrs Ross up the stair, a good person; and the boy was called after the minister her man worked for, so the twins were Isabella Ross and Andrew Donald.

My father was now failing. He was 81, and at that age he qualified for the parochial relief of 10d a week. Everybody who turned 80 thought nothing of taking it. He said, 'I have paid my taxes all my life. It is my own.' It was scandalous he did not get a penny for his two boys who died in the war. Britain is such a mean parsimonious nation to the lower classes, yet they pay huge pensions to descendants of the Duke of Wellington and folk like that. My father liked going into the Broch to collect his tenpence. I saw he had plenty of wholesome food, and I gave Ross the gardener a stick of bogey roll every week. On Saturday night he would give my father a bath and change his shift, so he was aye spotless clean. There is nothing to recommend living to old age, for when you are young you think ilka happy day will be followed by another one like it, but when you are auld ye are glad of any little kindness. My two elder boys, James and Peter, were very fond of their didy and did all they could to help him. When he was still going out in the yawl, and did well at the ripper, he gave both boys a Gordon kilt with complete Highland regalia; their photo was taken in them.

We had only been seven months in our new house. My father had gone in to the Broch that day. It was February, and cold and icy. I told him not to go.

At suppertime I sent Peter over with a fried yellow haddock for his tea. He came back, saying, 'Didy is not there, his fire is black out and cold.' Nobody had seen him. I went straight to Broadsea, and he was lying in his bed, trembling badly. He had had a nasty fall on the ice. The doctor said no bones were broken but he was badly shocked. Mrs Ross looked after the other children, I took the bairns with me and sat up two nights with my cousin Mary. My father was quite conscious and said, 'This is the last of me, how thankful I am you are with me.' I told him not to talk like that, but he went on, 'I am on my journey steadfastly, trusting in Christ the hope of Glory.' That was at quarter to nine on the morning of 10th February. He passed peacefully away at 10 o'clock. He was buried on 13th February 1868. My two brothers were abroad so my two sons James and Peter walked behind the bearers as chief mourners. I watched the funeral go up the brae and knew I had lost a good, kind friend. I had done my duty and had no regrets at all, save that I had wanted my father to share my home at the end of his days. So old 'Piper' was laid in the dust beside my mother in Kirkton Kirkyard.

He had a large funeral as all the fishermen were at home, and, 'The place which ye knew shall know ye no more.'

My father's death is registered on 11th February 1868. It has always been in my mind he died on 10th February, yet he was buried on the 13th, and it has aye been customary for the dead to lie at least four days. I remember my cousin, Mary Watt, put on his fire and went to the Broch for the doctor when he fell on the ice. The next morning I mind on her saying to him, 'You will soon be up sheeling your mussels.' He replied to Mary, 'Lassie, my mussels are a' sheeled.'

My cousin, Johnnie Noble, who folk call 'Babbie Fyte's Jake' registered the death. I'm sure he must have given the wrong date. Because my father had tenpence a week, 'Pauper' was put on the lines. I told the registrar, 'That is the meanest thing you can do to the poor, especially a man who gave two sons for Queen and country.'

My Auntie Betty laid claim to the house, and a legal haggle went on for two years after my father's death.

The same night as my father's funeral I remember – when Jimmy, me and the two boys walked back to Sandhaven. A full moon was in the sky and sleet stung our faces. He said to me, 'I am never going to Broadsea to live, so you can put that out of your head.'

My daughter Nellie was born at Sandhaven in 1869. I was furious to learn my Auntie Betty had sold 35 to Sandy McNab for £7. It was hers to do what she liked. I had given it to her; how I wish our Sandhaven house had been built on that good site. Sandy McNab made a fine house of it. The court said I was unquestionably the owner of 72, and the lineal representative of the constables of Broadsea who descended from the ancient earls of Forgan in Fife.

My Auntie Betty and her daur went to 35 Manse Street in the Broch. She put all kinds of curses on me. but became ill and sent for me, I forgave her and she lived a few years. She was kept like a queen by her daughter, who had never had a lad in her life. She gave everybody a surprise. Within three months of her mother's death she married a fine man, and at the age of 41 had a son who turned out to be a charming young man and one of my favourite relations. They had been nine years in 72. I paid half the taxes and all of the ground-rent for all that time. It does not pay to oblige folk; I had a huge bill for legal fees which need never have been. All this had been a strain on my nervous system. My husband had gone to Barra to the great lines. I flitted myself, the boys loaded with what they could carry, past the Glenbuchty distillery, then the Mill burn and the darkies' graves where the crew of the *Bonaventure* are buried, and Joseph Mather's croft, and Cauld Wallie and home. In no time the but-and-ben lums were reeking and I was happy. My husband was furious, but we had seven years of happiness and great sadness. All things work together for good for them that love God.

The Sandhaven house was sold to William Pirie for £65. He put down £25 and the balance of £40 was paid over seven years. It was on the agreement that my husband's sister would look well after their mother in her old age should she be spared to do so. The £25 was eaten in legal fees. I had left Broadsea comparatively wealthy, but I returned with not a penny, for better or for worse.

# CHAPTER EIGHT

# A Time of Sorrows (1871–1878)

Christian did not leave an account of exactly how matters were settled with her husband – beyond saying that he was furious at her 'flitting'; but thereafter she had returned, with her family, to her ancestral home. It was there that the last three of her ten children were born.

My son Watt was born in 1871 and Mary in 1874. She was called after my cousin Mary next door.

There was something good about cousin Mary. She had been so kind to her old mother, Anne Pirie, and so often had little to do it with. Her man, Johnnie Crawford, had died two years before my father and she was left with a young family. When my father was mending nets at 72 she would put one of the quinies in with tea and scones for him. Annie Laurie, the eldest, was a nice lassie. Like everybody else she had to go to service at the age of ten. Poor Mary was badly let down. She had a laddie in her widowhood, but I was prepared to stand by her to the uttermost, which sadly was not for long.

My man was very hard on the boys. He gave them some awful hidings for hardly anything. He so much wanted to force his will and to bring them up in the fear of the Lord. A lot of unnecessary suffering has been caused in the name of religion throughout the whole world. I said to my man, 'Christ never drives folk, he leads. You are doing the boys no good by thrashing them so much.' I have seen Peter flee into Mary's next door on a Sunday morning, and dive into the butt bed, down between her two daughters who were considerably older. His father would not hit him without hitting them. My husband's intentions were good, but he had no bending in his nature; absolutely honest and upright and one who walked daily with his Saviour, but he lacked a sense of humour. He would not allow the boys to go to the fair on the Broch Links and he had to know thoroughly the company they kept. Unknown to him they would go to the Broch for paraffin for folk who would give them a bawbee which they spent on the links. Jimmy Brave was well liked by the Broadsea folk. Being literate he filled valuation papers and other things for old folk who could not write. He was extremely well-mannered and tidy, and exhorted the boys to be the same. He would point, 'Your jacket – hang it up'. James brought a yellow mongrel from Castle Bay. The poor thing was spoilt but my man was very fond of it. It was his faithful companion and often went to Pitullie on its own. We had Ranger about eight years; he was the age of my son Watt. My husband spent a lot of time teaching the children English. He wanted them to be able to speak to anybody properly, but to respect Buchan Doric as their mother tongue.

We now had to work terribly hard, for herring prices were so poor. Fishermen chaved their guts out for nothing but to line the curers' pouch. The herring boom hit the Broch like a thunderbolt. They were gutting and packing on the streets. I have seen the pickle running down the back street to the Auld Kirk; I have filled up to Bain the curer on the fishcross. It was a scandal folk were so poorly paid; we managed to give our bairns a pair of shoes and a rig-out for Sunday, but they had to go barefoot to school through the week.

The 1870s were a bad time for the working class. The industrial upheaval was well under way. As fishers we felt the pinch, for most folk had gone over to herring fishing completely. You could not barter herring for dairy produce the same way as you could do with white fish. A new race had risen up, the fish-curer. Formerly, fishermen bought the barrels ready-made and cured their own. Now there were big curers who had real money. Small curers were in it in a much lesser way. Penny curers were usually the sacked foremen of big curers. They knew the trade inside out and through intrigues they managed to keep afloat; poor curers started in a small way on borrowed money and often made good. The latter usually lived in rented rooms with a big-minded wife to ginger them on; she usually engineered the mixing with society and by knowing the right folk often helped them over a stile.

Coopers' wages were on the breadline, and if they were out of work in the winter their bairns, poor things, were forced to go to the soup kitchen. I have often seen coopers gathering welks in the winter. After the railway came, welks became big business. All the Broadsea bairns spent the summer gathering welks to help shod their feet. The railway was a blessing for the fishwife, I could go to Strichen and New Deer in a day, and I still bought fish at the Broch though our folk were at the herring.

I went regularly to Strichen House. Mrs Baird was a kind woman. The staff all liked her and the garden and grounds were beautifully kept. Near the house was a large monkey puzzle and two high holly trees which at Christmas were a show of red berries. They had been there in Lord Lovat's time.

We certainly were very poor in my childhood, but my own children had far less to eat than we had, for times were now geared to put all the profit into the curer's pocket. We had now running water on the street at Bredsie. The taxes rose, so one had to save for that. In truth we had been robbed of our independence, but yet that noble pride and defiance of countless generations still shone in the faces of the fishers and the cottar folk, and in fact a more stubborn and hard breed ensued who could stand up with courage to their employers. Whatever is said of the Victorians in the future, be they Empire builders or what have you, they were certainly not champions of humanity, as so many shall one day have to stand before an angry God and testify. It seemed hordes of bullies had been rounded up to take on foremen's jobs in gutting yards, to drive the women as hard as they could. I have told some to wash out their mouths for the filth they used. My two old neepers, Annie Rogie and Suffie Noble, were both married long ago: Annie to Isaac Noble and Suffie to one of the Watsons from Smiddy at Pitsligo Meer. She had now a mansion in Saltoun Place, but Annie and me still went to the gutting. We were arled to the Bruces for four shillings. We helped to build the mansions at the top of Commerce Street. I was gutting with the Lows after that. (My cousin, John McLeman, the minister, was married to Sarah Low, a daur. They went to America, but came home.)

Curers were all now wanting huge houses with a staff to match. The Parks were the only real gentry in the Broch. All the others were pretenders. Unfortunately folk knew all their history, so it is not so easy to hide your sair bits. Snobbery is such a sinful cruel thing; one section is purposely making the other as miserable as possible. Not all curers were greedy money-grabbers; a few were decent employers and would come and go with you.

There were many peculiar tramps always on the trot. Once a poor man, quite mad, all tied in strips of clout like bandages, was sitting on the cradle stane at the front of Fittie Belle's door, gabbing some kind of discourse. Belle said, 'I am sorry, I am only a poor woman, but if you would like a bit of fish for your dinner you are welcome.' He said, 'Fish, fish, I haven't eaten fish for forty years.' He ate it greedily. In fine weather it was amazing the amount of these folk who stepped around. May Duthie's Jeanie was a devout Christian spinster who did a lot of good among the poor of Broadsea and the Broch. She belonged to the Faith Mission. Her mother was blind as was my mother's cousin, Jean Lascelles, who had a Braille bible; she lived with her mother latterly at 36 Broadsea – her brother and his wife, Betty Scott, lived in the other end. Mary Duthie's daur, Jeannie Noble, died in my cousin Dougal Noble's house at 18 College Bounds, Broadsea. 'Heaven is already rich from her ungathered sheaves.'

Rising high behind Broadsea was the green gallowshill, and between Kinnaird Head and it was the beautiful green Castle Braes with the high green Caird Hill croft through the Trochie from Back Street and the big farm of South Broadsea, occupied by McCallum: the steading is still there. I can mind on the farmhouse being a singlestone butt and ben before it was heightened. The Broadsea toll house was demolished to make Denmark Street. My mother could remember the University tower at the head of Back Street – many of the buildings were still there till recently, and some of the stones went into the new Free Kirk. The remains of the College are the buildings next to Bobon's Geordie's daughter's house in Back Street. A doos' dookit belonging to it stood where Lang Jim's house is built, much further up the Court Road. An old maid kept a little school in Wordie the Carter's close. You used to be able to go in there and come out at any of the little lanes on the Broadgate. When we were young, between Back Street and the Middle Street, most of the houses along the Broadgate were gable on to the road, with a lot of little lanes swarming with humanity.

We never made up to the town folk. We always thought them very greedy. The shore types were different, for they were on the same footing as us. The bit called the Garvage was the fishing section of the Broch; along the harbour south of George Lind's brae you were into a different territory, and the folk were different also. When the herring started proper, it seemed that man was bent on cleaning the sea of its spawn; one wonders how the sea has stood up to it for so long.

Barrasgate was opened up and all these other streets and yards and huts and smoke-houses in such ugly array covered the whole of McCallum's farm – and came right to Broadsea. The Rumbling Gwite a beauty spot (deadly to young loons) was completely ruined. All the smoke-houses spewing out reek, and on a wet day the black stuff from them fell from the sky. My granny used to speak of the Braun Seere who foretold when we saw black rain to watch out, for this was undoubtedly a sign of the times. Neister's Annie, who lived at 1 Broadsea, said 'To be born amid beauty and to die with such ugliness around you!' When Ptolemy, the great Roman map-maker, sailed round Kinnaird he called it the majestic headland, 'Taixalon Akron'. If he saw it today, with open sluices for herring guts and the local rubbish dump!

I have often asked myself why my own childhood was so vastly different from that of my children. We were going through the sad process of an old culture breaking up and disappearing forever. We were now at the mercy of industrialisation and firmly in the grip of a well organised capitalist machine. I had no hope of sending any of my bairns to university, for we did not know where our next breakfast was coming from. The 1860s saw the sea full of dogfish which ate up the herring, more dogs than had ever been known in living memory. When the Klondykes paid the curers at the end of the season then the curers paid us. So under the new system folk had to resort to a tick book for the whole summer. It meant both the house and boats' victuals had to go on the slate. The 1870s were lean years too, the year my son Joseph died[45] we went deep in debt, I tried hard to keep afloat in the old way of 'pay as you go' and went with many a hungry belly to achieve it.

Under the bounty, boats were engaged to leavers for £20 and £1 a cran for the first 200 cran, thereafter they got the herring at their own price, often as little as two shillings a cran in a glut. Not until the rouping of herring did the fishers get anywhere. Curers tried their hardest to stop this. The salesman was a new shark who saw the chance to make a lot of cash with little effort and without fouling his hands. The year the Franco–Prussian war broke out scarcely a curer honoured his bargain and many fishers were out at the door. We were engaged to 'Dirtinbreeks' Davidson. Later, when he got his money from the Germans, he never paid our boat their due.

Many of the German agents were Christian believers and during the season attended the Congregational Kirk, which had a Lutheran flavour to their taste. After service on a Sunday night my man would ask the Dinesmanns of Stettin or the Gunters of Hamburg back for a simple tea of fish done in butter with meal bread and milk. They often came to our house and dined and spoke of the Lord's coming. The German bairns would sit on the fenderstool and wait patiently and mannerably with my son for their elders to finish, and they sat down to the second sitting. I could aye lay a table fit for any class. Looking back over the years when I think of those intelligent, scholarly, Godly people, it makes me shudder to think of the part that nation played in bringing about the destruction of civilisation as we knew it; but we must not carry any unwarranted hatred in our hearts to anybody. My granny used to call the old college building in the Back Street, 'Proctor's Lodging'. Lady Saltoun told me Proctor was a mannie like 'tak' a' who chased truant students. Hedging lined the road from South Broadsea farm toll house to Mains of Broadsea up the Court Road, where Jim's house stands with the old doos' dookit. It was long a landmark at sea. Foreign sailors called it the 'Torn', in our childhood. It was a heap of grass-grown stones, and many confused it with the university itself. Behind this the big herring boats were drawn up for the winter, when we resorted to the small lines for a few months.

'Proctor's Lodging' – the verbal tradition referred to an ambitious chapter in Fraserburgh's history. When the founder of Fraserburgh received his charter for burgh and regality he was also granted leave to found a university and started to do so. The project – like Fraserburgh harbour and trade – attracted hostility and jealousy from Aberdeen. But the ultimate demise was probably and perhaps solely due to lack of funds, for Sir Alexander Fraser sold off many lands to finance his ambitions, and died in 1623, with a reduced estate and in straitened circumstances. In spite of a grant from the Scottish Parliament in 1597 Fraserburgh University was probably not functioning after 1605. But certain old buildings associated with it retained by name an echo of an ancient and honourable idea. It was at this time that the estate of Philorth was diminished by the sale of Inverallochy (to Lord Lovat, and given by him to a younger son, the first Fraser of Inverallochy) of the old Philorth to Alexander Fraser of Durris, and of certain other inland parts to Thomas Fraser of Strichen, cousin of Lovat and ancestor of 'Mormond Tam'.

There had long been a custom in fishing villages to help ease the food situation. Older bairns of large families would live with somebody else, girls as servants to rock children and boys to help with baiting lines. Often these children were overworked by their guardians, and completely taken advantage of; they could not get enough work out of them. I had no room at Pitullie to take such a person, but back at 72 I let it be known I would. The first to ask to live with me was Onty's Jessie. The lass did not get on with her stepmother. I had just engaged her when Epp's Jean asked me if she could stay with me. When I looked at the quinie's shabby shoes something went round my heart and I said yes. Epp, or Elspet McLeman, her mother, was a widow with a big family. She was always the essence of cleanness and had been married to my cousin. Both Jessie and Jean lived with me for seven winters running. I gave them half a crown a week, for they were well worth it. The work they did among the bairns enabled me to go oftener to the country, and I could make their keep and help ourselves foodwise. Both lassies have remained my lifelong friends and fortunately both got good husbands.

I asked my husband why his mother disliked me so much. He said fishing was not her idea of success. He had a junior Master's ticket. It was the height of her ambition for him to become a captain in square rig and to mix with the well-to-do. He said that was no life for a married man, most of his life on the sea. We took the bairns out to Pitullie every Sunday night to see their granny. It made no difference, completely ignoring any tension that might arise. We had a better relationship, and she was genuinely fond of our Peter who was always up to some devilment and yet had a way of getting round folk by his funny sense of humour. He and James and my daughter, Mary, had all brilliant heads. All my own honest endeavours in Pitullie had failed, but now when my mother-in-law came at a turn to see us I went out of my way to make her welcome. My husband made-over 13 Pitullie in her name. We still paid the taxes and ground-rent, for after all she was his mother. My husband realised we should have stayed in Broadsea when we married, but the mill will never turn with water that is past. We could have been well off, but the money was gone on that white elephant of a house in Sandhaven. My mother-in-law was too straight-laced. She was a very respectable woman, nearly twenty years younger than my parents, but I think genuine Christian believers should break adrift from creeds and sectarianism and go out and practise what they preach. For world events clearly show the Lord's coming again is drawing near, because we must remember no particular sect will judge us, but God himself. So many are in fact afraid of what their fellow church members think of them. I have heard men pray to the audience with lots of fancy words and scripture and they, in fact, think they have kidded folk on as to how good and sincere they are, while in God's sight it is as the contents of an orra slops pail. Many are called but few are chosen; before your first sark gets over your head God knows who are going to be his.

Old Clarke came with our milk from the Broch at five in the morning; often it disappeared. My son Peter rose for the milkman one morning and put out a jug of whitewash. Many folk were missing milk. The culprit quickly spat out the whitening, and folk saw his shoes covered that day. It was a loon from the south end of Broadsea going to the scaup in the early morning. When we knew who it was we could deal with this malefactor; Geordie Gunner's Nanse dished him a real clout on the lug.

My son Peter was always up to some kind of tricks. There was an old wifie, Maggotty, one of the Wattecks. She lived in the little housie in front of Cockie's door. Her man had ran off and left her not long after her marriage. She had become a man-hater and would sweep her doorstep if a man passed, and no male was allowed to enter her dwelling. It was customary to give all these poor souls a gift at Hogmanay. I aye sent Peter up with a quarter of tea, and he got in; she would give him a jammie piece. In the season everybody made enough berries to last till the spring, and sometimes I grated an apple into my rhubarb.

What a struggle to bring up a family! We were going through the labour pains of changing from a rural to an industrial nation. The sea was far too good a thing to remain unexploited. From time to time there had been a lot of trouble with the Highlandmen, all over wages. When the boats were engaged by the curers they had promised the hired men a bounty like the boat-owners. A failure to carry out their bargain resulted in riots and mass violence. Once it was so bad the police had to call in the military from Aberdeen. All the windows along Broadgate were dang in. The truth was never brought out in the papers, for the hired men had a point; the curer should have kept his word.

On the night of Saturday, 1 August 1874 there were some 2,000 Highlanders, largely Lewis men, in Fraserburgh, seeking employment as hired men on the boats. Christian ascribes the riot which took place to the hired men being cheated by the curers of their share of bounty. A historian of Fraserburgh has attributed it to the fact that they had just been paid (as was usual on a Saturday late in July or early in August) their share of the curers' settlement with the fishermen for the 'early fish' – that is, all catches up to 20th July. Whether from resentment at what they reckoned unfair settlement, or simply from whisky, when the public houses closed the streets of the Broch were quickly full of violent and drunken Highlanders; the doors and windows of the Town House were smashed and preparations were made by the mob to set fire to it. The police were insufficient in numbers to do anything effective and the situation was soon beyond control.

Some of the local volunteers drew their arms and ammunition from the armoury in order to oppose the rioters by private initiative – a move which, probably fortunately, was quickly checked by the chief constable of the county who was in the town and at once directed that the volunteers disarm. The rioters were eventually dispersed by heavy rain: a detachment of Gordon Highlanders was sent to the town to support the police; a number of ringleaders were ultimately arrested, and prison sentences ranging from one to two years were imposed.

After this system was scrapped, when the big gluts of herring came in and they were not all sold, some owners would wait like vultures and hyenas. They arranged rows of empty kits along the pier and lay in wait, and when the skipper of an unsold catch gave the order to go out and dump them in the bay, some greedy curers with a sweet smile would say, 'You don't need to go to the bother of going out to dump 36 crans, there is 30 crans of empty kits lying on the pier, you can fill them.' And often the men were so tired and disappointed at not getting their catch sold they would let them have the herring for nothing. But my husband had a determined nature, and always dumped an unsold catch, for he would not justify the curers' greed. A favourite trick was to hold out they had run out of barrels and salt and often at the last moment got a catch for next to nothing, while the railway sidings at Lonmay, Rathen, Mormond and Philorth Halt, and especially the junction at Maud, were crowded with trucks of barrels shunted in, and also wagons of salt.

Many farms from very far away sent horses to cart the herring. The curers built bothies and stables for the men and beasts along the back of Saltoun Place. The country carters were usually a jolly crew.

Broadsea has aye been a progressive place, and we got ourselves organised to meet the new order of things. We were determined we were going to lay down the law to the curers, and in any decision it was solidarity to a man. There were now so many bairns in the school it was overcrowded. My man was one of the committee who proposed to erect a new building on the same stance. They wrote to the General Assembly, who said they would pay a third of the cost. The Society for the Propagation of the Gospel gave us a third, and the village had to raise the other a third. All the women worked hard to achieve it. They had bazaars, and bring-and-buy-sales, but my husband never lived to see the school built, although he was one of the folk who pushed the business.

My son Peter was crazy on the sea. He had an old bark tub which he paddled with two oars about the shore: folk called him Peter the Rover. At the age of eleven he went to work on the *Isabella Anderson* of Banff. They were shipping herring to the Baltic.

My daur Mary was born on 11th May 1874. She was my eighth[46] child – far too many, for many reasons. At the end of 1874 my son Peter had left with a cargo of herring for Prussia. I was making the pottage on the fire on the morning of the 7th August when I distinctly heard his voice calling me. He was buried at Königsberg in Prussia on the 13th August. That was the start of the breakdown of my mental health, for I am sufficiently conversant with drowning to know that no drowned person is found floating, and this cost me many a sleepless night.

My husband was not content with being told. He got some of the German Klondykers to get us the full information and all the translation of the inquest and everything he could find out of Peter's last moments. He was only thirteen. Captain Cowie came to us and brought us Peter's wages, which were eight shillings. I could never have spent it, and when we settled up after the fishing my husband gave that sum to the children's hospital in Aberdeen. Later my son James erected a headstone on Peter's grave; several Broch folk have seen it.

My heart was broken. My husband was very kind to me. We had a definitely different relationship; never once did I see him hit the boys again. He had been brought up to think men superior to women, that a woman's place is in the home looking after bairns, that the man is head of the house and the wife must be subject to him. I refuse to accept this; both are equal and in making decisions that should apply also. My own personality had been submerged in Pitullie, but I had quickly reasserted myself on home ground. I lost my last two brothers the next year. George had married in Angus; some of his children returned to Buchan. Andrew married in Caithness. I wondered for what reason I should be spared as the sole survivor and to live so long.

My last child was born in 1876. The poor soul was to have the hardest life of the lot. She was called Charlotte Murison, after Lady Saltoun and Mrs Murison the howdie wife. My son Joseph was quiet and a middle-of-the-road scholar; he had been called after Joseph Simon in Leith (he was my husband's last cousin, and had been brought up with Jinna. His mother died in the first cholera epidemic). My son Joseph had been working during the school breakdown. He was carrying lime for the masons who were building the houses on College Bounds. He was eleven years old and had tuppence a day. He was going back to school the next week, but that did not have to be. While on the scaffolding a stone fell on his great toe. Foolishly he washed his injury in the nowts' drinking water and caught tetanus. I nursed him three days. It was heart-rending to see the sick child in convulsions. 'The Lord giveth and the Lord taketh away, blessed be His Holy Name' – even now it is hurtful to me. Joseph was buried on 13th September. I was furious at a society which forced bairns to work. Having to put by a funeral set us back financially, and it was the worst year the fishing had ever seen. Our boat went into debt. While I was in the country, all winter my husband made nets and towed them and we put in awful hours working together, to get the nets ready to sell to the chandler, but by February we had cleared our feet of debt; but what an effort: I had gone to the Broch to do washing for would-be toffs, and my man had gone to the welks to make an extra shilling, but once again we were free.

My husband had four cousins married in Broadsea. They called them the Rollie sisters. All were tall, proud women and spotless clean. In the winter of the same year as Peter died, word went round that the *Veteran* of South Shields was sinking. My Aunt Annie's grandson, Joseph Taylor, 22 Broadsea, a lad of eighteen, dived into a terrific sea with a running line and attached it to the ship. He saved many of the crew. Sadly we saw many perish. Saltoun honoured him by having a silk banner embroidered to commemorate the act. It was carried by two folk in Broadsea Walk.

The Broch was an interesting place during the fishing. You

could hear the Fife accent, the Shetland, the Gaelic and every other, 20,000 folk crammed into anywhere, washing houses, garrets, lofts and outhouses, the Patiences of Avoch, the Callys of Nairn, and efficient girls from Hagiesund in Norway. They were streets ahead of us; they wore for the gutting white rubber aprons and white boots. The Highland folk would send the most droll things by the post, dead unplucked hens, and cows' paps filled with oatmeal. The girls would wear red, blue and pink shawls and stockings of the same colour.

Philorth was greatly added to, in the fashion of the times, by the 17th Lord Saltoun. When he died, he bequeathed a 'broken estate' to his elder son, and Christian describes at least some of the reasons why:

> I went regularly to Philorth with fish. Lady Saltoun was a strange wifie. She was penny wise and pound foolish. When the Waterloo Saltoun died, she and her husband 'Big Zander' came north. They were jubilant when they returned. You would have thought it was a marriage they had been at instead of a funeral. She straightway let the wind into the Saltoun purse, which according to her behaviour seemed to be bottomless. It would have done Lady Saltoun the world of good to have been earning money for a year instead of spending it. I was sorry she completely destroyed the old Philorth House; the first bit, and the next built at an angle, held sufficient room for them. When I heard of this before it started I said to them, 'Would it not be better to replenish the old Castle of Pitullie, and Cairnbulg,[47] which belonged to John Gordon, one of the numerous stray bairns of the 3rd earl of Aberdeen?'
>
> Lady Saltoun built on a wing at Philorth. It was a mansion in its own right. They say the Sutors' School was copied from the same plan. It did not match anything there and looked out of place. Later she had Dickson the painter lying on his back on a scaffold for weeks picking out the plaster flowers in gold

on the ceiling. She had Tommy Strachan forever changing the Chinese wallpaper, and one month Webster would be painting baskets of fruit between the picture rails and roof; next month he would have it blotted out, then pastoral scenes would appear instead. At Christmas she sent presents to all her coneevitors in the south. I have seen the ribbon from her camisole go round one of her Christmas boxes; I have seen the girl Ruddach the cook put a dumpling in the kitchen into a blue flowered bit of lawn which I had recognised as a piece of her Ladyship's bedgown I washed regularly twenty years before that. Coming in the road I have taken one of the postboy's bags on top of my creel. I said to him, 'Does her Ladyship give you tuppence for your Hogmanay for taking all that stuff in for her?' He said, 'Never a brown bawbee.' She often asked my opinion, for she knew she would get a straight answer; I would never hunkersleed with her. I told her instead of making their sons professional soldiers, they should have made one a lawyer, another an articled banker and kept control of the running of the estate themselves.

She spent £100,000 on the house and garden. I told Lord Saltoun he should have started his own shipbuilding company at Fraserburgh. Then Scotland was leading in shipbuilding. They could have trebled the vast sum they foolishly spent on the house, but he was a scholarly but stupid man who thought when he had inherited the title he was initiated into some great mystery and that folk owed him a certain deference (which I for one was not prepared to give him), and that his ideas were infallible. He played into his wife's barrow all the time.

The girl Ruddach often gave me tea, and if she was about the grounds her Ladyship would ask me through to her private parlour to drink it. Often in the house you were greeted with the most amazing and incredible sights. Fire-irons would be flying but-and-ben amid a terrible din. Once I saw a bronze horse scuff past Tomlin the butler; had the ornament hit him it would have split his head. The Honourable Charlotte would set herself up by the drawing-room chumbley-piece which provided a plentiful supply of ammunition. She and her sister Kate May would keep up a regular fusilade. Often the Annie May one joined in the battle, and depending on whose side she was on Lady Saltoun joined in also. She would enter this hullabaloo like the haiver oot in a low drinking dive. She would grab Miss Annie Mary by the scruff of the neck and drag her over a settee. Her Ladyship dipped her hand in the water of a flower vase to make it more potent, and as she skelped her daughter you could hear the slaps ringing through the building with Annie Mary skirling and yowling like a scalded cat, and little wonder, for the weals must have been like half-crowns on her honourable dowp.

Before Peter died my husband and I were invited to Miss Annie May's wedding. A huge marquee tent was set up. Fishwives and cottar wives and duchesses rubbed shoulders on the lawn. It was a lovely concern; she married Lord Zook![48] It was a lovely hot day and grand summer. Three weeks later, when I went to Philorth, through the trees I saw Annie May lying on a wicker recline; she was reading in the sunshine on the green. I said to Mrs Birnie in the Lodge, 'I thought she was on her honeymoon in the South of France.'

Mrs Birnie had a natural belly laugh, Then folk did laugh for none thought the world would be engulfed in strife and bloodshed. Mrs Birnie said, 'Did you hear the latest?' and she laughed again, 'When the bridegroom showed her his credentials she was so scared she ran home to her mother.' At first I did not catch on! After a year of marriage Lord Zook was given a divorce because his wife refused to sleep with him. Kate May, the young one, was married to some of Lord Pitsligo's relations.[49] Before her marriage Annie May had fallen in love with a boy Macdonald, the first horseman at the home farm. Eventually her folk found out. Her Ladyship told me; I told her such a union would have been an asset to themselves. The boy came of good Lonmay parents; he was extremely handsome, intelligent and keen on farming. He was far too nice a chap to have been a factor, but when a large farm became vacant she could have put her daughter and man into it and gone in for beef cattle. Fast steam-driven ships were now running between Aberdeen and London, and with all the big hotels and things they could have made a lot of money. Her Ladyship said, 'How vulgar to go into trade.' I said to her, 'The Master of Saltoun married you, and you were nobody. Now the farms are being sold to raise capital to live on.' She might have done well at my suggestion.

Charlotte was married to a nice fellow, Willie Keppel. He was the same folk as one of the wifies who took up with the late King Edward. One day I walked into the Broch with Willie Keppel. He newsed all the way. He asked if I had known his in-laws long, I could see he was trying to pump me to know the more boisterous side of Lady Saltoun's nature, but I was guarded in my answers. The staff were very loyal, for few in the Broch knew of their fighting and oncarry, neither did I reveal it to anybody. I told the girls, 'You have far too much time on your hands. The world is the harvest field. The waving grain is waiting for you to reap it. Go along the fishcross and you will hear the anguished cry of a bairnie greeting who has had nothing in its belly for two days. They are not the children of lazy folk but of vrichts and stone-masons and others who are out of work because of the winter, and who during working months did not make enough to lay by for a rainy day.'

They did not get up till about 10 o'clock in the day, these girls, but they were nice lassies. The young one sometimes came to see me with a nice girl from Rattra House, a girl Cumine. Poor lass had a bad kersehad and was conscious of it. She was very interested in taking photos and did a lot of good likenesses. She did all the groups of bairns in country schoolies. But still the battles went on, and days later you would see her Ladyship with the gluepot sticking heads on figurines.

Lady Saltoun was aye changing her London houses; she was like the Broch folk who flitted every May and November. She would be in Brook Street, then Cavendish Square, all in one year. She disposed of all the old stuff from Philorth to furnish her many moves, and in its place she filled the house with marble washstands, parlour suites and all kinds of new-fangled trash from the London shops. She had shooting lodges at Ullapool and Wester Ross and even the Outer Isles, and in many of these places she left the ancient stuff from Philorth. There used to be a black varnished deece that stood in the entrance of old Philorth. It had four panels of deeply carved strawberry leaves with a cluster of three berries in the centre of each; also a low wooden armchair which I always admired. It had a carved panel of the Covenanters signing their names in blood on a tombstone in Greyfriars Edinburgh. And many other things – all these things were sold in London with her Ladyship's temporary houses. I was flaming at Big Zander, her man, for allowing these acts of vandalism, for these things should have been preserved for posterity. It was as much my heritage to admire as it was theirs.

One night at a prayer meeting in Dunkie's house her Ladyship came in humility, and on her knees gave her heart to the Lord Jesus. That was not long before Lord Saltoun died. It was a pity her salvation came so late, but even though her tongue was still as sharp and dangerous as a broken eskalade bottle, her shortcomings pointed in the direction of virtue. She had asked of Rachel Watt, Dunkie's wife, 'Why are you always so happy Mrs Noble?' Rachel replied, 'My Saviour is always with me.'

Her Ladyship also found that happiness, and she led her man to the Lord, for he left a record to say he trusted the Lord with his soul, so in marrying her it was the best thing he ever did. I was in Aberdeen at the time. They had been to Philorth for Hogmanay; they went south early in January. Lord Saltoun was a dying man. He lived only weeks after that. He told me he had made his peace with God through the precious blood of Jesus. Her Ladyship will not go empty-handed, for to stand before the judgement seat of Christ and bring one soul with you is worth far more than the vast sums of money she squandered. Her daur Annie May later married Lord Trevor, and her first lad, the loon Macdonald, went off to Canada (folk said her Ladyship had paid his fare). Today his children own huge wheat ranches on the prairie. When the Saltouns built the huge house, I said to them of the staff, 'One day these slaves are going to revolt, and who will you get to clean a place of that size?' They just laughed, but I said, 'Look at the trouble with the Highlanders' riots in the Broch, and it is all over wages!'

But the Victorian age was one of complete selfishness and immorality in high places.

Although I did not know it the die was cast. My sister-in-law and her husband William Pirie paid out the £40 they owed us on the house in Sandhaven. That was in April. We were glad at the time they bought it, for we could get no other buyer. Lord Clinton gave them a feu charter in May, so we were finished with Sandhaven for good.

The fishing of 1877 was not a bad year and we were just about to settle up before the boat's departure for the west coast. It was one of those strange days in August, starting bright and sunny, when all of a sudden the sky was black to its farthest reaches, across the Moray Firth. I had washed all the boat's bedding and with other folks' things they were along the dykes at the Wasten right beyond the Badlaw Head, and with the rain threatening I hurried to take in the blankets, which were dry. The sea had risen mountains high.

I had a grand sight then. I saw our own boat and that of our cousin Dougal Noble, 18 College Bounds. Then a cluster of boats and intuition told me something was wrong, and after nearly an hour with the rain lashing down, the boats went round Kinnaird.

The Congregational Minister came to the door. I asked him which one of my folk was lost, he said, 'It is the husband.'

It was the 21st August, exactly three years and two weeks to the day since my son Peter was drowned and in that time I had lost five of my nearest. I could only ask the Almighty for strength to carry on, but how I was going to feed so many mouths alone I did not know. It was a delayed-action shock. My husband's and sons' clothes were round the fire, and when they came in they related the sad tale. It was a common practice to take the sheet or end sail between the knees while hooking in a little block and tackle before hoisting the sail. Several careless folk had lost their lives in the same way. The wind filled the sail as it rose with force, whipping my husband overboard into the sea. He was a powerful swimmer, and in the direction of the prevailing current which carried him away, quickly made for Dougal Nobles' boat, which was quite close. As he was about to hoist himself aboard, a huge wave swamped him, and he disappeared completely. He perished beneath the breakers. My sons always thought the force had dashed his head against the boat, knocking him unconscious. The heavy leather boots with iron heels would have filled quickly, carrying him to the bottom.

I had loved him, though often we did not see eye to eye, but our last seven years were reasonably happy and sad ones. My son James was seventeen, so maritime laws would not allow him to skipper the boat, which meant I would have to pay somebody to do so. Shortly afterwards I was to lose another son and daughter, but it was not easy to carry on. I could only say to God, 'I was dumb because Thou didst it.' My eighteen years of marriage had never at any time been a bed of roses. A mean character drew the butt window and stole two new herring nets. He came to see me with a fine face; I hit him so hard with a baking bowl over the head. Then I was in the awful haggle that goes on after a death. The inquest was in the Town House. It was equally painful for my sons who were only children, but all these formalities must be gone through. I had nothing but my faith. My husband several years before had made a will leaving everything he had to me. Foolishly he made Crookie the Broch lawyer his executor. One should never give a lawyer any power. It was said Crookie had sold his soul to the devil. Satan must have given him a big price, for he was very wealthy.

Crookie the lawyer was one of the biggest blackguards ever born. He owned much slum property in the Broch and Peterhead, for which he drew exhorbitant rents, and on failure to pay he would call in Porterfield the peening mannie to lift their stuff and put the man in prison. I have witnessed many such transactions, and they would make your heart bleed, for ordinary folk could sympathise, but were in no position to help anybody financially. Porterfield had a cripple leg, and he nearly got another when he went to peen Annie Catheid. Then the poor were so meanly treated, and folk in authority turned a blind eye to it. Porterfield said to Annie, 'That is a nice fire you have Miss Cathead,' (Noble was her real surname). She said, 'Yes, Mr Doghead, they are in this house that will sleep in it.' He thought he was going to be thrown into the fire. She barred the door and gave him a terrible hiding with a spiletree.

So far I had found nobody willing to take the job of skippering my boat the *Ocean Foam*. Many thought to take on such a charge was unlucky, so for that winter the boat was laid up on the brae at Broadsea. I had to work like a slave with practically no money. I seldom could buy fish and did not get often into the country. My sons were going in inshore grounds, so what fish I had I got from them; Andrew was ten and George fourteen. His father's death had a traumatic effect on my son James, who became silent and moody. I realised he needed a change so I got him fixed up on the Parks' ships to see the world. He left me an allowance of four shillings a week and for about the next five years, some weeks on end that was all the money we had. We were now very poor. I cast the peats with the bairns. Derby Ha Moss was poor quality peat so we had always in my mother's time rented a leet from the Boyndlie Moss; it was hard work.

Crookie the lawyer finally settled up. One should never sign anything from a lawyer without first taking it home and reading it, and if the lawyer shows signs that he is unwilling to give you the document to read then you know you are going to be swicked. I went to the office demanding to read thoroughly what I was going to sign. The lawyer was out, but his clerk turned up the books which did coorspart with my statement. Twice a 'one' had been added before a figure. He was cheating me of £20. Fortunately my cousin Mary was with me. I made Crookie shake in his shoes, for it is amazing how a letter to the Lawyers' Guild in Edinburgh can shatter the myth of their invincibility. It is never what comes up but what comes out, and folk should never hesitate to report them. Folk are born blind. They have accepted greed and all the other evil things as much as they have tea and coffee. There is a right and a wrong way to steal, and the former is more heartless than the latter. A hasty retreat was made by Crookie, and Munro, the advocate, found a skipper for my boat. He was a Baxter from Fittie who had a wife and bairns. He was a likeable and deserving young man who treated me absolutely honestly and his family have remained my steadfast friends. His wife was connected with the Otties of Inverallochie, so the boat went on loan to Aberdeen for six years. Later a son, Andrew Baxter, was a cook on my son's boat.

For a long time I suffered the terrible pain of the loss of my husband and family. It was an appalling grief. I now had to be father and mother with so little and no prospects of any betterment, for though you worked your fingers to the bone you could not save a penny, for the returns were so poor. I had been fortunate in living in the years after teind and duty on fish were abolished, and before fishing became big business to the merchant, for then we were producers, wholesalers and retailers, and there was a simple honest living for everybody.

At my husband's death our house was blinded four days, as was the custom. With so many children I had no time to pity myself, but had to hackle tee and get on with the job. It is commonly believed the body of a drowned person rises on the ninth day after the tragedy. This almost always occurs if the person is in a harbour. Often men lost on the Rosehearty side of Kinnaird have been found about the estuary of the Philorth water, so on the 10th May I went over the Broch sands on a fruitless search. My sons went in the opposite direction. When I reached the Philorth water I carried on to Cairnbulg. Brandesburgh is the first little village. It was founded by Patrick Ogilvy, a son of the earl of Findlater. He coaxed some of the folk from Cairnbulg to start a new tounie on his land in order to cut in on the sea's bounty.

I eventually reached Cairnbulg, frozen with cold. It was a Monday morning. My cousin's daughter lived in a hoosie on the banks of the Allochy burn. My cousin Isabella Watt was a tall, graceful girl with a beautiful profile; she had been illegitimate and the chap she married was the same. He had been brought up in this hoosie by his grandparents – both I remember, for I had been in it as a little girl with my mother. (They called the mannie 'Codlin Fite' and the wifie 'Kirsty Yalla'. My Uncle George was married to their daughter, Barbara Whyte; they lived at 21 Broadsea. Another daughter, Betty Whyte, was married to Mosley at 65 Broadsea. She had had a tragic death by falling into a pan of boiling bark. The other sister was the mother of my cousin's man, who after his mother's death lived with his aunt at 21 Broadsea. My cousin lived at 22, and from the moment they met it was a love-match. The boy Whyte was married out of 21 Broadsea, but they went to live at his grandparents' hoosie in Cairnbulg; he was broken-hearted when she went to an early grave.)

Their daughter was a nice lassie. She said to me, 'My goodness Kirsty, what brings you here so soon after your sad bereavement?' I told her my errand, and she said, 'Leave that entirely in the hands of the Almighty. If your man's body turns up it is meant to be, and if not it is not meant to be.' I warmed my hands at her nice fire. The kettle was boiling and she asked me to stay to dinner which I was loth to do as I must return and make our own. After a nice hot cup of tea I set out for home. My cousin's girl was a kindly lassie, she put a baking of scones in my creel and took my arm all the way to Philorth Briggie. In the background was the ancient castle of Cairnbulg, like my own life now sadly in ruins. In our time we have seen this estuary completely silted up. When we were bairns on a Sunday we would go out there. The mouth of the Philorth water was so deep you could not possibly wade across – I don't know what accounts for this change.

My cousin's daur kissed me, and we parted and waved to each other across the burn. I thought on what she said. As it was, my husband's body was never found, but I asked God to help me. Instantly I knew a second work of grace had taken place in my life. Going over the sands at a place called Maggie's trink (a cleavage in the bents through which the Philorth Water may have flowed a thousand years ago) I was baptised with the Holy Ghost and fire, and knew God had some purpose for my life. I reached Broadsea knowing all would be well.

A fortnight after my husband was drowned, over 200 miners lost their lives at Blantyre coal-pit disaster. A collection was taken in the Parish Kirk for their families. I put two shillings in the box. It was all I could spare, but I thought 'it will give somebody eight loaves who is in exactly the same position as myself and maybe worse', for hundreds of children were made fatherless. We had a memorial service in the Congregational Kirk. My mother-in-law came, for it was the only funeral service her son would have. The Minister ended, 'And the sea shall give up its dead.' This tragedy shattered me but it ground my mother-in-law to powder. I had gone to Pitullie to see her. She put her arms round me and would not let me go. We must forgive people, for God has to forgive us.

I counted my blessings. I had an owner-occupied house and a boat, though no money, but I had to be grateful. The house, 50 Pitullie, now became my property. My in-laws were furious when I transferred the ownership to my husband's aunt, Jean Breenie, who had nursed and maintained her aged mother, Jean Ritchie, one of the Orams of Rosehearty. I do not believe in the law of the eldest son grabbing everything, for in most cases they are married and many do so little for their parents. Jean Breenie should have got that house in the first place; she was single and had two illegitimate children, Nancy Rennie and William Spence. No. 50 Pitullie had been built in the 1620s by a William Sim and his wife, Marjory Noble, a daur of the traveller of Zetland. Again, in the 1720s, a Barbara Noble from 76 Broadsea had married a Patrick Sim at 50 Pitullie; so twice my husband descended from my own family. Barbara Noble frequently gave shelter to the hunted Lord Pitsligo, a brave man.

# CHAPTER NINE

## *The Breaking of a Mind (1878–1879)*

My elder son was at sea, but I had still seven bairns to feed and clothe. I wore myself out with hard work. In buying fish at the Broch market I could not compete with the fisher-merchants, so I got little to barter for food in the country. I was sick with worry, neither eating nor sleeping, for I had no money except my son's allowance of four shillings. I know now I should have gone to the Parish for help, but I was far too proud. It may be wrong but that was how we were brought up; and selling your possessions is a degrading game.

Eppie Buchan, a St Combs woman who lived up the New Street at Broadsea, commented on my growing so thin. I said, 'It is hard to be a provider.' She gave me a bag of tatties which were most welcome, for I had been raking in the sea for everything edible for us to eat. When the bairns had gone to school and the little one was still asleep, I would put my arms round Ranger the doggie and break my heart crying. If I had been spared one brother – but I was grateful I had my cousin Mary, whose health was rapidly failing. We would never see each other stuck; she also had dragged a heavy harrow in her life.

There is a time to laugh and a time to weep, a time to mourn and a time to dance. These were the second great tears in my life. How I missed my mother, who had also known grief. Sixty years have passed and I see her now, resting her heavy creel on a dyke to get her breath. Both my parents are safe within the veil of salvation, but how I wished I still had them when I lost my man. I had my trust in Christ the Man of Sorrow, and knew what he felt as he stood before Pontius Pilate the Procurator of Judea, knowing full well he must go to Calvary to die and rise again to redeem mankind from sin.

For the doctor had asked me to go for a rest to Aberdeen Royal Mental Asylum. After a great deal of thought I consented, for something must break. I worried so much about my hungry children and who would look after them. My sister-in-law had no room, and her mother was over seventy. My cousin Mary said she would keep an eye on the bairns, as my daughter Isabella was only ten – but she kept the house, washed and baked, cooked and put the young ones to school clean while I was in the asylum. Charlotte the youngest was not quite two, but past the worst stage.

The world is so unwilling to accept that the disturbed mind functions in exactly the same way as the normal one. It is a tremendous problem the mind is trying to cope with; perhaps if I had been less of a thinker and a more dull person it might not have affected me in the same way.

I boarded the train at Fraserburgh. My cousin Mary and her daughter Annie saw me off, also my daughter Isabella. It was a sad day in my life. We passed Kirktoun kirkyard. The tall lums of Philorth House stood above the trees. I could see the kitchen and parlour ones reeking. Rounding Mormond Hill and Strichen several folk I knew came on the train. We passed through Brucklay station, and as I went up that line to start my life sentence little did I dream that later so many of my grandsons would go up that line on their death sentence.

Then Cornhill was on the outskirts of the city of Aberdeen amid a large garden. Forbes, the Laird of Newe, had generously donated £10,000 towards the building of the new asylum. I entered by a small gate set in a high granite dyke, and was admitted. The nurse who gave me a bath commented on how clean I was. We went through endless corridors, and in each section I noticed the door was firmly locked behind us which gave me an eerie feeling. Finally I went to bed, tired after my journey.

We were washing our faces at five o'clock in the morning, for breakfast was at six. Not even the pangs of sheer hunger could have forced me to eat in the dining-room. That was a sight the King and Queen should go and witness, for if you are not humble before, once you have seen it you will be, and you will value good health and every other blessing you have got from the depth of your heart. Patients were gulping and stomaching their porridge in such a slovenly and distasteful manner. Today I would think nothing of it for I realise that he that is sick hath need of a physician; one needs healing for the body as well as the soul. Then I feigned some excuse to skip dinner. The sister said, 'If you work in the kitchen you can eat there.' The Physician Superintendent was one of the Sibbalds of Balgonie – a well-to-do Fife family. He was a kindly, skeely man, genuinely interested in his patients. I spoke with him for an hour, and then I was fixed up with a job in the kitchen. I did not want any of my children to visit me, for it is not the sort of place bairns should see, especially if they are very young.

Never did I love anything so much as that spring, when the trees burst into leaf and the primroses came out. How glad and grateful I was when I was told I was going to be discharged. I came home, and my bairns were so glad. Isabella, only a child, had the house beautifully clean and everything in good order. I had previously arranged with Munro the advocate to give her five shillings per week from the rent of the boat, and with four shillings from my son they just got by with barely enough to eat, for the taxes and ground rent had to be paid. Being in the asylum is a terrible stigma. It should not be, for the same hand who put it onto me can put it onto anybody. Mental illness should not be confused with mental deficiency. They are whole worlds apart but equally sad. When I came home I found folk constantly trying to shun me as if I had leprosy. The usual pattern was to smile and be pleasant for a moment, then make some kind of excuse that they were in an awful hurry to do something. I went to the farms in the country, and in many places where they could see me coming I found the door barred in my face, once it got around I had returned from the asylum. It was a terrifying experience. I had only Christ who dined with publicans and sinners, and who is a real friend to social outcasts.

I was told at both Philorth and Strichen House, that in my absence somebody else had taken their custom. I have gone as far as New Deer selling hardly anything. It was a sad defeat to have to return with a full heavy creel and a heavy heart. I could see it was not going to be easy to make a living, and it seems impossible for the public to be sufficiently educated to the fact that a mental disorder is an illness. Probably the most tragic factor is that the person can be as right as rain one day and tragically sick the next.

So now so many doors were closed to me that it was hardly worth my while going to the country, but I plodded on. Though I was 'sodger clad' I was 'major minded'. It seems that under great mental stress insanity takes over. The odd thing is that in many cases the patient knows all that is going on. I called at Witchill House, as I usually did, by the back door. There was a narrow courtyard between the kitchen wing and the steading; you went through the stillroom before the kitchen. I asked the housekeeper if she wanted fish. She said, 'I must ask Madam', whom they call Her Ladyship. The house was occupied by Lord Saltoun's factor, Sir Alexander Anderson, who also had a beautiful town house with the stairs and pillars at the corner of Frithside Street. In Witchill a long lobby like a street ran the whole length of the interior. The housekeeper had to consult Madam in the drawing-room at the far end. I had tip-toed in to hear Lady Anderson's reply which was so loud I heard it all, 'Tell her we are supplied by a Rosehearty merchant since she went off the round and it is not necessary to come back.' She added, 'Under no circumstances give her tea or anything that might encourage her. We can't have a mad woman coming about the place.' I retreated to the back door. They were none the wiser. The housekeeper delivered her message and I thanked her with a courteous smile, just as if nothing had happened. I had a strong urge to go back and hit the wifie. My husband's grandmother on his mother's side had been Christian Anderson. She had been an aunt to Sir Alexander Anderson, who was my mother-in-law's first cousin, and from there she took her empty pride, and from there my husband took his. Another cousin's son was Sir George Anderson who was Governor of the Royal Bank of Scotland. He had been born in the Fishcross in Fraserburgh.

On the Ugie side of the road, halfway along the Strichen High Street, was a hoosie occupied by Mary Hogg, the Ettrick Shepherd's daughter. This had been the Andersons' ancestral home. They were folk who worked very hard and did well for themselves. Christian Anderson had married a Gibb Sim in Pitullie; she had the westmost house face on to the street, but I have nothing to thank them for in spite of their honours. Often Lady Anderson visited Jinna, my mother-in-law. Once she was waiting for the horse-bus to start. Sitting opposite was a wit, a Pitullie mannie called Aikey. The horse gave a series of loud noisy farts. Aikey said, 'My, that is gey crackers.' Indignantly Her Ladyship answered him, 'I did not come here to be insulted.' Aikey replied, 'Neither did I and if it dae it again we will baith gang oot ower.' That story may be credited to the upmaker but nevertheless that was how she was held in esteem!

Witchill was long occupied by the factor of the Philorth Estates, but Christian gives an inadequate impression of Sir Alexander

Anderson. He was descended from a farming family long established near Strichen, and was a great benefactor of Fraserburgh. As Chairman of the Harbour Board he was responsible for much of the modernisation of harbour and town which went on in the 1870s and '80s. Previously he had had a long and distinguished career in business and in the service of the city of Aberdeen. On the completion of the new Balaclava Breakwater in 1875, Anderson inspired a major ceremony for the laying of the foundation stone, when a hundred Broadsea fishermen drew a boat in procession. On board were Lord Saltoun with his guests and his family, and manning the boat were many of Christian's relatives – Nobles, Taylors, McLemans – Broadsea skippers all.

At this time, certain key appointments in the government of Fraserburgh were in the gift of the Superior, as they always had been. As the Harbour Board Chairman and as 'Baron Baillie' of the Burgh, an office in the hands of the Superior and generally associated with the duty of factor of Philorth, Anderson acted in all things as 'Commissioner for Lord Saltoun'. Until 1840, indeed, the town was entirely governed by the old Barony council, nominated by the Superior. A number of local government reforms were initiated in the second half of the nineteenth century: Lord Saltoun granted to the council the right of election in 1875; and in 1892, under a new act of parliament, the Barony council ceased to exist, and Fraserburgh was henceforth governed by an elected Provost and town council. The Provost was thereafter *ex officio* Chairman of the Harbour Board.

In time I became accustomed to folk shunning me. I have always been far too observant a student of human nature to imagine the situation was worse than it was, but I quickly knew who were my real friends. Mrs Moir, the blacksmith's wife at New Deer, made no difference. She gave me tea and bought my fish, and Mrs Murray in the cottar house at

Auchmaleedie always gave me eggs in exchange, and a Mrs Napier in the village, and two cottar wives, a Mrs Wright in Crossgicht and a Mrs Gill in Old-What. Davidson, the butcher in Strichen, was always kind. He gave me a good measure and aye threw in a big bone to make soup. Mrs Ewing, in Strichen Lodge, said, 'I have always known you.' So did Mrs Rennie, in the Mormond Inn. She knew my real story and always gave me a better dinner than what I paid for. Three cottar wives, a Mrs Knox in Adziel, Mrs Park in Mill of Strichen and Mrs Coutts in South Redbog all remained my friends as before, and these were now the sum total of my country customers. I made the journey as long as my health held out, but it was a depressing business. I had practically no customers left in the Broch, and none who would give me washing.

Rushmore, the chief Sheriff Officer – he styled himself, 'Queen's Messenger at Arms' – first he had the huge house at the corner of Love Lane on the Fishcross. A door in the gable led to the office of his auctioneering business, and a bigger thief was never born for taking bids out of the wall and wheeling things up himself: he stooped to a very low level. He had a bonnie and nice lassie, Anne Rushmore, who died in the cholera epidemic. I had taught the lassie to read in Woodman's School. I had been very sorry for she was only sixteen. Later he built Blofield Cottage on Charlotte Street. His wife had died; another daughter kept house. They fancied their onion, and were far in with the Philorth estates in every department, for Rushmore measured off the feus and did a lot of work for the estate office in finding suitable folk as tenants for the farms. He was aye rouping among cows, so he knew everybody and their financial standing. He larded the Salt-ouns with flattery, like basting a walk-day hen, and was behind all of Lady Saltoun's harebrained schemes in spending huge sums of money to the extent of taking the estate out at the door. The Waterloo Saltoun left £184,000 as his published estate: Rushmore left £36,000, and the Saltouns he served so faithfully left £23,000. It does not take anybody with a head for sums to work out that one.

This day I went to Rushmore's back door. The cook said she would ask Madam if she wanted fish. I could hear her reply, 'Heavens no; that is the woman who has just come from the asylum.' They were not in the habit of buying from me, but I always went in before, because on the gate a notice said, 'No hawkers, pedlars or beggars'. On the opposite side of Charlotte Street the Strachans from Cairnbulg had the same notice on their gate. I went in there also, for no other reason but to shame them. Fortunately such people cannot close the gates of heaven to those who want in there. I told the girl Rushmore to take care what she was saying, for the same thing could befall her. Rushmore knew when the Saltouns were not in residence, and by having his palm crossed with silver permitted curers to stack empty herring barrels on the platform at Philorth Halt, which was Lord Saltoun's private station. Trains did not stop there, but only to serve the laird.

Ellen McLeman, my Aunt Nellie's granddaughter, if she saw me go past would give me a fish for the bairns. I appreciated her kindness, but my friends were few and far between. Charlotte, Lady Saltoun, came to see me. After she married for some reason or other she took to me – not in the sense of a servant, partly because I could speak good English and partly because of my ready tongue. I had known her over thirty years and never did she do what she did that day. She sat on a row of chairs in front of the box bed, almost out at the door. I asked her to come ben to the fire, but she said she was all right. I knew what was going through her head. If I acted peculiarly she could make a quick exit. She did not take tea and I felt very sad, for nobody was going to trust me anymore, even my bairns' chums at school no longer came.

It was a problem to know how to earn a living to support so many bairns. I put in a terrible winter of hard work and near starvation. I fainted and nearly fell in the fire. Dr Mellis asked me to go to the asylum in Aberdeen for a rest. I readily agreed, for it was a blessed haven of peace as it has been a haven to so many, and the lassies who look after the patients could not be kinder. The nursing profession is to medicine what a pair of glasses are to failing eyesight. It is scandalous those quinies are paid with sweeties for doing such a noble job, and in some places they have to put up with awful inferior food. At Cornhill it has always been good. The superintendent assesses what a patient is capable of doing, and they are put on a suitable job.

I was in the laundry and in no time I was allowed into the town. There was a Rosehearty woman I was friendly with and I took her arm all round the harbour. We were given a shilling for working in the laundry, and we used this to buy a panjotral when we had a cup of tea in a café in George's Street. The Rosehearty woman's folk had owned a frachting boat which carried goods regularly to Aberdeen and Leith.

In the Seatoun of Rosehearty was an old house with a stone stair up the gable leading to a large loft. In the season farmers would come down with corn and other goods which were stored in this loft ready for shipping. The boat went down and one of the sons was drowned. This resulted in the mother landing in the asylum. She was a nice person and we found a great deal of comfort in each other's company. It is tragic to hear folk joke about padded cells and make fun of mental illness, but if they gave one thought to the thousand tragic things that have led to a person being in an asylum, they should hang their heads in shame. We were joined by a woman from Turra; she was a cheery type, and the three of us would go window shopping, admiring everything but coveting nothing, for we had only a shilling each to last us a week. My daughter Isabella had again to do the needful at home. She was a bit older, but a big responsiblity for a young lassie of eleven to take on.

In the hospital laundry we did a lot of work for the big hotels and boarding-houses in Aberdeen. This helped to bring in an income towards running the place. I got to know the manager of the Palace and many others. At the back of my mind I constantly thought of what my bairns were doing. I had always been good at needlework, and they set me to teach other patients how to pick out open work on linen. I taught the Turra wife, and a girl from Huntly and a woman from Insch way.

There was an excellent book library. There I met two young boys who could have been my sons. Both were to be of great help to me businesswise. One was a doctor who failed his exams, the other a lawyer who took too much drink. Many folk go into the asylum to hap their sins and to evade the law, but the young doctor and lawyer showed me how to keep a journal, and to make notes as something came in my head to revive my memory, and to write it down before I forgot. They do not encourage writing with quill pens, as if one went missing it could be a dangerous weapon with seriously affected patients; also such people are liable to drink the ink – the same with sewing needles; they are strictly in the care of the Sister. All writing had to be done in pencil. The two boys kept sharpening my pencil for me, they were fascinated with my travels abroad. I was so glad to see both these chaps discharged and thanked God they were clothed and in their right mind.

There was a ward which we had no part or parcel with, it was called the 'GPIs'. They made a lot of noise at night; what a terrible thing to happen – 'He that soweth to the flesh shall reap corruption.' The tragedy, they say, had been brought about by the bad trouble, with a duration of twenty years. Often for long periods those people are perfectly sane, then they take delusions and speak a lot of dirt about being the sons and daughters of dukes and earls and other famous people. All their laundry was done in a separate place and their dishes boiled. Nobody can ring down these people, for many an innocent person has been smitten by an unfaithful marriage partner. It is not the kind of subject folk would want to speak about, but here you were aware of the existence of this dreadful reality. The saddest part of all was the number of young loons and quinies who you would have thought had nothing wrong with them. There was a nice lass from Unst in Shetland. I cheered her up a lot by speaking of the places I had been to and some of the folk I knew. She knew the Tamsons, on the north side of Baltasoun. We once spent a winter there at the great lines, and I knew Sandison's shop at the head of the loch, also Haroldswick and Ronnesvoe. When she went home the lassie sent me a bonnie shawl, so fine you could have pulled it through a gold ring. I have been to Flugga, but what a place in the winter!

To my surprise Charlotte, Lady Saltoun, came to see me, passing through Aberdeen. She had a lot of good bits about her. I got on with her because as a servant I had never regarded the situation as 'them and us', but 'us and us' and I would have told her off as quick as she would have told me. I had always liked old Ness Madgie best. I remember working there as a child, and the staff were speaking of the French Revolution, and in my mind I said to myself, 'Had such a thing happened there I would have smuggled old Madgie out to our house, and blackened her face with soot and sat her down at the fire with a poker to dunt the peats and if the revolutionaries came in I would have said it was my dottled old granny.' Old Madgie had lived to a great age with a sheltered existence and never knew what life was all about. I had great respect for her, and also her son the Waterloo soldier. He had a keen ear for music. I have played the fiddle with him in the Masons' Hall on Broad Street at a kirk soiree; but his successor lived in a different age with rampant snobbery on the upsurge.

Charlotte, Lady Saltoun, constantly asked me to unfold the

scriptures until God showed me I was to cease feeding the heads of those unwilling to do the word spoken (Ezekiel 33, 30–33). She was certainly a born-again woman, but my counsel was but a sweet lullaby in her ears (James I, 21–25 points out we have to be doers and not hearers only, and that it is only in doing that we are blest and are not defeated when the storms of life arise).

I knew my landing in the asylum was all part of my fiery trials. It is the fining pot for silver and the furnace for gold. Job is our finest example. He knoweth the way that I take. When He hath tried me He will bring me forth as gold, or as the silversmith skims and purifies until He can see His own image. I have had the experience of both the fining pot and the furnace of affliction in Isaiah 48, and no matter how fierce, he will eventually come forth unhurt.

It was all part of God's plan, in the prophecy of Daniel concerning the Jewish captivity and the four great world empires which commenced at that time, continuing until after the birth of Christ. The Roman Empire was the last of these until the time of the Reformation, and by knowledge and understanding of these things do we realise where the Throne stands in God's sight and purpose, not the Throne of England as so many wrongly refer to, but the Throne of Great Britain. And I think 'not till the day of the Gentile is past will Scotland regain her independence', and as I have so often said to Lord Saltoun and, since my own baptism of the Spirit, to many Members of Parliament, that 'Whosoever enters into a parliamentary career in this nation will one day have to give an account unto God, as to how far he has furthered God's purpose in by and through his own mouth, and this nation.'

Although Christian did not describe exactly the length of each stay, it is clear that in the first three years after her initial admittance to Cornhill she periodically returned home. Her first discharge was in the spring of 1878 and must have lasted until the 'terrible winter of hard work and near starvation' in the same year, after which she returned to Cornhill for a rest. She referred then, however, to being grateful to be home again, clearly for a second time and clearly in the early summer of 1879. It was at the end of that period at Broadsea, in December 1879, that the final break came, described by Christian without affectation or self-pity.

I was grateful to be home again, but now I found several folk scorned me more than ever before. Aberdeen folk have a far greater tolerance of mental illness than have the folk of Fraserburgh and Peterhead, for in the hospital a Buchan-haven wife told me she met with exactly the same treatment. The doctor advised me not to go to the country as it was too much of a strain for so little return. He asked me to go back to Aberdeen for a check later in the summer, but what a hard struggle to earn a shilling to help make ends meet. The fine weather was not so bad but I dreaded the oncoming winter. I got a job splitting fish in Sandy Meek's fishhouse. I knew folk did not relish my presence. Then I overheard a woman say, 'I think it very wrong a woman out of an asylum should be working with knives.' It was not the man's fault, he had no option but to sack me.

There was nothing left for me but to gather welks from the shore. At least there were plenty of them, and I got fly and watched the receding tide, then made my appearance first, for nobody came near me for about a quarter of a mile on either side, so I filled my bucket quickly with all the big shellfish. It was a sad and lonely existence, but I had my faith and went into Aberdeen towards the end of the summer. I got a terrible shock when I returned to find my dearest friend, my cousin Mary, had died of cancer while I was away. Nobody told me for fear of upsetting me. It was a tragic loss of a real friend. Within a month of her death her eldest son and his wife, a Pitullie girl, claimed the house and put Mary's single daughter and laddie out. Annie, the eldest lassie, gave them a home, bless her. Such is the justice of this world! So now there were new folk next door, and I was like a castaway on a desert island alone. My cousin's daughter, Annie, was married to 'Jock Rochie'[50] and lived at 65 Broadsea. She was kind to me, but being of another age group we could not have the same feeling for each other. I put in three[51] terrible years of sheer hard work and poverty and living on my nerves. It is difficult to describe the atmosphere, but I could only liken myself to the black population in America who are scorned. These poor unfortunate souls expect it from people, and I had now learned to do the same. They cannot help the colour of their face any more than I could help my mental illness.

It was a freezing day getting towards Christmas. I had been breaking ice on the pools of water on the shore to get at the shellfish. My hands were absolutely lifeless. I could hardly hold the pail. I had applied to emigrate to America with all my children to start a new life where nobody knew us, so here at last was the reply. My frozen fingers tore open the letter.

My spirits sank as I read. My medical exam for sailing had not been accepted by the consulate, because of my having been admitted to an asylum. I was told I would have to be put onto Ellis Island and then deported back to Britain. It plunged me into a deep depression.

I had half a dozen hens who were not laying; they could not, for the poor things got hardly any food, so had to forage about for themselves. I knew the exact moment my reasoning broke. I struggled to hang onto it, it was as distinct as a butter plate breaking on the floor. A bottle of paraffin lay near the hen-house. I remember pouring it over the small shed and my son George struggling with me. Onty's Sandy and his wife put me to bed. I heard like a tune playing in my head – I was absolutely worn out. I was not responsible for my actions. The doctor gave me a sedative and now I was on my way to

America. I was lying on my bunk on the ship, I could hear the sailors singing as they shifted the sails.

I felt so much better in the morning. Two doctors and a policeman came and I was certificated as insane. I was to go to Cornhill by the three o'clock train tomorrow. The authorities would come and assess the whole situation. Folk dreaded having anybody certificated for they could be taken out at the door. Many insane peoples' estates went to the Crown to be administered by Chancery. Several folk put my children wise to loot the house before the receivers came in, and they did get a lot of things, but were really too young to know what was of real value. The bairns got most of the photos and family papers; somebody put them up to it. The fishery officer was also the poor inspector. He called together all his commissioners, who had to inform the Lord Chancellor of the Government the extent of an insane person's property. The Crown had power to recover expenses and to seize and sell personal property on behalf of the commissioners.

My eldest son was yet a minor and could not be allowed to accept responsibility for seven children. It was decided the young ones were going to Aberlour Orphanage, and the house and contents would be sold towards their keep. I heard all this going on from my sick bed. Then I really knew who were my genuine friends. When she heard the bairns were going to an orphanage Mrs Annie Crawford, 41 Broadsea, came down and offered to take the three youngest ones, Charlotte, Mary and Watt. Nellie was ten; she went as a houseservant to folk in Inverallochy. Andrew was twelve; he went to live with Benff's Kitta until she died. He then went to live with Madgie Noble at 18 Noble Street. Isabella, Andrew's twin, went off to Lowestoft at twelve to work for Maconochie. When she came back she made her home with Mrs Elizabeth Noble at 10 Broadsea. They were very good to her. My son George, who had prevented me setting fire to the hen-house was fourteen.[52] He was not fixed up with anybody and was the last to leave 72 before he handed over the key to the commissioners.

They put the house up for sale, and God works in mysterious ways. It was the 30th of December 1879, the nineteenth anniversary of my mother's death. A terrible gale swept Scotland. The whole back of the roof of 72 was lifted by the wind and landed in the sea and remained there. The hurricane resulted in the tragic Tay Brig disaster. Huge snowstorms followed, and one night, as darkness was falling, Willie McLeman, 34 Broadsea, was returning home from sea-fowling with his gun, when he noticed movement under an upturned boat. He was amazed – it was my son George, who had no home after 72 was vacated. He was too old at fourteen for the authorities to take an interest in him. Willie McLeman took him to his home where his wife, Liza Cardno's Jeanicky, made him welcome to stay until he married. Willie McLeman's mother was Barbara Sim, a first cousin of my mother-in-law. Although she did not profess to be, Liza Cardno's Jeanicky was a sincere Christian who will one day be justly rewarded for her great kindness to the poor and downtrodden. She gave tea to all the tramps and food to the aged, often leaving herself with hardly any. She had a lot of waifs and strays under her roof at one time – Johnny Hendry, Bobby Rhymer Duthie, my son George and a quinie Janet Summers. All were given a good comfortable home.

Everything that was left in 72 was sold by public roup in the mart in Cow Lane. All my own and my brothers' school copybooks were sold with other stuff for 2d. Rushmore the auctioneer was a slimy character. He got a good haul to himself. His house, Blofield Cottage, was full of bankrupt curers' stuff.

I often wonder what my eldest son thought when he came back to find his home was sold and everything with it. The gold watch my husband got for bravery was also sold and my children have tried without success to trace it.

No offer of help came from the Pitullie side. My mother-in-law sold 13 Pitullie to Beelie Mitchell and his wife Annie Gatt. I don't know who did it but the partitions between the rooms had been demolished. I think they were afraid my children might go in and occupy it. The Mitchells divided the rooms, starting with the bed coverings. It was cruel of Jinna to sell the house when her grandchildren had no home, but it was her own to do whatever she liked with.

The commissioners for the poor sorted out the situation. They could not take the boat because Baxter still had a four-year lease on it. Nobody would take the dog Ranger, so he had to be done away with. That morning the gauger came and shot the doggie. The boys buried him on the brae and the children were in a dreadful state of tears because we had had it since my son Watt was born.

A cab drew up at the door. I was dressed and ready. My young children were screaming murder and clinging to my skirts as I was hustled out. Annie Laurie and Betsy Buchan were at the door and waved me off, but I was too ill to care whether I lived or died. It was lack of food and sleep, for I had gone hungry to give it all to the children. I reached Aberdeen and never was the asylum more welcome. I cannot have enough praise for these doctors and nurses who give so much of their life to heal the sick. With nourishing food and rest I quickly recovered.

My eldest son was still at sea. He wrote to me regularly. Christmas came and some local bakers in Aberdeen generously gave us a treat. I did a lot of baking myself, but my heart was at home with my children. My daughter had brought several garments to mend, and as we celebrated the birth of the Child of Bethlehem's stable straw, I thought 'how magnificent there is still hope for man'.

# CHAPTER TEN

## *Cornhill (1879–1892)*

Christian now began a period of her life – in fact the last forty-five years of her life – as a permanent inmate of the asylum. The years could have been wretched to recount and to read about. Instead, she made of them a rich experience, richly described. She was fascinated by the variety of persons admitted to Cornhill and she gave her impressions of them faithfully. She worked hard at tasks she knew well – as fishwife and laundrywoman, buying fish at Aberdeen Market, cleaning them and delivering them to Cornhill. She was determined to save money in order to buy back her house or a share in it. She made herself a notable character and an influence on those around her, as she had always been. She worried about her family, recording their unfolding lives, and all too often their early deaths. She reflected bitterly on the dissipation of her inheritance – the proud house of the Constables of Broadsea and their family possessions. Above all, she felt herself called to preach – and preach she did to all and sundry – a message of Divine Providence and salvation through the Cross, always salted by pithy observations from her own very human experience.

> One day, about six weeks after my entry, I noticed the doctor was wearing my gold keeper ring on his cranny. I told him it was mine. He said, 'What would I be doing with your ring?' Another day he handed me a batch of letters, maybe twenty. He asked if I would look for some addressed to himself. I

found three, and to my surprise I found one from my son who was somewhere in the China seas. The doctor said, 'You will soon be given a job.' The superintendent had a long chat and said to me, 'If you are going to be under the threat of mental illness, you would be far better to come here and live a routine life in Aberdeen, where you can get help at any time.' I had been certificated and must live under parole.

In the spring I started as the hospital fishwife. I went to Aberdeen Market three times a week, bought the fish and gutted them. The porters were all so kind to me – what a difference from the people of Fraserburgh and Broadsea! The wifie from the fishmarket cafe always gave me tea and a roll for nothing. I said, 'I am not a beggar.' She said, 'It is coming off a braid boord.' I would have paid for my tea but she would not have it. She said, 'We dinna miss a cuppie tay tae a puir wifie frae the asylum.' I am greatly in the debt of all those market folk who helped me more than ever I can thank them.

I got to know the trawl skippers and their wives, and all the shore-porters and stevedores and gutting quines down the point law, and I spoke to them all of their never dying souls. I worked very hard and sewed by hand dozens of patchwork quilts, and I did a lot of embroidery for Aberdeen shops, besides working in the hospital laundry. We were fortunate in having so many skeely doctors in the asylum.

Dr Jamieson, the Super in the asylum, was a kind man who tried to help his patients in every way. In my heart I planned my escape. I mentioned this to a schoolteacher lass, an intellectual with not much wrong with her. She had lost her mother. They had been close and the girl only needed a suitable time to rest after her tears. She mentioned what I said to the Super. He pleaded with me not to run away – it would only hinder my progress.

My house in Broadsea stood roofless for months. It was on the market. The commissioners tried to roup it but there were no takers, so they would sell privately for money towards my children's keep.

Anne Taylor had married at nineteen a well-to-do chap from Barton across the river from Hull. He was lost at sea the following year, so she was widowed at the age of twenty. Her mother was Mary Johnstone, up the road at 55 Broadsea; her mother had married Bouff's Jimmy shortly after his first died, he was drowned at the Lintern fishing, leaving her with half a dozen little bairns. Mary Johnstone had taken her old parents to look after – the wifie was a Third from Cairnbulg, and the mannie lived a long time. He must have been about ninety. He had been on the field as a private soldier at Waterloo (in his old age a grateful nation gave him ten pence a week as a pauper). I remember them being in a cottar house at Techmuirie. He was a Johnstone from Crovie.

Mrs Garden (Anne Taylor) came to me in Aberdeen and said she would buy my hoosie, if I was agreeable, on the heading that if I was to come home I would be given a corner and could have it back if I wanted at the purchase price. Her sisters-in-law were two spinster schoolteachers in Hull. They would help her pay the money and put on the new roof.

I said, 'Anything you like, but it will never be my hand that will sign any document saying that I sold it.'

Anne Taylor came of a family who swore like troopers. They were bold and impudent, nobody would have sat on them. Their mother had a hard time bringing them up. Sometimes I would have given her a bit of butter from the country. The daughter minded on my kind acts, and said she would repay me by taking my hoosie off the market. I discovered she had many kindly sides to her nature in spite of a brash and forceful appearance. She had been one of the few folk who had treated me as a human being when I came home from Cornhill the first time. So the house was roofed, and Anne Taylor moved in with Maggie Noble, who married a man Lovie from Whitehills. Mrs Garden had a five-year-old son who lived with her mother. She had paid the commissioners £35 for my house, and what a strange sequence it all had.

My son James became a confirmed agnostic, bitter towards the authorities who sold his birthright. He hated McLaren, the minister, with the white flame of hatred. He tried to recover some of the stuff that had been sold at the roup, and discovered the best of it had been bought by the lawyer and his click at their own valuation. An oil painting on canvas, depicting Christ entering Jerusalem on an ass was bought for five shillings: it had been given to my mother as a wedding present by Catherine Thurlow, the wife of Lord Saltoun. It was signed 'J. Runciman', also a heavy silver tassie was inscribed 'Alexander Fraser and Mary Gordon 1707'[53] (it had come from Fraserburgh Castle), and many other valuable things. Under such circumstances it was not ethical for a lawyer to acquire a client's property. The way some of these make money, they are lower than the lowest prostitute, but one day they must all go to a deathbed, and what then? Often their conscience gets them; that is why several have been found hanging from the beams in stables and outhouses. What a terrible thing to become a disciple of the devil, all for the greed of gold.

Mrs Anne Crawford, 41 Broadsea – folk called her Annie Bogie – her mother had been a first cousin of my mother. Both Annie's parents had been Nobles – she was paid a sum each week for my three young children's keep. She was kind to them. It is hard to lose both parents at that age for a gien bite is easy eaten. I had to bring up my family from a distance, no easy undertaking.

In 1881 my son Watt died of scarlatina in Annie Bogie's closet. I went through to the funeral and felt very sad, but somewhere in my heart I was grateful. He was ten years old and he had been coiling and kettle-boiling on a fishing boat that summer. He had four pounds in a bankie by his bed and the trustees' commissioners paid the rest of the funeral from the proceeds of my realized estate. I spent the night in 72 and went back to Aberdeen next day. My son Watt was free from the cares of a loveless upbringing. Thy will be done.

I worked very hard for I was determined to pay back the money on my house. The Lord Chancellor wanted my boat also, but I managed to get this confiscation stayed off until my youngest child was sixteen. The lease on the boat ran out in 1884, but it helped a lot to keep my children from being paupers, for I had £15 a year rent. The tax gatherer took a shilling per pound.

The lease on the fishing boat, *Ocean Foam*, ran out, so rather than renew it I agreed to sell it to Aberdeen. The commissioners for the Lord Chancellor had the main say, but with the help of a little persuasion on my part, I suggested we take the money realised and put on a new one which was built by Forbes of Sandhaven and called the *Union Jack*. My brother-in-law, William Pirie, had a 50 per cent share only till my youngest child was sixteen, for under the Act of Lunacy my whole estate was administered by the Crown. My youngest daughter was now eight. I was extremely happy to know that they still had a source of income, though the commissioners would not permit any of my sons to work on the boat.

My son George married very young a charming girl, Jane Noble, a daughter of Alex Noble (Rochie) 41 Broadsea. Her father had married a second wife, and evicted from the house his large family by his first wife. Like my own children they were scattered to the four winds. Jane Noble had been given a home by Sottie's folk, so to marry young was the best thing for both. She made him a grand wife. I was very fond of her. Anne Taylor had let them into the butt end at 72.

My mother-in-law died in 1883, the year before the new boat was built. I went through to her funeral. She had lived latterly with her daughter in Sandhaven, which was now a very busy fishing port. I was amazed at the transformation. A new road was cut from the Meal Mill to join Pitullie with herring stations all over the place.

My son James stayed in the seamen's mission in Aberdeen when he came to see me. He was a firm agnostic, fed by the fact that the authorities had appropriated everything belonging to us, but the poor have always been so greatly wronged, yet we must abide by the law. He came to me and said he would like to marry the widow who bought my house. I said, 'If it's to recover your heritage that is not sufficient reason for marriage.' She was three years his senior. I was not against the idea, for she came of strong-willed folk: the Taylors were proud and stubborn. (My didy, Alexander Watt, had a Taylor grandmother on one side and a Greig from Cairnbulg on the other. The first Taylor came to Broadsea in the seventeenth century. Folk still speak of 'waiting a Highland moon'; when the moon was high everybody was on standby during the seventeenth century. The Gordons of Huntly gave the allied pass to the Macphersons and Macintoshes to cross their land to raid Buchan. After such a raid a Broadsea woman, a tailor's wife, found a laddie who had been left behind weak and hungry. She had him in her house, which today is 73 Broadsea, for the authorities would have hanged the boy. The tailor and his wife were a childless couple and kept the boy, who spoke Gaelic. He was known as 'the Tailor's boy' and that was the name he took. I often heard my old didy relate this story.) My daughter Anne Taylor wanted to go through a Christian marriage ceremony. She was not the wrong one. My son wanted no such thing; he said why should he be a hypocrite and go through this when he did not believe a word of it. In Scotland if a couple declare their intention of marriage to the Sheriff in the presence of two witnesses it is perfectly valid, and my son intended to do this.

I was shocked and horrified beyond anything that human words can convey. It is almost impossible to think that one brought up as he was could have done that. I asked the girl what she was thinking of. She said she wanted him. I said, 'You are both going to mar two lives and probably several more, for this is the result of my son's bitterness and can only lead to heartbreak, and I can only remind you Jesus died on Calvary that the sin of our past might be cast into the sea of forgetfulness.'

They went to the Sheriff to declare their intention. I was furious at my son Andrew, who, along with her youngest sister, witnessed this pagan union. For ten years I prayed earnestly and it was my joy to know my son had found the Saviour at Stornoway. His wife also was converted, and they went through a Christian marriage ceremony, and my son Andrew and her sister were again the witnesses. She was the youngest and the only one I really liked of Mary Johnstone's family. The poor lass made a marriage to a wealthy man but it ended on the rocks, for he was an out-and-out cad. Passing through Aberdeen she often called at Cornhill to see me. When she introduced me to her aristocratic Edinburgh husband I was not taken with his shifty eyes. He was engineer on the Shetland steamer.

My son Andrew was now drinking heavily. He had a very likeable pleasant nature. Folk called him Donald Brose, why I don't know. His marriage to Mary Duthie, from Inverallochy, a fiery character, steadied him up a lot. My son George folk called Geordie Ra – why I don't know either.

Dr Reid, who had been an assistant, took over at Cornhill. He was a wonderful man with a great love for suffering humanity. Following the death of my son Watt I had a fit of depression and was confined to bed for two weeks. Then I was back on the rounds with my creel. There was no hope of being discharged, but after she was older my daughter Isabella, during the slack time in January and February, always took the butt end of the Forbes House at 14 South Square, Footdee. I went there every Friday night with my four daughters. It was something of a home life to stay till Monday. We did this till Isabella married John Mackenzie, Rochie's stepson in Broadsea.

My daughter Nellie told me she was getting married to a fellow McLive. She said she was expecting his child. He was a cooper to trade and came of a proud family. Later she came into Aberdeen in a woebegone state and showed me a terrible letter from her boyfriend stating that since her mother was in the asylum he could not consider marriage. I told her she was far better rid of this blackguard. In due time the child was stillborn. She was living with my daughter Isabella, who had a set house up the back stair in John Lawson's House on Broadsea Road; it is now called Noble Street. My poor lassie died of puerperal fever three days after the birth. I went through to the funeral, and stayed a week. I was greatly depressed, but waited thirty years to meet the cad McLive. After the war[54] one Sunday I was having tea in the refreshment room with my granddaughter Kirsten Sim and her husband Andrew Crawford, a Christian fellow I am very fond of. My granddaughter told me who the folk were who were sitting beside us. It was this McLive who was visiting his wife, who had been admitted as a patient to the asylum. I unleashed my tongue on that one – 'The mills of God grind slow but exceeding small.' I always spoke to the woman of many things and to pass on the word. It was my joy to see her discharged and to return to her folk.

My elder son was constantly at loggerheads with the authorities. He refused to try and make things easy for himself. They would not release their hold on the new boat, the *Union Jack*, so he got no say in the matter. McLaren, the Parish Minister, was one of the commissioners for the Crown. He would not give an inch, and suggested to the Registrar that my son's children should be classified as illegitimate. My son had three beautiful daughters, who, poor things, had to suffer by having their father's folly cast in their faces: in fact the teachers at Broadsea School took an ill will to them for no particular reason. A Miss Buchan, a teacher in Broadsea School, once said to my granddaughter when the school term started, 'Oh you're the girlie whose parents are not properly married,' before a class of forty. Fate has a strange way of repaying those with a ready tongue. This dame took up with an officer from a foreign boat and was left in the lurch with a child. I knew the folk in Aberdeen where she went into hiding. Then she returned as if nothing had happened, until one day she was making a fool of a dunderhead lassie. They were talking about a cat. The teacher said, 'You know the pussy cat says meow, meow, meow.' She got a shock when the girl replied, 'But the foreign doggie says bow, wow, wow.'

There was a lassie of about sixteen came into the asylum; she was depressed when she discovered whom she thought to be her parents were in fact her grandparents, who had lavished an abundance of love on her. I told the lass not to worry, and to be grateful to have had such parents who really loved her. They had a beautiful house in Bon Accord Terrace. The folk were nice to me and the lass was soon home. She married a chemist in Edinburgh, and never a Hogmanay has passed but she sends me some little gift. The lassie was depressed when she found out about her illegitimacy. It is a word that should be erased from the English language.

My daughter Mary married Robert Davidson, a person I disliked on sight, but I said nothing, for I was not going to interfere in any way with my children's choice of partners. My own husband had been a mother's boy, and I had first-hand knowledge of what this means. My youngest daughter Charlotte married Hugh McKay, a Highlandman from Sutherland. He was the son of an evicted crofter from Kildonan. Strangely enough I disliked him also but kept my counsel to myself, so now they were all gone to homes of their own and I no longer had the worry.

I was now happy to be the fishwife and laundrymaid at the asylum, which had been home to me for years. Following my daughter Nellie's death I was quite ill for I missed her a lot. She was a laughing cheerful girl, so full of fun with an infectious mirth. It was all part of my fiery trials. Many young mothers after their first childbirth come into the asylum with nervous breakdowns. It is a condition and penalty of civilisation for in primitive tribes there is no fear of labour pain, which makes the mother relaxed and birth is comparatively easy. I tell these girls I had ten and to start to worry once they have passed forty. Mostly they are very young. By far the majority get over it quickly; only two or three have I seen return for further treatment.

Dr Reid often asked my advice on people from our own quarter. He asked if I had any suggestions to help a Cairnbulg man who was admitted. I said, 'Yes, give him a job to make white nets in some of the stores down the Pocra Dock.' The man went to his job every morning and was not long in getting home. Later his two sons passing through, having come from Yarmouth, and gave me a beautiful cashmere shawl. They were both Christian boys. One was a beautiful singer. I asked him to sing 'When I survey the Wondrous Cross on which the Prince of Glory died'. The whole staff in the asylum kitchen stopped work to listen. It was very moving, especially in a place of this kind, but I could see God's purpose for my life was to speak to the medical profession, for so many doctors are atheists. The universities often are responsible. I knew a lady doctor who had found the Saviour at fifteen. When she went to university, her colleagues said, 'We wonder how long you will remain a Christian.' She was saved before her entry and held on to her faith, but she was astounded at the unbelief among doctors and specialists and nurses. I have seen some nurses abandon their faith simply to keep on the good side of a doctor who is an unbeliever. There is a kind of status symbol among nurses that it is the thing to marry a doctor, and then they feel they have made the grade.

Until the Great War nurses were generally the daughters of business and professional folk. Many, after marriage, kept in touch with me. One lass became a devout Christian and labourer in the field. Now happily married in England she has led many to the Lord. She was the daughter of a Glasgow boot manufacturer.

A wifie who lived near Cairnbulg school came into the asylum. She used some scandalous language. Dr Reid asked me to find out what she was saying. I would like very much to know the origin of the Cairnbulg dialect, they are a distinct ethnic group. In the Philorth charter room mention is made of the fishings of Cairnbulg in the thirteenth century. The wifie kept saying, 'The Whore Buggers Breedir'. I got out of her that her sister-in-law's brother had appropriated her savings and she hadn't a hope of getting them back; this put the poor wifie off. I was kind to her and she followed me about and was soon well and home again. I was grateful.

Many folk come into the asylum to dish out religious tracts. Often they are doing a lot of harm, for many of those people are not prepared to acknowledge the help of medicine and lay people have no proper guidelines which qualify them to administer to the sick. Many of the Open Plymouth Brethren seem to think they own the publishing rights of the gospel. There are, I agree, many folk of strong character amongst them but there are also some very weak ones.

A very snooty wifie came in from the swank area of Devonshire Place. She was boasting of her son who was the captain of a liner. Nobody could have cared less though he was the donkey man! How stupid of people, for what is your life? 'It is even as a vapour that appeareth for a little time and then it vanisheth away.' We are all actors with a part to play. Even King Edward was but an actor playing the part of Macbeth. Lords and Ladies are but likewise human beings playing to a greater audience. Even Queen Victoria, who must surely have been the most venerated woman in the world, could sit down to a glittering banquet in the Guildhall, but the Queen could not but be constantly reminded of her mortal day, for in an hour, like all others, she must go and have a bowel movement. If we have health we have everything.

A patient came into the asylum under a fictitious name. I knew by his eyes that he was a psychopathic type. I knew immediately who he was; I had seen him as a young laddie at Strichen House. He was the young laird, who only came during the shooting. He never stayed there as in residence. He had been admitted to Cornhill for attempting to shoot somebody. He spoke to me and said, 'How long have you been in the asylum?' He went on, 'I only came into the private home for a rest.' I thought it funny – because I was Kirsty Watt I was in the asylum, but because he was George Baird[55] he was in a home! What is the difference? My nephews sent me newspapers from America regularly, and often they linked the name of George Baird with that of Mrs Langtry, the Jersey Lily. She was said to be the friend of princes and millionaires but the American papers said she was something else. Baird was not long in being discharged.

When somebody appears in the Broch with a lum hat and English accent, the folk are bowled over and play into their barrow and in no time the incomer is on the crest of the wave; yet they are so ready to ring down anybody belonging to the place. I am not against English folk coming to the Broch. It is a healthy exchange of blood to marry outsiders, but be it an English labourer the Broch will not want to know him – only a person they think is somebody.

Aberdeen was now a very busy port. English emigrants were pouring into Torry by the thousand to man the steam trawlers. Local folk resented this very much: rows of beautiful granite tenements were going up everywhere, constant fights took place between the locals and incomers, and the breach never healed until almost all the sons of both laid down their lives in the war – then they realised how we should strive for the brotherhood of man.

When I came back to the hospital from the Aberdeen fish market, on a Friday, I aye came by way of the Castlegate, for here I could pass on the word of God to the wayfarer. When I was young, in the fine weather deep in the Grampian mountains when we were selling our fish, often we would meet wandering Jews who had fled persecution from Germany, Russia and the Balkans, and from all over Europe. Britain had opened her door to such people and she prospered in so doing. We would have a heavy birn of fish on our backs on the hills; the Jews had large packs often consisting of bales of cheap cloth. London folk speak of this as the rag trade. Sometimes my mother bought from them, and over the years we got to know them, for they eventually made their appearance at the coast. Some of the old men were those same Jews who traversed the hills, others were a second generation with stalls on the Castlegate. I loved to speak to them, for the word is to the Jew first. After my own baptism of the Holy Ghost and fire, no human being but God Himself began to teach me of Abraham, hence the twelve tribes of Israel, God's giving of the law to Moses, then their travels under him and Joshua's leadership, right on to the possession of the Promised Land under God-given judges and kings, their wars and troubles and on to their captivity in Babylon; then their release by Cyrus the Persian. At this point it was obvious that obedience to God's word is the only way of having His blessing. Our God is a dreadful and terrible God outside of his love towards us in his beloved Son Jesus. The Israelites in their day were overshadowed by God under His, the coming Saviour's shadow. Everything in their rituals, ordinances and sacrifices was the shadow of him who, in the fulfilment of time, would fulfil them in Himself. In the keeping of the law during his earthly sojourn, His death on the Cross as the Lamb of God without spot or blemish, His glorious resurrection and ascension, back into the Heavenly Holy of Holies, there to fulfil the Levitical High Priesthood, and to become our own High Priest, to those who have come unto God by Him. In Galatians God clearly showed me the law is our schoolmaster to bring us to Christ.

I always spoke to the Jewish traders on the Castlegate, subjects from the Old Testament, never from the New. In Aberdeen, so far from their own land, I realised what God said of them, that they were disobedient gainsaying people, arrogant, hardnecked, impudent and rebellious. So they were and still are, besides their love of making money and putrid business methods. I met with all these things in the Castlegate, yet God put His own love in my heart for these people because of what Abraham, Isaac and Jacob stood for in His sight, confirmed in Romans XI. It is sad that so many believers are influenced to a great dislike of Jews because of their impudent and arrogant opposition to any and everything concerning Jesus. I certainly got plenty, but I have proved they can be very lovable and kindhearted, for when they discovered I was a patient from the asylum they could never do enough for me. Often I got a very cheap remnant to send to the Broch to make dresses for my lassies. In Romans XI the Jew is blinded in part only; it is our business to prevail with God to open the other eye.

My eldest son James had become so atheistic in his outlook, and he had a burning desire to educate himself. I could only pray to God to help him in his unbelief. He said, 'God created the world: then who created God?' God is, and does not require any creation. Time and space are meaningless, for a thousand years are as a day, ten thousand years are as a drop in the ocean. My son believed in the Darwin theory and totally rejected his Christian upbringing. Strangely enough he did not smoke or drink, and kept on saying one can be as moral as an unbeliever. I told him he was a miserable sinner; he said I was being ridiculous.

After ten years God used a Faith Mission preacher's faithfulness to convince my son of his need, at Stornoway in the Isle of Lewis, but not without a great deal of heartache in the years between. But, 'Be ye not weary in well doing, for in due season ye shall reap if ye faint not.' God is long-suffering, long-forbearing and has long patience, and we must be likewise until he gives repentance unto the acknowledging of the truth, knowing full well the God of this world blinds the minds of them that believe not, lest the light of the Glorious Gospel of Christ should shine in unto them, II Corinthians, 4.

I have always had the gift of really knowing and seeing through people, all but the man I married; but then the heart will always find its own reasons for blinding its owner. I have never been taken in with fine speeches. I never regretted turning down any of my suitors. The Master of Lovat married when he was about forty. Murray Fraser of Philorth never married. Later I was glad I did not accept him and go out to India, for in the 1857 Sepoy Mutiny they were fortunate to get off with their lives. Jamie Fraser gave me a first-hand account of what happened; they lost all their furnishings and personal gear and two-thirds of the European population in India were mercilessly slaughtered – but then what were they doing there? Much as I hate violence of any kind, the Indians were trying to regain control of their own country.

In my own marriage my husband was the exact opposite in outlook and disposition to myself. He had accepted Christ as his Saviour when he was twenty-five and married me two years later. I was converted myself before my marriage. I was expecting my first child, and through that I was saved by Grace, 'Suffer little children to come unto me and forbid them not for such is the Kingdom of heaven.' Stepping out as a

Christian we must be as little children feeding on the milk of the word, but as we grow older we have to be weaned and go on to stronger food. Not until after my husband's death did I receive the Holy Ghost as the Comforter, as a second work of Grace wrought by God, according to John 14. I was no sooner a widow than God showed me very definitely I must never be unequally yoked, not only in the matter of marriage, but in friendship or in business. One must come out and be separate. To do so brings a greater fulfilment, just as Christ is received by us as Saviour and friend, for God the Father receives us into his presence. Marriage in the first instance was a state between a man and a woman ordained by God, and when those who have become His children enter that state, God expects them to live up to his standard, for it and in it. The marriage bed is honourable and undefiled: therefore shall a man leave his mother and father and cleave to his wife and they shall be one flesh. It was said of Adam and Eve (a state which Jesus verifies in Mark), 'So then they are no more twain but one flesh. What therefore God hath joined together let no man put asunder' – that was his answer to the Pharisees on the matter of divorce.

Verses 10 to 12 plainly show that a divorced person who has remarried has committed adultery. For a long time in this land it was not lawful for a divorcee to marry again. It is not so long since the bill was passed to make it lawful to do so. Moses gave the bill of divorcement because of the hardness of their hearts, which means an unforgiving spirit. Matthew, chapter 18 clearly shows how often we must forgive, and if we don't forgive we ourselves will not be forgiven by God the Father. The bill Moses gave was to be for only one cause, fornication. If two people do not get on they are far better separated, for nothing can be more soul-destroying than living in discord. Divorce is an easy thing nowadays but it is not of God. Until the war some women put in dreadful lives, keeping silent and tolerating drink and bullying. Rightly they will no longer do it. God's standard says 'Husbands love your wives and be not against them' (Colossians, chapter 3), 'Dwell with them according to knowledge' (This means a knowledge of God and his ways), 'Giving honour unto the wife as unto the weaker vessel, and as being heirs together of the Grace of Life.' No man or woman after marriage can live unto themselves or have their freedom as before. The first two years there has to be much give and take, with bearing and forbearing patience until moulded into a complete understanding of the one with the other's difference in disposition and outlook on life. God showed me by the spirit of revelation concerning my mother-in-law, that I, with my disposition, was just as trying to her as she was to me. This brought a greater understanding and peace of mind to all concerned.

We are first accepted by the Beloved, because of the finished work of Jesus Christ, but we must get to the place of being accepted for ourselves, because we have become willing and obedient in that which is acceptable to Him, in our daily life and our contact with others. To this end God puts us into circumstances to prove us, and that is where so many fail to become acceptable, yet we are enjoined to prove what is acceptable unto God, Ephesians, 5. First we have to learn to suffer in God's will, I Peter, 3, and in the middle of our tribulations we must learn to commit our souls to him in well doing when in the midst of it, and when we have done well and suffered for it we must take it patiently. I proved this after I let my Auntie Betty into my house at Broadsea, an action which ruined us and took us out at the door financially. I took that patiently. This is acceptable to the Almighty, again as a born-again lively stone in the holy priesthood, we are built up to offer up spiritual sacrifices acceptable unto God by Jesus Christ. We must offer up joy and the singing of praise in the time of trouble, because of his hiding me at such a time in his pavilion, so too we are to offer the sacrifice of thanksgiving. These I have learned in my fiery trials and afflictions. As Jesus said, ' I came not to do my will but the will of the Father.'

The Master of Saltoun[56] married a nice Irish girl, Lady Grattan Bellew. I had not a lot at the time but bought half a yard of strong lawn and I picked out three fraises. She was delighted. Shortly afterwards Lord Saltoun died.[57] My son Andrew was at the funeral, and told me his Lordship's riderless horse was led in the cortège. His Lordship loved his horse as one of his own bairns. I was sorry for his wife. Her husband's death took a lot out of her. When she came north her hair was quite grey. I noticed her head was dusted with white lead powder. I said, 'Your Ladyship, if you put that stuff on your hair you will raise some kind of skin trouble.' I should have held my tongue; next time she appeared she was wearing an awful white wig, for all the earth it minded you on a besom mop for putting beeswax on a floor. She seemed to think it was more becoming and respectful for a widow to have white hair.[58]

In 1892 my boat was claimed by the Crown. Strangely enough Munro the advocate died that year so thus ended another chapter in my life. William Pirie got his own fifty shares. The lawyers who handled the thing took eighteen of my shares, and Reginald Macleod of Dunvegan, on behalf of Her Gracious Majesty received my other thirty-two shares. They required a copy of my husband's death register. For keeping my children Annie Bogie was paid nothing like the sum my whole estate fetched, so who got the rest is one of those many mysteries of government business, but I went on with my work, glad to be well able to do it with no bitterness to anybody.

# CHAPTER ELEVEN

## Public Tragedies and
## Private Reflections (1892–1918)

I heard Keir Hardie and Cunninghame Graham in Aberdeen. I was greatly impressed with their oratory and radical politics.

The British Empire is probably the greatest the world will ever see before man all but destroys himself in a series of unthinkable conflicts. We have seen the first in 1914, but there are bigger and better things to come. Keep your eye on Jerusalem, when the Jews return to their own land – that which precedes the coming of the Messiah Jesus in clouds and great glory.

The scriptures must be fulfilled. The year 1914 was the time of the coming of sorrows, the first Great War.

Britain was foremost in technical things and successfully launched the industrial revolution on medieval pay and conditions, practically still prevailing. This gave a lead over other nations and accounts for the vast fortunes accumulated in the nineteenth century. They treated their own folk in exactly the same way as they did their slaves. Had they been a little more human and introduced legislation for a decent pay and working hours, embarking on so great a venture, they could have created a measure of lasting peace and worthwhile influence over two thirds of the earth's surface, but greed, pride and other deadly sins took precedence over decency. But the scriptures must be fulfilled.

As trawl-fishing hotted up, inshore fishers complained of the sea being cleaned of fish. Many urged the government to step in and take strong measures to protect the spawn. Bigger places grew as smaller ones declined, when families flitted to the large fishing ports. Torry was now a conglomeration of different accents. Fittie[59] did not change so much partly for the reason that farmland round it much earlier had been developed as shipyards, but the folk changed. Fittie wifies no longer wore their particular style of mutch, which they called a cockleronie bonnet; some were edged with fine bobbin lace. After the Inster fishing in the winter, Broch boats called regularly at Aberdeen. Often I had tea with a ship's crew in the market café whereby I could watch as a winner of souls; also I kept up with news of home.

One day I met Gilbert Noble who is married to Dunkie's Jock's adopted daughter. With him was Joe Maclean who said to me, 'Do you mind when you put the paraffin on the hen-house?' Gilbert Noble was furious at him and said, 'Joe, you should have left that alane.'

It did not worry me, but I replied, 'Yes, and do you mind when you used to piss your breecks when you were a great big loon who should have known better, and the lave of the bairns in the school were scumfished with stink?'

Joe was totally illiterate. He could neither read, write nor tell the time. I am sorry for such people. I had long since become so accustomed to snubs and insults that they ran off like water on a ducks' back.

In 1886 the Broadsea folk began to collect funds for the building of the Fishermen's Hall. I have grown to love Aberdeen, but I love home best, so like the lave I wanted to give my own contribution. I did many fancy tea-cloths and sold them. I got the linen very cheap. I sent the money to Kirsty Rollie's son, Isaac Noble, who always acknowledged it by letter. Daily every Broadsea boat gave a box of fish and in seven years or so the hall was built and opened by Lord

Saltoun and his Irish Lady. I went through to Broadsea for this big day.

The new Lady Saltoun had an awful time with Charlotte, her mother-in-law, who had refused to give up the reins at Philorth. Maids and gardening boys would be given a job, then Charlotte would take them off their job and send them on her errands into the Broch. The new Lady finally put her foot down. When Charlotte, the dowager Lady, died I missed her letters from St George Square, her last residence. She had a nice side to her nature if you could find it. She would have been better on the stage rather than a stately house. She would have helped me but she knew I was far too independent to accept anything I had not worked for. She died submissive to her Redeemer, and God has promised we will meet in the Glory.

John Noble ('Jock Rochie') died at 42 College Bounds. He was married to my cousin Mary's daughter, Annie. I had aye regarded her as my nearest relation and went through to Jock's funeral, one of the most impressive, for Templars from Rosehearty, Cairnbulg, St Combs and everywhere, wore their sashes. It was my turn to comfort Annie, who was left with half a dozen bairns. She has been my friend in all our joys and sorrows. Jock was thirty-five; he died as the result of an accident.

The last years of the century were happy ones for me. I went to Aberdeen market and worked in the laundry and had a great measure of peace.

I am sure the Boer War killed Queen Victoria. Something did not ring true about the whole thing. It was a war of London society. Debutantes and duchesses were trooping out to South Africa as nurses, dames who have never teemed a chanty po in all their life. They were having a braw good time at the expense of those laying down their life. It it not difficult to see through those folk. As usual, Winston Churchill wanted to blow his own trumpet. Everything he says, does and writes is to advertise his glory. I have followed his career, because I worked for his grandmother in Brooklyn. They were nice folk.

The British had been falling behind, and many colonials and Americans came to the aid of the Colours, including my own nephew who came as a medical volunteer. Single and in his late forties, he grabbed the chance to pass through Britain. He visited 72 Broadsea and spent two hours in the Broch between trains. He later met my husband's nephew, Richard Pirie, a Gordon Highlander, in Capetown. I saw him off at the station with a large contingent of troops. A brass band was playing 'Goodbye Dolly Gray' – this land of many partings. He wrote me regularly, and said the Boers were magnificent soldiers and brave. I myself was pro-Dutch, for when we travelled the fishing we often met men and women off Dutch boats. They were straight, honest to deal with, hardworking and so like the Scots in temperament; and I am sure their Dutch Reform faith has not made them any different by their sojourn in Southern Africa.

My nephew said conditions in hospitals and places were terrible and all kinds of diseases raged. He was working among soldiers and civilians, and caught dysentery and died at Upper Tuggella about twenty miles from Ladysmith. His mother and stepfather were dead, but my other nephew was married with two sons in New York. I felt very sad, for I looked forward to my nephew's return.

This century started in hatred and bloodshed – Kitchener with his shocking scorched earth policy and deplorable concentration camps, where thousands of people died while the real issue was the glittering prize of the gold and diamond mines. I was sorry to hear David Fraser of Philorth's two boys had also died in the conflict.

On their way south to Great Yarmouth long special trains loaded with fishers from the Broch and Blue Toon stopped for an hour at Aberdeen. I loved to go and meet everybody I knew; my son James was in a carriage with his two daughters, and my son George's daughter. Two days later I was shocked to see my son and his two lassies back in Aberdeen. Mary, his eldest girl, had died of meningitis. She was nineteen and possessed that china-like beauty of those who are destined for a short life. It was a blow my son has never got over. This upset me very much, for the girl always reminded me of my second youngest brother. Then Jane Noble, my son George's wife, died, leaving a young family. They had both worked very hard to build a beautiful house at 5 George Street, Broadsea. I liked her and mourned her loss. My son never got over it.

Dr Reid was kind. He arranged for me a working holiday. In the asylum we did a lot of work for the railway. They had just recently built at Cruden Bay a huge granite hotel like a castle. Many wealthy gentry came and built private houses for the gowff. I went down for a few weeks to work in the hotel laundry. I liked going down to Port Erroll to see some of the fishers I knew. We used to call it the ward of Cruden. I knew the Taits, the Taylors and the Massons. Spunkie's folk had a house up a close. This diversion helped me a lot to get over our recent sadness and the dreadful Boer War.

I did not go near the Broch for it would only upset me. In a baker's window loaded with cream cookies I saw a blue ashet identical to the dinner set I got as a wedding present. Mine were sold at the roup when my house was plundered. It made me wonder where were the dishes? Were they distributed in kitchens around Buchan, or decorating the fake Welsh dresser in some of the would-be gentry's houses?

I was now seventy years of age and still doing a full day's work. Dr Reid had wrought wonders in the asylum. I had seen the garden extended and the beautiful entrance lodges built round the corner, and the refreshment room. Houses had now gone out the whole length of the lower Stocket road.

We now had radiators and electric light and baths like the one in which the mannie drowned the brides.

My daughter Isabella and her husband built a small half house in Rochie's Close, at New Street, Broadsea. She was too near her in-laws and did not get on with them. They should have got a stance somewhere else, for relations are best well apart. My sister-in-law, Mrs Pirie, died at Sandhaven, which more or less ended my contact with it.

My daughter Isabella came to see me and said, 'I do not know what is wrong, but I feel absolutely done.' She had little energy. Then she learned she had cancer – it played on her nerves. It was one of my saddest days to see my daughter admitted as a patient to Cornhill. She was soon home, but the cancer progressed. Then her son James died of consumption: he was nineteen. She took this very badly, and landed in the asylum again. It seems under mental stress scholarly people are affected to a greater extent. My daughter was bright, but had married for a home.

My son Andrew had a new drifter, the *George Walker*. When the new harbour was opened the *George Walker* sailed in with Lady Saltoun aboard. She cut a ribbon as the boat passed between the two piers. My son James called his fishing boat the *Venture*. I asked why he called it that. He said to me,

'My soul is now united,          Soon as my soul I ventured,
With Christ the living vine,      On the atoning blood,
For long his grace I slighted,    The holy spirit entered,
But now I claim Him mine.         And I was born of God.'

Three times the *Venture* turned turtle, and at High Skare lighthouse a Highlandman was lost. On another occasion all the fishing gear was lost. My son was very grateful to Jock Mosley's son, William Crawford, who gave him a few nets to start again that fishing.

I liked the American newspapers for they gave you all the truth of things that no British paper dare publish.

The peace ushered in that dreadful age of every known vice. King Edward was a very bad image for Britain. What a pity Leopold or Arthur had not been King, for they were far superior. American newspapers gave all the truth of what went on in some country houses. King Edward was fly. He held his carry-ons in other folks' places, so it did not cost him a brown bawbee. Looking back it is not surprising that decade ended in slaughter.

In 1913 I had a slight stroke which left my mouth a little thrawn, but I am so grateful to have all my faculties restored and my memory not damaged at all. I was soon back in the laundry but at eighty you have to be grateful for every hour. I no longer went to the fishmarket, and I miss it.

Dr Reid started me writing, to swacken my fingers, and all the students and everybody encouraged me and helped me. A Newcastle quine who had part-time work in the kitchen would say, 'How ya henny, can a shappen y' a pencil?' They were all very kind. I have written reams and reams.

As regards the Lord's coming I must go through the grave, but in this short century we have seen so much scripture fulfilled.

There was so much talk of war it made me feel ill. There were stories of strange things flying over Aberdeen. I saw two myself, shining in the sun as they flew over the Foresterhill. I am sure they thought me mad. I corresponded for years with the Wingates, a Scottish army family who settled in North Woolwich. They were friends of my cousin, Jessie Noble, who lived there. The Wingates were believers and wrote me enlightened letters. They were sure war was inevitable.

A chiel flew from Port Erroll to Norway. Folk thought this wonderful, but they did not think it would be used to kill innocent women and bairns in England.

The Great War of 1914–18 marked the end of the world of which Christian wrote so much. That world had changed greatly during her lifetime, and she observed the changes with an often caustic eye. It was a world of closed communities, in which families had followed the same calling for generations. Relationships were sometimes harsh or oppressive, generally inequitable, but seldom impersonal or outside a certain established tradition of conduct. Now too many of the *dramatis personae* of Christian's long story were to pass, early and suddenly, from the scenes she knew. She had known them all, introduced them with her pen to later generations: the descendants in America or Australia of brothers, long dead, the children of her own children, themselves the survivors of hardship and suffering. Now many of their stories ended abruptly, at sea, at Gallipoli, or on the Somme.

Sometimes I wonder if the war was all a terrible nightmare. On a fine summer night you could hear the distant thunder of the guns on the sea, and after the shelling of coastal places and the Zeppelins, we had to do drill for air attack. Those who could were to seek solid shelter in the corridors, and patients lying were to be put under the beds. I hated the blackout, for you could no longer see the last rays of the sun. On a dark mark night Aberdeen was not a safe place to be in, for breaking-in and stealing were rife. All the papers were full of it.

Never did I think I would live to see the day when the enemy would be coming out of the sky. They were flying in the air like birds and going down in the sea like fishes and the world was running with blood. All my sons' and daughters' boys of an age had volunteered when war broke out. George Sim was in the Navy. He came with his father, my son George, to see him off. John Mackenzie was very badly wounded at Ypres. My nephew in America had two sons who both came over to enlist and help Britain. The elder was killed at Beaumont Hamel: he was twenty-one. The younger went down on the *Lusitania* on 7th May 1915: he was nineteen. My grandson was killed at Gallipoli on the same day, while his brother was killed the same week in Flanders. The two sons of my Australian nephew also came to help Britain. They came with the Anzacs: they were coming to Broadsea for leave. My young grandson, Peter Johnstone Sim, was delighted to meet them and both wrote me till their letters ceased. The elder was killed at Cape Helles: he was twenty-four. The younger was killed at Suvla Bay, he was twenty-one. A young maid who polished the floors sang a beautiful song about Sulva Bay; it never failed to bring a tear to my eyes, for now all my connections with both America and Australia are completely severed. My family tried to hide all this news from me, but I saw it in the papers. My young grandson was lucky to come back from Gallipoli alive, only to find himself in the thick of the fighting on the Somme. He was badly wounded; a shell had shattered his shoulder. He set out to walk to the dressing station and with the loss of blood had probably fallen down. He was in the company of a lot of Broch loons, and while visiting a friend here a Broch boy, Jock Summers, who was present, gave me a first-hand account unknown to my family. My son was astounded years later when the War Office sent the boy's leather wallet with several decaying but readable letters. Anyway they laid him as an unknown warrior in Westminster Abbey among the Kings. He was twenty-one.

My daughter[60] Anne Taylor died from the shock of all this. My family had been wiped out, and above the calamities I had the worry of my daughter Isabella, whose health was rapidly failing. She had a tumour. It was not easy to detect. She refused to go to the doctor like everybody else because they had no money to spare to pay him. I think medication should be available to everybody without such a high price put on it. My daughter's personality changed. Dr Reid told me it dependend on how the tumour pressed on the brain. It did not affect her speech and I had tea with her every morning, and a prayer. In the asylum I have met with many similar cases who appear to behave with disorder: fortunately they sleep a lot. I have found this particular condition affects the intelligent and well-educated folk to a greater extent than dull and unread folk. They seem to be more disturbed and self-conscious.

My son James volunteered for the Royal Navy at the age of fifty-seven: he rose to be a warrant officer. After his wife's death he prigged with me to come home to 72 Broadsea and stay. This I declined. His sons were gone and the single daughters had to travel the fishings to earn their living, so how could I possibly sit alone in that house with all those memories? To sit by myself in the same neuk where I had seen my granny, my parents, and my son pass away, and of the former not one of their sons followed them to the grave. No, my life was among the living; my job was in the asylum which was quickly filling with shell-shocked young loons. At night it would be silent as the grave; you could hear a preen fall. Suddenly there would be a cry, and in no time one affected the other and the din was dreadful, and trying for the nurses. Some patients were so bad they had to be put in pads; cunning is a characteristic of mental illness. I often saw a patient tear an orderly's face.

Karl and Hans were two shell-shocked German prisoners of war. They quickly came round and were put to work in the garden. Everybody kept well away from them, but I spoke to them. One had little bits of English. They were young loons from Munich and Hamburg. They would have done anything for me and always called me 'ooma'. If we are to follow in the Master's footsteps we must love our enemies. Since the war ended I have had a Christmas card each year from those two boys.

A grandson of my cousin. Johnnie Noble, 21 Broadsea, William Noble, got the DSM for bravery on the drifter the

*Gowanlea* which was engaged with an Austrian cruiser. At the same time George Noble (Sottie) 40 Broadsea, his stepson, Joe Watt, got the Victoria Cross.[61] Wm. Noble is now married to Jeannie Masson. Sometimes she comes to see me. They live in Laing John's hoosie at 74 Broadsea.

My cousin Mary's grandson, Alex Noble, was also decorated for an act of bravery. He is married to a very nice Inverallochy girl; they live in old Mosley's hoosie at 65 Broadsea.

No person wants to kill another. It is politicians who start wars and expect others to fight them. The greatest tragedy was that all the crowned heads of Europe, extending as far afield as the Russians, were the offspring of Queen Victoria. They threw in the muck pail, the one and only chance that folk with real power had of getting round the table in a joint effort to work to civilise and develop the world for man's good. Instead they were more concerned with pomp, and show, and levees, and etiquette and protocol and other such dirt, or how one could outshine the other in grandeur.

Kaiser Willie is a shade of the Anti-Christ, and should have been tried and punished accordingly. When he made a visit to Palestine, a gap was made in the ancient walls of Jerusalem that this Anti-Christ might enter in splendour in a grand coach driven by six white horses, even trying to outshine the King of Kings who did enter on the back of an ass on his way to die for sinful man.

My son had been engaged with the enemy. Their ship went down and several Broch men were killed. He came to see me. He was with a Peterhead loonie, Buchan, and a Broch boy, Duthie, a son of Kindy's Jimmy from Inverallochy. They were fortunate to get off with their lives. I saw them at the station. The girls had returned from Yarmouth. It was about 7th December. What a sad crowd compared to former years! There was hardly anybody who had not lost a loved one, or had somebody to worry about at the front. They told me nearly sixty lads had been killed from a little placie like St Combs.

The war dragged on and the country became so short of men. Recruiting folk turned a blind eye to loonies who faked their age in search of adventure; many enlisted at fifteen. The head gardener constantly rebuked the butcher loonie for coming in by the front avenue. He just kept on whistling, not in the least put out, and the baker loonie who came daily to the back door with a cheery smile; both fell in France at the age of sixteen.

I was sorry to learn that Philorth House was burned to the ground. I cannot conceive how this could possibly have happened. It consisted of three separate oblong blocks forming three sides of a square, barely touching at the inside corners. It was said the cook was pro-German and set the house on fire. She had sent a wire to the honourable William Fraser,[62] who was coming on furlough from the front, stating he would have a warm welcome when he arrived. I heard this with much sadness for today it would be interesting to see inside a Roman centurion's villa and in time the same of a Scottish ha' house. Philorth was too far out of the Broch to make a hotel, so could only have been an orphanage or poors' house as most of those places will one day be. With fast trains and ships, and now flying, the world will grow small in distance.

If you have a country to defend you need an army to defend it, and to run that country well, you have to gather taxes in order to do so. Even though they take half the working-man's pay they scarcely will have gathered anything, so the wealthy eventually have to carry the burden. It is clear as daylight. In a way it was maybe better Philorth went quickly rather than a slow malingering death like a hovel. Now there is a railway station leading to nowhere, but in my mind's eye it will remain the same, of how a young officer of the British India Co. and a laundry-maid experienced the joy of first innocent love as beautiful as a clump of snowdrops in the wood. From the garret window come the strains of 'Annie Laurie' floating over the trees, sung by Bobby Wilson the strapper at the pitch of his voice, or Mary Ritchie singing the 23rd Psalm. One day somebody may again build there, but I am doubtful if they will capture the happy ghosts that flit about that place.

In my time I had seen the laird in Scotland representing the Kirk, the law and the county council rolled into one. Squiredom in England was a different thing. Something got lost on the way. Partly by their pandering to Westminster's domination of Scotland, today they are as any ornament on somebody's dresser. I met Lord and Lady Saltoun in Union Street. They asked me to have tea in a refreshment room; my daughter Mary was with me. The Saltouns were very sorrowful about their son Simon[63] who was killed in France. I told them to cry to the Lord and he would heal their hearts. Poor things were now homeless and living in lodgings at Witchill. Lord Saltoun reminded me of something I said to him many years ago: 'No matter what we have, own or possess it is only on loan. God can blow on it and it can be as it never was.' This applies to human relationships also. I could hardly think it was nearly seventy years since I used to hurl Lord Saltoun into the Broch in a little wicker carriage. My mother once gave him black sugar. I had to wash his sarkie and borrow another till it was dry. It must make myself very old.

My granddaughter came from Fife to see me with two of her bairns, Annie and Andrew. He was about seven and said he was going to be a soldier. They were coming home to live in Benff's hoosie at 73 Broadsea.

We were told there was going to be an Armistice at 11 o'clock on 11th November. I have seen Britain rise to the peak of her glory or shame whichever, so I wanted to witness this, for though man will not believe it, it marks the beginning of the end of time, the commencement of such a time as never was before – murder, theft, slothfulness, infidelity, disregard for the sanctity of marriage, filth and carnality, disobedience to parents and a complete disregard for law and authority. Race will rise against race and brother against brother. God's word says that is what is in store for us in this twentieth century. As a little girl I had seen Lord Lovat's massive bonfire light up Buchan from its lofty peak on the crown of Mormond Hill, in honour of Queen Victoria's coronation, and fulfilment of the lifting up of this land by God, so that the word may go to the utmost ends of the earth.

We went on the tram. Nellie the cook took my arm so we could get a seat on the low window at the corner of Belmont Street to avoid the press of the crowd. The bells of St Nicholas boomed out eleven, and in that first two minutes' silence I prayed that God himself would take of the things of Christ and open man's eyes to his own folly, as he unheeding heads for disaster; that God would help the maimed and sick and bereaved in Britain, Germany, America, Turkey and everywhere, and that they would seek the saving grace of Christ.

Led by a pipe band the most heartrending parade came down Union Street. Nurses were pushing dozens of bath chairs – soldiers, sailors and flying loonies – some had legs missing, others arms missing, two had no legs at all; some had the deathly appearance of those afflicted with that inhuman weapon – gas; some had their noses and lips blown away leaving an unsightly hole for a mouth. A woman beside us fell away and fainted at the sight of these boys, unrecognisable as human beings. It was not a victory, but man's greatest defeat.

At the eleventh hour James Keir Hardie tried hard to avert it but was howled down. He was absolutely right and the government was wrong. All the carpet-slipper Field Marshals in the War Office, it showed how childish and immature are the minds of those privileged to rule countries, bringing their own petty squabbles to this degrading extent. They direct wars and expect other folk to fight them, the whole blasted bunch. Winston Churchill has to live with the conscience of a mass murderer. I have yet to hear one say he was sorry for Kitchener's death. Haig is one of the greatest butchers the world has ever seen, and the aristocracy have boosted him into a hero. They have bonded our freedom to America to spend millions on slaughter, yet they would never declare war on poverty and hunger. With my own eyes I have seen the slums of Glasgow, London and Liverpool, and Cardiff, with white women with black bairns at their breasts, in dire starvation. But for his vanity man would rather glorify war. Whenever one can detect the smell of a warmonger in a politician's make-up, the public should vote him out of office at the first opportunity, and rightly so, for human life is nothing to them. How any of the directors of war on any side can sleep soundly I do not know.

During the Crimean War the government promised the poor a better deal. It was a lot of ballyhoo. The same was said during the Boer War – again a parcel of lies. And during this terrible last war we have heard so much mouth about a country fit for heroes to live in. In nearly five years we see nothing but mounting unemployment and more making-ready, strikes, disruption and disorder, and a multitude of lies in high places.

How I wish I had never lived to see such a terrible slaughter. I am certain many found Christ in the battlefield; there is a life for a look at the crucified one.

And these pension committees, set up and recruited mostly from the middle classes or would-be gentry as we call them; they do all in their power to swick a poor widow and bairns out of a sixpence. My grandson left a widow with three bairns: she was awarded seven shillings and sixpence per week. My son has a pension of two shillings per week for his sons. King George offered him an MBE. He thanked His Majesty but said he declined to accept, since that was the value put on his sons' lives. So many members of parliament are cowards and hypocrites, and most are institutional Christians which is meaningless in the sight of God.

I have nothing but my old-age pension of five shillings, which goes to the asylum for my keep. It is wonderful to know in old age that you have at least a shilling when the other one goes down. God bless Lloyd George, adulterer though he be!

# CHAPTER TWELVE

## *Evening (1919–1923)*

About ten days after the Armistice my daughter Charlotte died in hospital from the terrible flu which swept the world, said to be caused by rats living on corpses. I had only seen my youngest daughter twice since she married to Sutherland. She was a fluent Gaelic speaker. I met her eldest laddie when he was a little boy; he is now in the Royal Navy. I have never met her other children. She was only forty-two.

Then my daughter Isabella died. Before she became ill I noticed she was growing thin. She suffered from indigestion and had a kind of herseness in her voice. She and her son James were both believers. I did not go to Broadsea for her funeral. I prefer to mind on her as a brave little girl who took on the responsibility of running a household at the age of ten. She was fifty-four. I have seen most of my children away before me.

The sinking of the *Titanic* was a terrible disaster and proved man cannot beat the elements: so many theories were given at the time.

My father used to tell my sons all about his trips to the Arctic whaling. He said in the spring the ice-pack came down and each floe was alive with wildlife. He could name most of the birds. What brought this to my mind today, an English doctor said to me, 'Ye must look after the old for they know so much.' It is fine to have a good memory, but you have all the little aches and pains that go with it.

The post-war world was profoundly disturbed. The sense of the end of an era was sharpened by the Russian Revolution, which seemed to some an unimaginable horror, and to others a millennium. Disease, exhaustion and civil unrest were everywhere. There was also a sense of fearful anticlimax: so much sacrifice, so much grief, so little real cause for triumph or even relief.

With the relaxation of the tension of war there was a certain slackening of moral standards – a feeling that anything could be done because everything had been paid for. Christian reacted to all these trends with characteristic vigour. She found immediate cause for indignation in the treatment of ex-servicemen and their families. The 'comradeship of the trenches' was followed too often by the bitter distinctions of the dole queues, and Christian's loathing of war was swiftly directed against the aftermath.

Like most of her generation she reacted to what would later be called the relative 'permissiveness' of post-war society. She felt that corruption was eating into the Western world, or part of it, and that the War had marked a significant advance of this corruption. But she also felt that this was ordained – the fulfilment of prophecy, however terrible. In this foretelling of ultimate disaster, Christian felt that the Zionist movement was playing an appointed part, that Scotland (unconquered as it had been by Imperial Rome) had its role; and that the immorality, as she stigmatised it, would culminate in a great and final disaster, of which the Great War was only the first of many preliminaries. But of world events, the Russian Revolution seemed to Christian the most significant. Many feared it would be imitated in other war-weary lands, and Christian's emotions were mixed. Passionately sympathetic as she was to the poor and oppressed everywhere, she felt that revolution was an understandable reaction. Her old pugnacity and patriotic fervour fed her radicalism when industrial unrest in Scotland in 1919 created a fear that worse might be coming. A letter gives Christian's mood, to her eldest son, James:

12 February 1919

My dear son,

I still have not heard from Mary, it is a very worrying time, we are passing through that place in Scripture such a time as never was before when men's hearts shall fail them for fear. But we must put on the whole armour of God and guard against the wiles of the devil who is seeking whom he can devour. No mails are getting through from Glasgow and I do hope they are all well and safe and that none of the children are hurt. It is said many innocent people were battoned by the police. On the Sat. the gates of the asylum were locked and a notice put up no visitors were allowed until further notice. We realise had the revolution spread this place could have made an excellent fortress. The little footgate on the Stocket Road was used for coming and going but the staff were not allowed out. A young doctor over from Woodmanhill told Nellie the cook what was going on. He had just got through from Glasgow on the Sat. morning before the Stirling road was closed. He told her of the terrible violence on bloody Friday. I am so glad John Maclean wasn't involved. He is a brave and courageous man with a mission which has worn him out through hard labour in prisons. His parents were evicted from the islands during the Highland clearances and it is to avenge this gross criminal injustice to Scotland that he has worked so hard for the working man.

It will not go down well with Glasgow under siege by English Troops and Tanks. The soldiers are still locked in to the Castlehill Barracks for there is an active Communionist [sic] movement in Aberdeen. Having seen Glasgow myself, and the terrible degradation under which some of the people live, it is not surprising that this has not happened forty years ago, for some of the poverty cannot be described, and something that should never have been.

After fighting that terrible war in which all the politicians promised so rosy a future and told so many shocking lies, now every other place is closing down and men out of work. In two weeks' time I will be into 87. How the years fly. I never thought to live in an age like this but we know in whom we have believed and have an anchor which will not fail.

This will be the slack time for the fishing. Margaret will look in when she comes home from Kyle. By then, I hope this terrible time will be over. You said your youngest daughter Christian was not too well. I hope she is much better, the fishing is too hard a job for a girl who is not strong.

Larry and Kirsten were in the Sunday before the revolution. He gave a word of prayer after tea. I find I am now getting a bit dull in the hearing. I have often to ask folk twice what they are saying. My Aunt Annie's grandson William Noble came to see me and all are concerned at the awful unrest in the country. The papers are guarded in what they are saying. I like to read at least three, and then make my own deductions of the truth.

Much of the debrette columns [sic] are responsible for causing a lot of unrest, for to flaunt wealth and idle, gracious living is only to cause trouble while half of the country is dying of starvation; and, again, if you are wealthy it is no use unless everybody knows. Pride is a system devised by the devil. God himself was the first Communionist [sic] in saying all men should be equal in his sight. That equality can only come through the finished work of Calvary.

Do not attempt to come in to Aberdeen till the weather is better and all the snow past. There is no point in filling your body with cold in travelling such a long distance, and coming off a hot train into the damp and cold of the city.

For what I pay I am so well fed here I would willingly share half my meals with some poor person if I could do that. Give my love to all my extensive family, and tell George and also Andrew not to come in till the Spring. This deadly flu still rages to add to the misery of our age, but be still and know I am God.

I commit you to the care of his overshadowing wings.

With love, Mother.

But the Russian form of revolution, the strident atheism of the Bolsheviks as well as their atrocious behaviour, was deeply repugnant to Christian. Her own radicalism was prejudiced, perhaps, but it was principled, Christian and humane. She saw in the Russian Revolution a great – perhaps the great – evil of all the evils of evil times. But she also felt that it had changed the world irrevocably, and that subsequent events would unfold beneath its shadow:

> Had there been a bite for everybody there would have been no French Revolution, and no Russian Revolution which was brought about by the German High Command who will live to rue the day: 'Rear a crow and it will not pick your een.' We have seen but a vision of a vision of the emancipation of the working man. It is every human being's desire for a classless heaven on earth, but how can it be when Satan is the prince and power of the air? How could it be possible with power of darkness reigning? Heaven is not here. The Czar and his family could have been given the sack peacefully. Russia may have exchanged one tyranny for another. Two centuries may pass and it may not have stabilised itself, but though the rest of the world is unable to do anything about it, never again will man trample on his fellow man without the rest of the world knowing. This is the rise of the impotent clay, or the day of the common man – 'impotent' meaning he formerly had no power, but 'except the Lord build the house they labour in vain that build it'.
>
> One must admire the brave Russian people, for from my own experience I know that being hungry is not fun. The fact the Russian revolution has coincided with General Allenby's entry into Jerusalem amply demonstrates that we are now at

the end of time. To understand and interpret the scriptures and bible prophecy one must be a truly born-again believer with a real and genuine experience of Christ, to have been tried and tested in a life of study and prayer. We have seen a great step leading to Armageddon. Great Britain has this part to play. Humbly, Allenby dismounted from his horse and entered Zion on foot by the Jaffa Gate, (Zechariah, 14, 'Behold the day of the Lord cometh for I will gather all nations against Jerusalem in battle.') As impossible as it sounds, in this century will once again the nation of Israel be brought together, preceding the coming of the Messiah.

James May in Cairnbulg married a Margaret Noble, one of my mother's clan. Their daughter married Thomas Gordon of Broadland. From them descend Gordon of Bourtie and Overboddom, ancestors of Arthur James Balfour who played a major part in the budding of the fig tree in Palestine, (Zechariah, 8, 'I was jealous for Zion'). God will bring the Jews back to their own land, not for the worthiness of the Jews but for God's own holy namesake.

The Russian Revolution is the rising of Gog. The Great War is the first of the terrible battles commencing at the time of the coming of sorrows, hence it is in three phases, 'When ye see these things look up, for your redemption draweth nigh.' A very nice man was Malcolm Hay from Seton. A patron and commissioner of the asylum told me he had been an intelligence officer working with codes, and that a wire from Lenin to the Bolsheviks had been traced, telling them to be patient, for they will one day rule the world. This will never happen, but for the restraining hand of God. Gog and Magog portray the greatest rejection of Christ, but much misery will be in store for the world ere the final battle, and those who have washed their robes and made them white in the blood of the lamb will be safe. For the final battle will be fought in the mountains of Israel. The earth shall see fire with pillars of smoke, and the slain shall be as dung on the ground and nobody shall gather them. It will be warfare greater than any of the vile things we have seen. It shall take seven months to bury the dead, but it is from the second death man must be saved. People do not like the truth, but it is the same yesterday, today and for ever.

In Revelation we read of the rising of the beast Kingdom. Everything within the domains of the old Roman Empire will be ruled by one body – Seven Kings must give up their crowns to this jurisdiction, and those who did not belong to the beast Kingdom shall be free: Scotland and Wales shall be free. The Scots as a nation have a definite part to play in the prophetic calendar of events; God for some purpose of his own did not permit the Picts to be conquered. Although they tried hard to defeat them, Scotland never came under the rule of the beast Kingdom. Antonine was driven out, and Hadrian built his boundary wall. He also built the defences of Jerusalem. He who refuses to accept the mark and number of the beast will be persecuted, and may have to die for his refusal.

I supported the suffragettes wholeheartedly, for why should women be regarded as inferior?

Working at men's jobs it was understandable that lassies should wear breeks, but now in tramcars I see some with a fag sticking out of their cheek, often on the end of a long pea-shooter, engaged in that foul and vulgar habit of blowing reek in other folks' faces. And crime is so much on the increase, one cannot give any skowth to criminals, they only turn round and laugh at you. But there are many worthy young folk about. Many a rough and wild-looking young loon has helped me on and off to tramcars. We must look for the good in everybody. The trouble in my own life was that I had wrongly expected everybody to have the same code of decency as I was taught as a child. But I did not find it, especially among Fraserburgh ministers and business folk. They erected a massive stone to McLaren the minister, so big it would not go into the kirkyard. Maybe outside the gate was the right place for it. We must tell the truth about everybody. Mrs McLaren was a nice woman who did a lot of good among the poor, but the first thing in Christianity is humility. What is a minister[64] needing a huge mansion for, only but to enjoy the fruits of a good job?

It was understandable in wartime that most things were scarce, but in shops I notice a marked deterioration in quality. In the high-class shops furniture is now so slimly built and craftmanship has deteriorated as if overnight. With all this unemployment in the country, and so many ex-servicemen starving, the government should set up schemes to train them and all the young loonies leaving the school to serve an apprenticeship in cabinet-making and other things, and give them hope, at the same time saving the old crafts. Scotland has a heritage in stone, it abounds with the stuff. Thousands of loons could be trained as masons to keep up the ancient tradition and save it from dying out. They could have schemes to train them by rebuilding all the old castles and historic places, not to revive a selfish way of life, but to encourage tourists and travellers to come and spend money to help the flagging economy all over Britain.

In the farming and fishing communities a lot of money has been made off the war by some who have invested wisely. I have often heard it referred to as blood money. By aspiring to standards they were not accustomed to many have spent foolishly. Many fishermen are now occupying curers' houses – and why not? But there is a midst in everything, for fishing has always been a precarious business, and one finds the fat and lean years go side by side. It is best to steer a middle course and be humble and remain solvent. Money-making, though, applies to folk at all levels of society, especially the armament companies.

Christian's final few years were tranquil. Half her life had been passed in Cornhill and she had acquired privileged status there.

She entertained a stream of visitors from her family; she watched the comings and goings in the asylum and, as ever, she reacted with humour as well as compassion, and with native shrewdness as well as with religious fervour. She was writing her reflections, her recollections and her reactions almost until her last day.

The old parts of Aberdeen are fascinating. I do always admire the granite masonry. Cumberland House, in the Ghaistrow, is a beautiful old house. It was the headquarters of the Hanoverian command in the time of Prince Charlie, when Aberdeen was looted. Then the infamous Lord Ancrum, a traitor to Scotland, took over and carried out his campaign of burning and looting north-east Scotland. The Gallowgate is a wonderful old place, it reminds you of the Royal Mile at Edinburgh. It is a pity the buildings have gone into some of the most abominable slums. In Edinburgh the Scots built seven-storey houses long before New York was ever heard of in the western world. The richer you were the further you went up the stair. The extreme poor lived on the ground, while dukes and earls lived at the top, all going in the same door. The Scots have always been a democratic race.

When I came to Cornhill first, when I used to go to the Aberdeen Fishmarket, often I would explore Aberdeen. There was much that was fascinating in the narrow lanes and wynds of the old city. Going up the Shiprow on the left-hand side from Market Street was a building which looked like a bit of the Abbey of Deer. In the close behind there was a maze of dwellings. I used to look at it going past.

One day an old wifie, who I had noticed before at the mouth of the close, spoke to me. In time she was very friendly, but terribly poor. Her feet were sticking through old bauchles of shoes and her clothes were raggy. A little further up the Shiprow was a very fascinating range of buildings, with coats of arms set in the wall: it was the town house of some dignitary in ages past, but now a slum, for a family occupied each room. Another old wifie in this spoke to me as I admired the masonry. She asked me to have tea; I did not take it that day, but another day I had a medicine bottle of milk and a piece, and soap crystals. I washed the wifie's cups and made the tea. The further into the building the stink was the greater, but I knew she would be offended if I refused. I did the same a different day with another wifie. They were lonely friendless folk and I asked a Faith Mission girl and a Salvation Army girl to call on both. One of the wifies was a Roman Catholic but she was still delighted to have visitors. I asked in the asylum if I could give them a bit of soap, for I think they had about two shillings a week as paupers. I enjoyed knowing these wifies. Both have long since passed on, but before they left the sad and sordid Shiprow, both found the Saviour. One can find sincerity in places where you least expect it. There is nothing dishonourable in being poor, for it is something you cannot help. It is not something you have done yourself, but society around you has created the condition.

Tea is such a wonderful institution, that miraculous five minutes when you sit down and drink it and banish the cares of the world for the time being.

I sat often in the garden doing my embroidery with a businessman's wife from Kings Gate. She could not speak, but after a lot of patience and love of my duty I could converse with her, though not a word was spoken. I found with much love and understanding I could get through to all those folk. A smile is so rewarding, and they could number their children with signs, or point to the sky for their loved ones who had gone. I am sorry I cannot chart that language on paper in the same way as music, for it would be such a help to medicine.

I have many many friends in Aberdeen. Kallie's son, William Taylor, my Aunt Annie Watt's grandson and his wife Anna, came from Torry to see me, and Annie's grand-daughter, Annie Taylor, and her husband Dad Campbell from Lossie. (They told me, from childhood, they had known Ramsay Macdonald was destined to make a name for him-self. He was howled down for advocating peace.)

Coming and going to Yarmouth I get many visitors, and a large box of rock which I distribute among the patients, doctors and nurses. My granddaughters bring their gutting crews. Peter Wilson's daughter, whose father came from the Sloch; Benjie, who lived at 46 Broadsea, was a brother of Dunkie; old Sanny Noble in Fatson's farm was another brother. Benjie's Jock's daughter had a boy and lassie before she married Wattie's Joe. The laddie is married to Barbara McLeman. He is a go-ahead chiel; I like having a news with him. Several times they have come to see me. They are very friendly with Alex Gordon, Dickson's adopted son at 19 Queen's Road. Their daughter Christina, a pleasant and bonnie red-haired quinie comes regularly to see me. She was neeper to my granddaughter since they left school. They are very comical, constantly taking the rise out of somebody. Christina Noble was telling me a nosey Cairnbulg woman counted all the other crews' barrels at dinner-time. This time she lay in wait, concealed, and as she began to count she struck her on the back with a stone, which to the curious wifie, seemed to come out of the sky!

My sister-in-law, Jean Pirie in Sandhaven, kept her daugh-ter Jessie's two orphan children. When she died, the governor of Peterhead Prison took the lassie, on the heading she had nothing to do with her relations. My son Andrew and his wife took the laddie, whom they called Rossie. He was good-looking and tidy. After he came back from the trenches his personality changed; he mixed with all sorts of droll com-pany. He comes in here to see me at an odd time. I have a soft spot for him and always remember him in my prayers. My son has no children and was pleased to take the boy. He would have taken the girl also, but the governor's wife is her father's relation.

The girls came home from Yarmouth, Grimsby and Lowestoft. My granddaughters had been caught in a coal strike, pickets had stoned the train all the way north to Berwick-upon-Tweed, where it was brought to a halt and not allowed to go any further. The Mayor of Berwick gave the fishgirls a high-tea in the town hall. Since the war trade-union membership has trebled and the day will come when they will be like the working man's House of Lords.

In order to raise money Lord Saltoun offered the Broadsea feus for about 30 years' ground-rent. My son wanted to buy No. 72. By right it belonged to me. It had taken a long time to do it but I had repaid every penny to Elsie and Jane Garden, the two spinster schoolteachers in Barton-on-Humber. They are Christian girls and have come north to see me twice. We have corresponded for about forty years. They arranged with their nephew, William Garden, my daughter-in-law's son by her first marriage, to give me a proper discharge, which he did. I like my step-grandson; he is knowledgeable chap with his feet firm on the ground.

I miss my daughter-in-law Anne Taylor. She was a cheerful person, full of good humour and fun, and the soul of generosity. She always wanted me to come home to live with them, but for reasons so obvious I did not consent to do so. I could not live looking on the sea which claimed so many belonging to me. I told my son he could have the house on condition he put the names of the single daughters in the title, for they are the ones who have to be protected. My son wanted to heighten the house by another storey. I told him not to make it too big, as small places survive longer and are less costly to keep up. They all want me for a holiday, but since I am so well it would only upset and depress me to go back to Broadsea. I am now at the closing of my days and will go back there when I pass away. I look forward to passing through the valley of the shadow of death, but I will not pass through death itself, for I feel in eternity I shall learn more and more about God. It is the second death and the lake of fire man must be saved from. We have the chance to accept or reject the finished work of Calvary.

I am indeed thankful to have been given the grace to bear up to the strain for I am better composed than any of my family.

Many interesting characters have come and gone in the asylum. Rollo, the mason's son from the Broch, is married to a Broadsea girl, Mary Jean. She is as broad as she is high and as round as a butterball: he told me of their fabulous wedding. Hundreds of children had biscuit-tins from the midden, beating them with a stick, and to this fanfare they marched to Broadsea Hall to dance. She comes in here quite a lot. She is a poor eccentric creature. That kind of person is a target for ill-tricked, hafflin boys. She lives in Gunner's Wull's house. She was telling me the loons are constantly blawding her hoosie, by putting a flock of hens down her chimney and aye rinking on the riggen. I always give her a sweetie when she comes. What is not given is not required.

When rationing was in force, and food was so scarce, a Cairnbulg woman, Mary May, told me she worked the black market regularly. I told her it was highly illegal to do such a thing. She came to see me now and again; she is married to my cousin Mary's grandson, John Crawford (Munty), a trawl skipper. Mary May would have made a good laird's fool if they still had such a person. She said to a woman here, 'Hoo long hae ye been vrang?' The woman, a nice mannerly person, is the wife of an estate factor.

An Inverallochy man, a victim of the battle of Jutland, and a chap from up Ballater way are two patients I personally feel should not be here. The Deesider was at Mons. I asked him about the angels.[65] He said no such thing ever was. It was the strange cloud-effect against the night sky illuminated by burning buildings. Impossible as it may seem in a place like this, both have a terrific sense of humour, and are perfectly sane.

It is heartrending on a visiting day to see an ex-serviceman's wife come in with maybe four bairns to see their father. The children are puzzled at the strange sight, and the wife will be crying, and there is nothing we can do to help them. That is the price paid for helping their country. We do not value good health half enough. It is not till one loses it you realise just how well off you are. Sometimes the thought crosses my mind when I see so many poor ex-servicemen, why have I myself been spared so long? A living sorrow is really a terrible affliction. Time will heal a heart but it will not heal a broken body.

Sitting on a seat at the railway station with Nellie Hacket the cook, I was waiting for my daughter Mary coming off the Glasgow train. Waiting for a train was a man beside us. Nellie said he was Lord Lovat.[66] He had a young curly-headed loonie with him, the Master – he was an exceptionally beautiful child. He was pleased to know I knew his father and grandparents. He said he always regretted they sold Strichen. He told me he was very interested in planting trees. Then who should appear in the station but my granddaughter, Eliza Noble Sim, beautifully attired. She had come to meet the fellow she was engaged to, a captain in the Royal Navy. His folk had a house on the Strichen Road in the Broch and his cousin was married to a brigadier. My granddaughter was surprised to see us. I was flaming when she said she was in too great a hurry to linger – I never see the lady anyway. Her real thoughts were, she did not want her lad to meet us; all this hurry is a lot of bluff! I am not ashamed of the asylum; Cornhill is one of the finest centres of healing in the north of Scotland. I never met the captain – she steered him out at the other exit. The rest of the family are all exceedingly pleasant and not in the least proud.

Dr Reid died in 1918. His death was a great loss to the asylum. His last wish had been that I would go into the place for private patients as a reward for my life of hard work. There I would have a personal maid. That is like an old horse being put out to grass! I have no wish to be waited on, I will die in the yoke: this morning I peeled a bucket of tatties at ninety. I am neither daft or dottled.

For my ninetieth birthday I had my portrait painted. I did not know I looked so ancient. I will have to spruce myself up a bit. A young chap came home from the front to take over the job as physician superintendent. Then Dr Dods-Brown took over. He is a wonderful person: he has those far-seeing and piercing eyes of a master of his craft and can read the minds of his patients at a glance. From time to time we have seen a nurse who is harsh to patients, but they are very much in the minority. Sarcasm is a horrible thing; it reveals a great weakness and insecurity in a person's nature.

Since the war it is amazing the progress made in the treatment of mental illness. No longer is it the close and secretive thing it once was. In Cornhill there are not many dangerous types, though from time to time I have come across them in transit to somewhere else. When a person has psychopathic tendencies one must always watch out. You can usually tell by the eyes. They are crafty people and it is a pity in many cases their fertile brain could not be harnessed to a good use to help themselves. If they appear in your company you have to keep on talking, and never let them think you are talking about them. To cross one of these people in any way is putting a spark to a hayrick, and once started is already out of control. I am sure a real breakthrough will be made; it would be nice to see that day and also everybody having enough to eat and shoes on their feet.

There is something pathetic about old folk in senile wards, with little better than a spark of life. I have seen them go from adult to a child calling for their fathers and mothers, and hence to an infant and even as a child before birth. It is like a reversal of the process of life, a purpose we cannot ever comprehend but, 'Thy will be done'. The girls who nurse those folk have to be saluted, for it is a labour of infinite love. One day they will be rewarded. We should be grateful from the depth of our heart for every moment.

I am indeed. I said to my granddaughter Margaret Taylor Sim, 'If I get like that would you still come and see me?' She said, 'No, I would take you home and nurse you myself.' And I know she means this, as she is one of those fiery straight folk, but that is in God's hands. I have seen many such persons about to pass into eternity and all their relations at their bedside clamouring round waiting for what they can grab. A nurse has to be two-faced. She cannot say, 'Why do you come here now? You had no time to come when the person was in the sittingroom; we never saw you after the person was admitted.' Instead they have to offer them a cup of tea. Some nurses have told me they felt like sluicing it in their faces! If there is something to be gained you will aye see plenty at the right time, but having to pay in is a different story.

The young speak about their sweethearts, the middle-aged moan about their husband's pay packet, and call their neepers everything under the sun, and the old speak of happier days in the past. I have tea every morning with a woman from the fishing village of Gamrie, and it is pleasant to go over the mutual folk we know and their relations, and we are back travelling the fishing. In those days the Gamrie folk walked all the way to the Broch. At arling time often we would see six lassies with their arms linked passing through Broadsea on their way to the Broch to get a fee. Dozens of them settled in Shetland. There is a character called Isorach who comes in to annoy the Gamrie woman and to beg money. He is not related to her, only a nuisance. She said he had been a coarse character since a child. He knows all the

Broadsea folk. These folk do not change easily. It is like lifting a stone from the street and demanding that it should be an amethyst, but Grace can change anybody who is willing to accept it.

My son James shook hands with King George. He is now harbourmaster at Peterhead. It is a repeat of history. My ancestor, Alex Noble, from what is now 76 Broadsea, was harbourmaster to the earl marischal when he founded Peterhead. I think he was the first.

I don't work much now. My three sons are very generous to me, but I like to feel independent. I do a tea-cloth (but not often) for I must earn a penny to put a stamp on a letter to many friends. I have a steady stream of visitors. Students ask me about subjects on which to write theses, and at ninety I have taken up the teaching job I started at sixteen. It is most enjoyable and I have happiness and peace. I can ask my guests to stay to lunch if they come in the morning. A lass who used to be a maid in Cairness House works here. She does my shopping, so I am like a lady of leisure.

I can mind on General Gordon's batman. He was a dark-skinned Armenian who used to come into the Broch on a white horse. He lived at Cairness in a chaumer; he was an imposing figure in a turban and red cloak. Lady Gordon at Cairness was an Armenian. They used to have a clever Greek doctor who practised in Lonmay. It is like yesterday to look back on all these things.

At the closing of my days I have encountered so much kindness. I am blest every time I breathe. My life has been hard but I would not say it has been a sad waste, for my purpose has been to shed light in a dark place, and I have kept the faith, for which we are told we will be rewarded with a crown of life. I deplore war and urge man to seek the Lord while he may be found, call upon Him while he is near. Jesus said (Mark 10, 29, 30), 'There is no man that hath left house or brethren or sisters or father or mother or wife or children

for my sake and the Gospels, but he shall receive an hun-
dredfold in this time, and in the world to come eternal life.'

Christian Watt, Kirstie, 'Piper's Kitta', died at Cornhill in 1923
in her ninety-first year. Three sons were at her bedside, and she
was conscious to the last and happy, as she told them, to be
going into the presence of the Lord.

# APPENDIX I

## *Relationship of some people mentioned in* The Christian Watt Papers

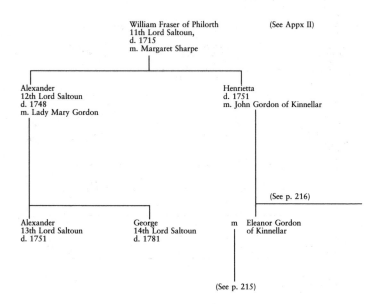

William Fraser of Philorth
11th Lord Saltoun,
d. 1715
m. Margaret Sharpe

(See Appx II)

Alexander
12th Lord Saltoun
d. 1748
m. Lady Mary Gordon

Henrietta
d. 1751
m. John Gordon of Kinnellar

(See p. 216)

Alexander
13th Lord Saltoun
d. 1751

George
14th Lord Saltoun
d. 1781

m    Eleanor Gordon
of Kinnellar

(See p. 215)

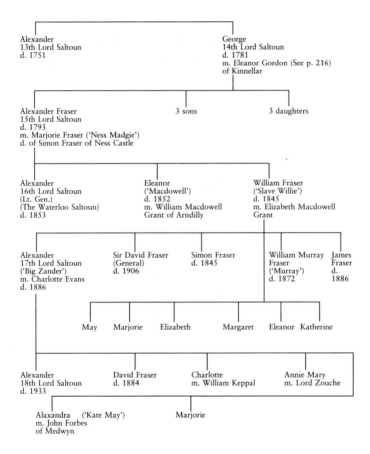

Alexander
13th Lord Saltoun
d. 1751

George
14th Lord Saltoun
d. 1781
m. Eleanor Gordon (See p. 216)
of Kinnellar

Alexander Fraser
15th Lord Saltoun
d. 1793
m. Marjorie Fraser ('Ness Madgie')
d. of Simon Fraser of Ness Castle

3 sons

3 daughters

Alexander
16th Lord Saltoun
(Lt. Gen.)
(The Waterloo Saltoun)
d. 1853

Eleanor
('Macdowell')
d. 1852
m. William Macdowell
Grant of Arndilly

William Fraser
('Slave Willie')
d. 1845
m. Elizabeth Macdowell
Grant

Alexander
17th Lord Saltoun
('Big Zander')
m. Charlotte Evans
d. 1886

Sir David Fraser
(General)
d. 1906

Simon Fraser
d. 1845

William Murray
Fraser
('Murray')
d. 1872

James
Fraser
d.
1886

May    Marjorie    Elizabeth    Margaret    Eleanor    Katherine

Alexander
18th Lord Saltoun
d. 1933

David Fraser
d. 1884

Charlotte
m. William Keppal

Annie Mary
m. Lord Zouche

Alaxandra    ('Kate May')
m. John Forbes
of Medwyn

Marjorie

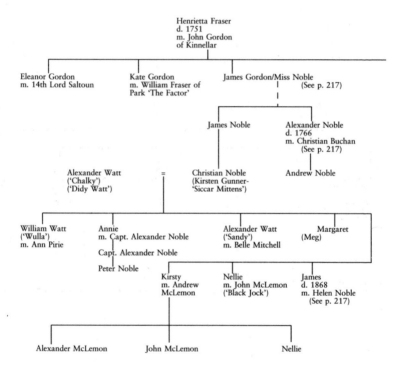

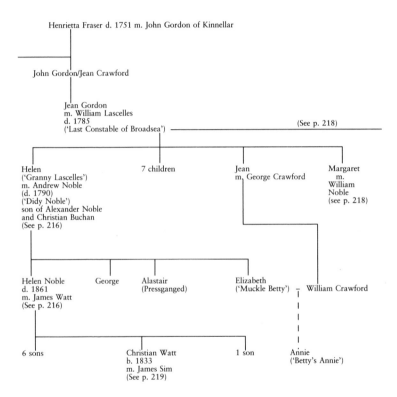

Henrietta Fraser d. 1751 m. John Gordon of Kinnellar

John Gordon/Jean Crawford

Jean Gordon
m. William Lascelles
d. 1785
('Last Constable of Broadsea') (See p. 218)

Helen
('Granny Lascelles')
m. Andrew Noble
(d. 1790)
('Didy Noble')
son of Alexander Noble
and Christian Buchan
(See p. 216)

7 children

Jean
m. George Crawford

Margaret
m.
William
Noble
(see p. 218)

Helen Noble
d. 1861
m. James Watt
(See p. 216)

George

Alastair
(Pressganged)

Elizabeth
('Muckle Betty')  —  William Crawford

6 sons

Christian Watt
b. 1833
m. James Sim
(See p. 219)

1 son

Annie
('Betty's Annie')

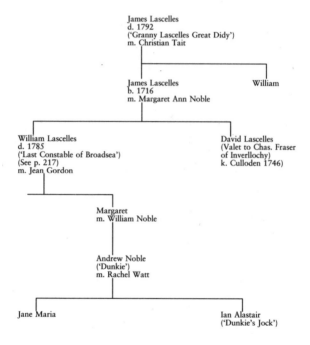

James Lascelles
d. 1792
('Granny Lascelles Great Didy')
m. Christian Tait

James Lascelles                                    William
b. 1716
m. Margaret Ann Noble

William Lascelles                          David Lascelles
d. 1785                                     (Valet to Chas. Fraser
('Last Constable of Broadsea')             of Inverllochy)
(See p. 217)                               k. Culloden 1746)
m. Jean Gordon

Margaret
m. William Noble

Andrew Noble
('Dunkie')
m. Rachel Watt

Jane Maria                                 Ian Alastair
                                           ('Dunkie's Jock')

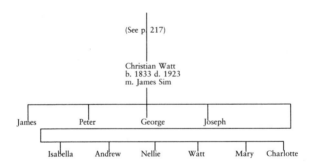

(See p. 217)

Christian Watt
b. 1833 d. 1923
m. James Sim

James  Peter  George  Joseph

Isabella  Andrew  Nellie  Watt  Mary  Charlotte

# APPENDIX II

## *Relationship of several branches of Frasers mentioned by Christian Watt*

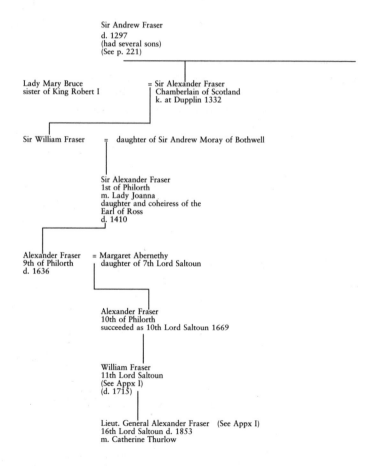

Sir Andrew Fraser
d. 1297
(had several sons)
(See p. 221)

Lady Mary Bruce
sister of King Robert I

= Sir Alexander Fraser
Chamberlain of Scotland
k. at Dupplin 1332

Sir William Fraser  =  daughter of Sir Andrew Moray of Bothwell

Sir Alexander Fraser
1st of Philorth
m. Lady Joanna
daughter and coheiress of the
Earl of Ross
d. 1410

Alexander Fraser
9th of Philorth
d. 1636

= Margaret Abernethy
daughter of 7th Lord Saltoun

Alexander Fraser
10th of Philorth
succeeded as 10th Lord Saltoun 1669

William Fraser
11th Lord Saltoun
(See Appx I)
(d. 1715)

Lieut. General Alexander Fraser   (See Appx I)
16th Lord Saltoun d. 1853
m. Catherine Thurlow

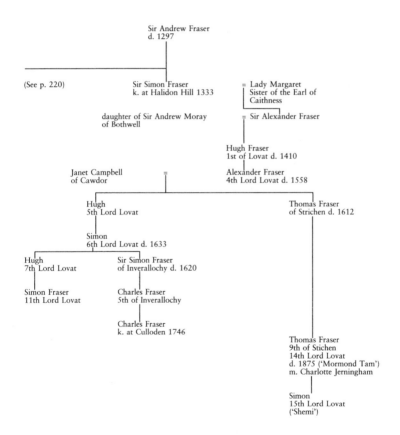

Sir Andrew Fraser
d. 1297

(See p. 220)     Sir Simon Fraser
k. at Halidon Hill 1333     = Lady Margaret
Sister of the Earl of
Caithness

daughter of Sir Andrew Moray
of Bothwell     = Sir Alexander Fraser

Hugh Fraser
1st of Lovat d. 1410

Janet Campbell
of Cawdor     =     Alexander Fraser
4th Lord Lovat d. 1558

Hugh
5th Lord Lovat     Thomas Fraser
of Strichen d. 1612

Simon
6th Lord Lovat d. 1633

Hugh
7th Lord Lovat     Sir Simon Fraser
of Inverallochy d. 1620

Simon Fraser
11th Lord Lovat     Charles Fraser
5th of Inverallochy

Charles Fraser
k. at Culloden 1746

Thomas Fraser
9th of Stichen
14th Lord Lovat
d. 1875 ('Mormond Tam')
m. Charlotte Jerningham

Simon
15th Lord Lovat
('Shemi')

# APPENDIX III

# Some houses and occupants of Broadsea and Pitullie

## Broadsea

*7 Broadsea*: Jean Crawford's home. Mother of Jean Gordon. Christian's great-grandmother; later occupied by William Watt, Christian's uncle.

*22 Broadsea*: Captain Alex Noble's home, *m.* Annie Watt, Christian's aunt.

*25 Broadsea*: Home of Captain Alexander Noble, Harbourmaster, Christian's cousin.

*27 Broadsea*: Home of Alexander Watt, Christian's grandfather, who left it, with Nos. 54 and 67, to his youngest daughter Kirsty McLeman.

*351/2 Broadsea*: Andrew Noble's home, Christian's grandfather, inherited from James Lascelles. Passed to Christian on her mother's death and given to her aunt.

*411/2 Broadsea*: Home of Alexander Noble, whose daughter married Christian's son, George.

*47 Broadsea*: Home of William Noble, *m.* Margaret Lascelles, Christian's great-aunt.

*48 Broadsea*: Home of George Crawford, *m.* Jean Lascelles, Christian's great-aunt.

*49 Broadsea*: Home of John McLeman, *m.* Nellie Watt, Christian's aunt.

*53 Broadsea*: Home of Andrew Noble, a tenant of Christian in No. 72.

*54 Broadsea*: Home of Andrew McLeman, *m.* Kirsty Watt, Christian's aunt.

| | |
|---|---|
| *63 Broadsea*: | Home of Alexander Watt, Christian's Uncle Sandy. |
| *67 Broadsea*: | Croft where two houses were built by Sandy Watt's sons, Christian's first cousins. |
| *69 Broadsea*: | Home of Crawfords. |
| *71 Broadsea*: | Home of Annie Gatt. |
| *72 Broadsea*: | Lascelles home. Passed to Christian Watt on her mother's death. |
| *73 Broadsea*: | Home of Taylors. |
| *75 Broadsea*: | Home of Annie Catheid. |
| *76 Broadsea*: | Noble home (the 'Noch' Nobles). |

## Pitullie

| | |
|---|---|
| *13 Pitullie*: | Home of grandparents of James Sim, Christian's husband. Christian's first married home. |
| *17 Pitullie*: | Home of Margaret Traill, formerly Watt, Christian's aunt. |
| *23 Pitullie*: | Home of James Sim's 'Aunty Betty'. |
| *50 Pitullie*: | A second house of James Sim's grandparents. |

# APPENDIX IV

## *Granny Lascelles' Account*

Seatown of Broadsea
3rd Julie 1840

Two gentlemen John and Charles Sobieski Stuart, came down from Strichen House to see if I knew or could tell them of any memory or actual piece of tartan pladd as might yet exist. They did find some in the Seatown, and some nice bits and patches and swatches in the bed kwilts, the 2 mannies and the guests of Mormond Tam the new Lord Lovat of Strichen.

Donald Macnabb the Taylor from Islay had in a kist a lot of nice old bits of pladd. They also sent over to the Tayloers in Cairnbulg and Cotton and the two towns of St Colms where they got plenty more pladd.

I also put them out to Pitulie and Rosehearty – His Lordship was very civil and gave me a fat hen which was hung for the dinner on Sabbath. The two men are grandsons of Prince Charles Edward Stuart. Their father was an illegitimate son borne by a Gordon girl, Allen, a niece of Lord Pitsligo's second wife, who sent her to France with the Prince's belongings left at Pitsligo Castle. Unwitting, the girl fell with child.

The two mannies are certainly Stuarts for they look so like all the pictures of Stuarts. They were so pleased to get so much Tartan pladd. His Lordship will look his Bealy estate for more. The two pretender princes told me to write a history of my family before it's all forgotten and on account of my own age.

My family's chief name was Noble.[67] The oldest recorded

was in East Lothian. He was married to Maria de Hales. He was William Noble who links in kin with the ancient earls of Dunbar.

The wife of Bernard Fraser was older and had a greater right to the lands. It would seem they had taken the side of the Cumines and lost their all. They seem to have come to Bredsie with the Frasers of Philorth. Randolph Noble, her grandson, was served heir to Maria de Hales. William Noble and Maria de Hales held the lands of Garlton under William de Vallibus.

In 1253 King Alexander III confirmed a grant of land from Randolph Noble and Thomas Noble, his son, to Sir David Graham of Old Montrose. Sir David's wife, Agnes Noble, was a daughter. Their daughter became Queen of Scotland, as second wife of King Robert II.[68]

Thomas Noble's wife was a Lascelles of Forgan. Randolph Noble, Thomas Noble and John Noble his son are in the Ragman Roll and did pay homage. In 1337 the lands of Garlton were forfeited to the Crown.

The said John Noble witnessed a charter to the Newbattle Abbey 1398. William Noble of Garlton was appointed Chamberlain and Procurator of the Abbey of Aberbrothock in 1463. William Noble was appointed Chamberlain and Procurator by the Abbot of Arbroath at Inverness in 1464. William Noble, his son, was tenant of Culcave in the Ardmeanoch. From him stem the Noch Nobles of Broadsea from whom my late spouse, Andrew Noble and I both descend.

They are not the principal line. The Revd Simson filled in the pages of our family bible with a grand pedigree embellished with barons and chieftains. It is quite wrongly done. The Bredsie line was inherited through Maria de Hales.

When I used to go to the big harvests south of Edinburgh and Glasgow I went to see the place of my ancestors at Rucklaw. Lord Belhaven had the nearby estate of Beal. We went regular from the north-east to the Glasgow Fair with a birn of fish on our back. A Noble was Constable of Dumbarton Castle. My father said they were the same Nobles as us.

Malcolm King of Cumbria had with other children a son, Gospatrick, Earl of Northumberland. The earl also had a son called Gospatrick, whose son Waldeve, the third generation, developed the herring fishing at Hexham – so we have long been connected with the herring fishing. Waldeve had a son Gospatrick, fourth generation. In 1120 he is described as Lord of Bolton and Bresscosthwaite. He also got much land from King David I of Scotland. He had the lands of Dundas on the south side of the Queen's Ferry. He was known as Lord of the Ferries. He had only two daughters. The elder, his chief heiress Christiana, married Duncan de Lascelles, son and heir to Alan de Lascelles, Earl of Forgan.

This Alan was created 'Comes de Forgrund' by King David I under whose patronage he founded the Kirk of Forgan in Fife. When we used to go down for mussels I have seen it often. It is a beautiful old kirk. The manse adjoining is very big. It used to be the Lascelles' chief residence.

Fifth Generation, Christiana by Duncan Lascelles had a son, Theobald, who married first Christina, a daughter of Maria de Hales. They had a son and a daughter. Theobald married secondly in 1220, Ada, the daughter of the 5th earl of Dunbar and Countess Ada, daughter[69] of King William the Lyon. They were given the lands of Rucklaw near Dunbar. By the first marriage his daughter Christian was said to be the wife of Gilbert Fraser, ancestor of Philorth.

Theobald had a son, Thomas Lascelles, who married Christian, daughter of Udard, son of Lord Crastyle. She later married Robert Bruce, Lord of Annandale, one of the competitors for the Scottish Crown. His son,[70] the earl of Carrick, was father to King Robert I. His daughter Isabella was Queen of Norway, wife of King Eric. His daughter Mary married Sir Alexander Fraser, ancestor of Philorth.

Alan de Lascelles, Earl of Forgan, and his wife Juliana de

Somerville founded the Kirk of Forgan in 1124. Their son, Lord
Alan de Lascelles was married to Annabelle, daughter of the
Cumine earl of Buchan, at Inverallochy. The second Alan had a
daughter, Marjorie, who married Peter de Hay. He gave them
the lands of Nachton, the seat of the Pictish Kingdom. His elder
son, Duncan, was married to Christiana. Their son died before
them, but they were survived by two grandsons, Henry, and
Lord Richard Lascelles, his heir. The earldom could be passed
on to the heir of their own choice but had to remain within their
own family. The above two sons had many sons, Walter, Henry,
James and others, but Lord Richard left his lands and titles to
his only daughter, 'Margeria Comitata de Forgan'. She was
married to Lord Alexander de Moravia. He was a son of the
people who had Fedderat Castle at Brucklay.

Their son and heir was Lord Richard de Moravia, soldier.
Richard de Moravia, Earl of Forgan, was married to Juliana, a
daughter of a distant relation, Radulph Lascelles who had land
in Buchan. They had a son, John Lascelles who is no longer
named as earl, for it seems they took the side of the Cumines,
being connected to them. But they still held Forgan, for he
witnessed many charters to King Robert the Bruce and Isabella,
Countess of Buchan, who had a house at Leuchars in Fife.

John Lascelles married Elizabeth de Nairne. John Lascelles
took his mother's surname and not that of Moravia. His son,
John Lascelles, was married to a Christian Sydserf who appears
to be a relation of his own. He witnessed a lot of charters to the
earl of Fife, later King Robert II, whose daughter, Maria,
married Sir William Abernethy, ancestor of the Saltouns. King
Robert's second wife was a granddaughter of Agnes Noble.[71]

John Lascelles' only daughter and heir, Mariota, married
Walter de Lascelles, son of Roger de Lascelles in Friarton of
Forgan, who was the direct heir male of Duncan and Christiana,
going by the surname.[72] Their son Walter had a charter of
Rucklaw and Howden, 1461.

Walter de Lascelles married Marjorie Noble of Garlton. They

had a son, John Lascelles, who married a de Nairne. They had a son, Patrick Lascelles, who paid his cousin Patrick Sydserf an annual rent. He was unmarried. His brother next in line, John Lascelles younger of Forgan, married Kate Mercer of Aldie. Her family for a time held the lands of Broadsea. The old wind tower at Kinnairds Head may have been their castle. John Lascelles and Kate Mercer had a son, John, who married Christina Crawford.

In 1587, this John Lascelles made over the lands of Rucklaw and Howden to his cousin-german, Patrick Sydserf. Their son, David Lascelles, bought back Inverdovet or redeemed the bond, witnessed by his father, John Lascelles, and his son, John Lascelles. David Lascelles married Anne Balfour. He made over the superiority of Inverdovet to his cousin, Patrick Sydserf, and his wife Janet Lander. John Lascelles, the son of David, married Magdalene Abernethy, an illegitimate daughter of one of the Abernethy sons. They were still living at Inverdovet, the Forgan dower house, in the year 1590. 'Lord Inverdovet' was the secondary title of the earls of Forgan.

John Lascelles had several sons. The elder was David Lascelles of Forgan, who had married an Anne Balfour. He was deeply in debt to his in-laws, who appear to have been the same family as Balfour of Burghlie.

They had a son, Patrick, who married Majorie Noble of Garlton. Their son, Walter, who was a Covenanter, married Margaret Fraser, believed to be a daughter of the 10th Lord Saltoun of Abernethy, by his second marriage, to a Forbes of Tolquhoun Castle.

There was no estate to inherit in Fife. It had been bonded or sold. The name is spelt Leslie, Lescell, Lassols, and any way as chosen, and so much confused as to the name of Lesslie.

Whether the father was killed as a Covenanter or died naturally it is not written, but he and his wife both died before their two sons were fourteen years in age. They were sent to live at Fedderate in Buchan with a relation. The elder son was

Walter, whom I will deal with last, as he represents the main line of my family. Both sons married in Broadsea. The younger son, John Lascells, married Mary Noble of the Ardmeanoch Nobles. They had a daughter, Grissel, married to a man by the name of Wilson in Rosehearty, and a daughter married to Jock Rowe in Inverallochy. They had a son, George Lascelles, who married but had no children. They also had my great-grandfather, James Lascelles, who lived to be ninety-eight when he departed this life. He married Christian Tait of Cairnbulg. They had several children who all died young. Their son James was married very young to Margaret Ann Noble. Their son, David Lascelles, was valet to Charles Fraser of Inverallochy. He died at a very young age of life along with his master at Culloden Moor.

The second James Lascelles had a son, William, who was my father. He was a good scholar and had a great desire for learning. He wore himself out fighting for what he believed to be right. He was honest and upright and godfearing and taught us all to read and write and never to covet. My sister Jean was only five when he died, fifty and five years ago. He was eight-years-and-forty when he departed this life. He was born to witness the dark age that had enshrouded Scotland. He tried hard but could do little to help the persecuted. 'We fight not for glory or honour nor wealth, but only and alone for freedom which no good man surrenders but with his life.'[73]

My father strongly opposed the Act of Union, and always had the forlorn hope to restore the Scottish Parliament. Also he fought hard to abolish teind taxes on fifth, and multures on the harvest. But he did not die a defeated man. It was beautiful spring sun. Fishermen came in their boats from up the west and as far as Ferryderm: also the cottar people came in their hundreds, for my father was a born leader. Many carried banners with the lion rampants. They were forbidden by the government to do so and I prayed there would be no skuffles nor rioting.

Following Culloden Lord Ancrum built military posts all over

Buchan. As the road left the Broch at the head of the Back Streets, a post was built opposite the College Tower. It is now the Corinthian Kirk who bought the building. I was chief mourner, and against custom I attended the funeral. When we reached the post we did not go through the small foot gate, but soldiers opened the carriage gates and we passed in a quiet and dignified manner; and again, when we reached the Barrack Guard House at the end of the Fish Crosse the soldiers let us through with great dignity. When the funeral was at Kirktoun of Philorth the cortège was still passing Derby Ha cottar houses. I took my little sister Jean to hold the tow with me at my father's head and my other sister, Margaret, took the tow at the foot as we had no living brothers. So thus was laid to rest one who gave so much in the cause of Scotland and freedom.

We had seven brothers and sisters who died in the flower of their youth. For years we had a lot of broiling hot summers which burned the crops, followed by heavy rains with scarce enough seed to sow the land next year. Everybody was not nourished.

My brothers and sisters all had long delicate fingers and the kind of beauty going with an early grave. Both my parents worked very hard but got nothing for it.

My mother was Jane Gordon, but liked to be known as Jane Crawford. Her grandparents had brought her up and she lived with them till she married my father. Her mother was Jane Crawford who had her to John Gordon,[74] younger, of Kinnellar, who lived with his family at Fraserburgh Castle. He had wanted to marry my grandmother but his own mother was very much against it. She was Henrietta Fraser, a daughter of Lord Saltoun of Abirnethy. Netta Fraser was a hard one, and a tough lady in business. She would make sleek of hard merchants, and make tradesmen dance for their money. When Hanoverian troopers searched the castle she supervised the opening of every drawer and press, and she told them if they stole anything she would have them court martialled. Her spouse was John Gordon of Kinnellar, a son of one of the Baronets of Lesmoire. He was a very fine gentleman, kind and helpful. He died at Philorth House. Their daughter, Nellie, married her cousin George Fraser, the Lord Saltoun.

She had a nature very much like that of her mother. George Fraser was a quiet man whose word was never heard. His wife had the stronger character. She had done the courting and the proposing but she made him a very good wife. They had inherited a greatly impoverished estate. Nellie rallied a dying horse and took it back on its feet. All the Gordon children had come over the Castle braes to Broadsea schule and by her mixing with the common dab she had learned much of the arts of survival.

George Fraser did try to help the sad lot of the poor. He died when not an old man. Nellie Fraser, Lady Saltoun, died in Edinburgh. It had been a scorching hot summer earlier that year. The Black Pox broke out in Edinburgh. The city corn-missionaries would not allow dead bodies to be carted through Scotland so her Ladyship had to be buried in Edinburgh.

John Gordon, younger, left my mother, his illegitimate daughter, £20. She took it as a gross insult, for she thought he should have been manly enough to defy his mother and marry her mother whom he let down badly. My mother refused to accept one penny and poor as we were, she stuck to her guns.

Another brother, James Gordon, my mother's uncle, had a son, James Noble,[75] whose parentage was questioned by Netta Fraser, Mrs Gordon. Again she meddled, but the couple lived together at his naval shore stations. Some said they were married secretly. They had no more children. My daughter Helen is married to their grandson, James Watt.

My mother was born and brought up in the house above the shore. It was left to my sister, Jean, who sold it to William Watt. My granny on my mother's side, who was in fact my great-granny, was a Noble from below the brae. That house was left to my sister Margaret, which was fair enough as I got my parents' and my grandparents' house. I bought the house below the brae from my sister, for my son George, so no question would arise over succession in the future.

My grandfather Crawford came of the Crawfords of Invernorth on the south side of the wood at Philorth. They are offshoots of the Castle of Fedderatte. My mother's mother later married Gilbert Noble but we always regarded her as an aunt. Her spouse was a fine man. I called my younger son Gilbert Alistair after him. Poor lad was pressed into the navy. I heard no more of him after two years' sailing: it has been a sad and sore heart to live with. Several have told me he died of a fever in Jamaica.

My other daughter, Elizabeth, is my other child of my four children.

Alexander Noble, who had a master's ticket, was married to a daughter of Andrew Fraser of Tyrie. He was the first harbourmaster at Peterhead to the earl marischall in his new port. He was a man of substance and property. His only child, Andrew Noble, married Margaret Gleny, a daughter of Peter Glennie in Broadsea, a tenant of Lord Saltoun.

Peter Glennie had forty head of nowt. Both Andrew Noble and his wife died before the harbourmaster, at Peterugie. Peter Glenny's wife was Kate Ritchie of the Tyrie and Techmeerie Ritchies. She had considerable dowry settled on her. They had several sons but by the eighteenth century the surname had almost died out.

Alexander Noble, the harbourmaster, was the scion of the ancient line of Garlton Noble. At his death his granddaughter, Christian Ritchie Noble, was served heir in 1629. She was the only child of his only child Andrew, who was Constable in his father's absence. This old office had come down from the time of Maria de Hales.

Christian Noble was very young when she inherited her grandfather's estate, which included much property and the house now occupied by Helen Noble, my daughter. The house is mentioned in Lord Saltoun's will. (This is an error on my part: he was Fraser of Philorth at this time, the one who founded the Broch.)[76] In our house at Broadsea was signed the Charter of the University.

My great-grandfather told me that this Christian Noble eventually married Andrew Noble, who had contested her own right to the arms of Noble, so obviously he was a close relative of hers but not a first cousin. He had a brother, Gilbert Noble, Burgess of Aberdeen, who married Mary Jaffrey, a daughter of the Laird of Corthes at Rathen. Her father was Lord Provost of Aberdeen. From Gilbert Noble descend the Alistairs, of whom was William Noble, who married my sister Margaret and had Andrew Noble – 'Dunkie'. He married twice and had John Noble, 'Bengie', and Alex Noble who married the heiress to Whetson's farm. From this line came the Nobles of Betty's Yard on Mormond Hill. From them come many of the Nobles around Strichen and New Deer.

Gilbert Noble, the Burgess, had a daughter Mary who married a Colonel Gillespie of the Dragoons. She surely had no family for nothing further is heard of her. Andrew Noble, traveller of Zetland, had the Mansion, Dennduff House, which was formerly outside Fraserburgh but now looks toward the Frithside Street. It was his father's place, but they always kept their house in the Seatown. It is presently occupied by John, 'Black Jock', the son of the Highlander, Donald MacLeman.

They were never too big to disown the Seatown. Andrew had that place, and his brother Gilbert had the house occupied by Dunkie. Andrew's wife, Christian, would not leave the Seatown to live in the Broch.

Gilbert Noble's familie took over Dennduff House. Andrew Noble and Christian Noble had six daughters. The elder was Grissel Noble, an exceedingly beautiful lass. She married Walter Lascells, the dormant heir to the ancient earldom of Forgan and the elder of the two brothers brought up at Fedderate. They had a son, David Lascells, who never married but left his possessions to his sister Anne who married Patrick Noble. Their only child was Margaret Ann Noble who is always referred to as Anne Noble. She had to marry at the age of sixteen her relation, James Lascelles.[77]

Anne Noble was the ringleader who led the Broadsea women at the dispeace when the Church of Scotland took over as the state religion, and wrecked the Parish Kirk on the Green.[78] At this particular time most Bredsie folk were staunch Episcopalian, and so strongly defended their faith.

Anne Noble and James Lascelles had a son, David, who died at Culloden. He was only a young boy. Then it was not unknown for children to be useful on battlefields.

The arms of Garlton Noble came to my father, William Lascelles, through his Mother, and then also the Arms of the Earls of Forgan came to my father through his mother, although on his father's, old James Lascelles' side, he was more than singularly connected. My father was never an easy man to please. He set such high standards for himself and wanted us to be the same. He could not abide anybody to be late for a fixed time, and he insisted on tidiness in our dress and good manners in daily living. Before his marriage he had sailed the world and had seen the penal colonies in Australia[79] and slave plantations in America, which greatly influenced his Whig outlook, and as a Christian he laboured for the good and well-being of mankind.

My father liked the ancient things. He would have greatly deplored the wilful destruction of the old castle of Philorth. Lady Buchan had kept it in such 'good trim'. She sold it to the Aberdeens. I mind on the daughter, Lady Dalrymple, living there before she sold it to Geordie Gordon, the bad earl of Aberdeen[80] who lived there for a few years with the English wifie, whose sister he married before they biggit Mormond House up at Corthes.

Lord Aberdeen was a go-ahead mannie who didn't lippen to the smooth flattering tongue of tyrant factors but did the job himself and made a lot of siller. He gave out a lot of short, improving leases on the sides of Mormond Hill for crofters, to the back-breaking task of breaking in land from the heather. The croft houses were roofed with the old slates and rafter beams from the castle of Philorth. The windows were used also. The same has happened to the castles of Pitullie and Pitsligo. In the village of Kyask you see finely carved doors now forming the shutters of bun in beds which have come from those old castles. All this vandalism was wicked, and commenced with the ill omen of the hope of restoring the Stewarts to the throne.

The following pedigree will show how we descend twice from the 10th Lord Saltoun of Abernethy. This laird is said to have been one of the best who ever lived. He died a few years before my old didy, James Lascelles, was born, but he told me his parents spoke a lot about his lordship, whose funeral took place from our house, which then would have been the home of his lordship's grandson, Walter Lascelles, and his wife, Grissel Noble. She was the heriditary constable in her own right.

I was born and grew up in an atmosphere of subjugation. From our earliest age we were taught to say to those in authority that we had always seen and heard nothing. I was born thirteen years after the rebellion, but by that time we were securely under the heel of Westminster, who carried out the most cruel, ruthless and brutal persecution.

The government built the barracks at the entrance to the Broch on the south road. In my time they extended it with the three-storey bigging at the back of the colonel's house to hold an awful lot more troopers. No young girl was safe to go about at night, and to cross them in any way was to bring the worst reprisals down on your head, for they persecuted the innocent for some small matter, which a schule boy had done. They built the post at the western entrance to the Broch, with a high watch toor to set all over the country; and so as not to be lazing about all day doing nothing they gave the soldiers a job at husbandry so as to keep them busy.

They commandeered the steading of the Fraserburgh Castle,

which was in the Saltoun Close in the back street known among the local gentry as the Kinnaird Head Garden. It was behind the steading where it is yet; and the big house which stood where the Saltoun Inn now stands was for officers. My didy told me the 10th Lord Saltoun died in that particular house on the Green.

From the back of the Broch, up the court-road to the Pitullie cross road and right up the Gallowshill to the back of Dennduff House was the links, and some ingrassing – many acres of rich pasture and good soil, dunged for centuries by hundreds of nowt. The military coveted this fine land and commandeered it for their animals. The beasts of the Broch and Broadsea folk were pushed into a corner. Sometimes you had to remove them altogether. This went on for forty years and the military eventually had the links all dambrodded into parks.

Lord Saltoun kindly gave the people a big part of the bents along the foreshore of the Broch bay. It was useless sand and scrub girse, but with dung the girse grew better.

What a day of rejoicing when finally the last of the Seaforths marched out the south road for the last time and all the barrack buildings went up for sale. Great Britain had now so many lands abroad they could no longer afford to keep so many troopers in Scotland; and as the troops left the Highland clearances began, which now have gathered such a spread and are still spreading.

My father did not live to see the military leave. He was dying of comsumption. He started to write those things he could mind and got to a few pages and took a bad bleeding and died. Seven of his children died before him, three at the same time with diphtheria of the throat.

I am nineteen years older than my sister Jean. I am the oldest, she the youngest, and Margaret is the only surviving child in between. My mother had a hard struggle.

My father on his death-bed said to me: 'Tell your own children and your grandchildren that you are Scots, and never to forget it.'

I was only a very little girl. I think there was a child wasseling and a child in the cradle.

A heavy snow drift was outside. An old tramp came to the door. A kettle was put on the fire both but and ben, and we all went but to my granny's end, so the old tramp had a dook in a wood tub by the fire. My mother gave the mannie a clean shift of under-linen, and then we all sat down to brose at my parents' humble board. They gave a prayer, for all my people had belonged to the Quietists. They were something like the Quakers, but believed in the new birth through the finished work of Calvary. The old mannie gave a dear and bonnie prayer.

My sister and I slept with my granny. My parents slept in the closet and the old mannie slept in the ben box bed. Again we sat round the table at breakfast. The mannie gave thanks and left very early, still two hours before day broke. The mannie patted my head. I think I had just started to go to school, and as he left in the dark snowy morning my father said: 'Ellen, memorise this day. You met the great Lord Pitsligo.' It is about five-and-seventy years. I can see the mannie now – poor soul, hunted like an animal for twenty years, but folk were so loyal they were determined the Hanoverian troopers would not get him, to take off his aged head.

Not long after a man came at night to our house to ask my father to the funeral of 'Sanny Brown', who was in fact the Lord Pitsligo, who used that name. My father took me to the funeral. He said: 'You must always mind on this.' As we went up the cassa at Rosehearty thousands and thousands had gathered in the park across from the Rathill Kirk. The service was said in the open. As they sang it was very moving to tears. Then they had a little private prayer inside the kirk, and he was laid to rest. The gathering was so dense the military did not interfere, for they marvelled at how they had been outwitted, and how in the midst of poor people none had sought to betray Pitsligo and claim the thousand pounds reward on his head.

The Act of Union had brought benefits to the peers who voted for it, but had reduced the poor in Scotland to greater servitude and poverty than they had ever known in the past.

My great-grandfather James Lascelles had a son Willie, my father's uncle, who married late. He had two bonnie daughters, Margaret and Isabella. Neither saw twenty. He and his spouse both died long, long before his father.

I married Andrew Noble, the third son of Alexander Noble, a kirk elder, and Christian Anne Buchan from St Combs. He was an exceeding handsome young man, well-read and sober of habit, with a besom of good fair curls falling over his eyes. We were first married into the hoosie below the brae where my son George lives, but I went up to look after my old didy. We were about five years married before we had any children.

My daughter Helen was born in January 1788. My son George in November of the same year, but not long after our marrage my father died, 3 November 1785; and on 13 January, two months later, my good father Alexander Noble died in the old croft housie at the far end of the Seatoun.

My daughter Elizabeth was born in 1789 and my beloved spouse died on 13 May 1790. It was exceeding hot weather so he had to be buried on 15 May. My husband died from the fatal abdominal pain: he was in the thirty-second year of his age.

My son, Gilbert Alistair, was born 5 months later so he never knew a wonderful father. I had four children all of equal age, and I had to be the breadwinner and the head of such a strange household: my great-grandfather James Lascelles, an aged widower, my granny Anne Noble, the heiress, a widow, my mother, Jane Crawford, a widow, and four infants.

They all worked very hard to help me, and I ran the two houses alone. I have seen my old didy spoon his pottage into my children's mouths because he thought they might not have enough. He was very fond of my daughter, Ellen,[81] and not to let her down he purposely kept himself alive to live to see her go to school, for he died a week later, at the age of ninety-eight.

My mother-in-law was kind to me. She had the nature of her

family, the Buchans. She was a good housewife, thrifty and good with money. She set up all the Littlejohn Nobles on a siccar footing.

Fortunately I got a lot of walking and a lot of work, and I went to the Brick Lodge to work to Miss Fraser.[82] She had a reclusive nature, always thinking folk were stealing from her, but the poor wifie was near a hundred. My cousin, Captain George Fraser,[83] was her nephew and favourite. She never lifted her heart after he died a very young man in the West Indies.

I went to Philorth House with fish, and my country rounds which my mother and granny had gone before. I also went to work to my aunt Kate, who was married to Wulla Fraser at Kirktoun House. It had been the minister's manse but they had extended it to a very grand mansion. He came as a clerk and got his foot in the door by marrying Lady Saltoun's sister.[84] He got the factor's job.

They had a nice family. Wulla Fraser did buy the Park Estate at Longmay, calling himself Fraser of Park, a cadet of Philorth. Nobody knew where he came from or anything about his origin. Park was bought with old John Gordon's siller, and what he skinned off the Philorth Estate, which I think should go back to the Saltouns. He roofed over the old kirk at Kirktoun and made it into the burial vault of Fraser of Park, but because he was factor nobody dared question his right. He put many grievous burdens on the poor, and what is it to him today if he is roasting on the branders of Hell in perpetual torment?

My sister Margaret married Wm Noble at Denduff House. They were wealthy. She was ambitious and had it beautiful, with crystal and siller vessels in the dining salon. They had the farmtoun of Upper Wachtouhill, where they went to live at the weekend, and the old croft at Betty's yard with a shepherd caring for a hundred sheep. Though I was a widow I was far too proud to ask anything from my sister, who was married for years before her only child, Andrew Noble, whom they called Dunkie, was born.

William Noble's sister was married to Wulla Alister who had the bonnie house at the corner of the Fishcrosse and Frithside Street. He ran their weaving business for William Noble. Then my sister died. I would have brought up Dunkie as my own but his father wouldn't let him away. Shortly Wm Noble married the servant lass, a young widow with the boy John Noble they call Bengie. She was also a Noble from Broadsea. They had between them the boy Alex Noble in Whatson's Farmtoun.

I have made no difference, and they all call me their aunt, and with their wives they come and see me. Not long after his second marriage William Noble went bankrupt. The Lancashire mills were sending boatloads of cheap cloth to Aberdeen at a third of the price. Up here, so far from the market, they could not run in the race. So small businesses went down.

But William Noble, late in life, became a fisherman and came down to his grandfather's house in Broadsea, where they got a living with the lave. His stepson, Bengie, got on well with his stepfather and built a house on their croft land at the Braeheid.

My sister Jean had a new house built when she married George Crawford, but she has moved into her good mother's house to let her son have more room. My daughter Ellen purposely did not marry until she was well over thirty, until all her brothers and sisters were up, and all the old folk in my care had departed this life; and she has been a generous and dutiful daughter, and my heir, for which I am grateful.

I had begun to write in the summer. It has now come round to the winter again. Twice I had been asked to marry again, but never would I put anybody in the place of my beloved Andrew Noble, with whom I await reunion through Christ our Saviour.

# APPENDIX V

# *James Lascelles' will*

Last Will and Testament of James Lascelles, Fisherman, in the Seatoun of Broadsea. At my death I give to the safe keeping of my Blessed Redeemer my soul and on the payment of all my just and lawful debts shall be carried out by my Executor Alexander Watt Chalky[85] Fisherman Broadsea. I leave and bequeath all my worldly goods and chattels whatsoever and wherever situate to my great granddaughter Helen Noble or Lascelles widow of Andrew Noble a White fisher and to her eldest child and apparent heir to the leadership of the ancient House of Noble, to be left in fee in her Mother's lifetime in time to be her own absolute property. My dwelling house and offices above . . . at Broadsea, consisting of 2 pine doors, 1 front door and 2 windows. All of the rafters, beams, none of which belong to Lord Saltoun, all my furnishings and plenishings. My great lines and my small lines, my kists and my blankets, my tea case and sugar bowl, copper wares and brass wares, kists and dresser and deeces, chairs and stools and clock and all my worldly goods of any kind and that my great granddaughter Helen Lascelles or Noble may be able to enjoy my presents in her lifetime.

The will is dated 2nd February 1792

# Notes

**Introduction**
1. See Appendix I.
2. Home of the Gordons of Cairness. Thomas Gordon of Cairness was a Major General in the Greek Service, who wrote a history of the Greek Revolution; his wife was Armenian.
3. Fraserburgh: known locally as 'The Broch'.

**Chapter One: Origin and Tradition (1833–1843)**
4. Dogfish produced oil for lamps, as well as fertiliser.
5. The principal tower still stands, as Fraserburgh lighthouse.
6. Didy – Grandfather
7. Christian wrote, 'For centuries they owned land in the Black Isle near Cromarty, they called them "the Armeanoch Nobles" but shortened to "Noch".'
8. For relationships see Appendix I.
9. For some of the Broadsea and Pitullie houses to which Christian refers by number see Appendix III.
10. Charles Fraser, younger of Inverallochy, commanded the Frasers of Lovat at Culloden. He was a cadet of the House of Lovat although his lands of Inverallochy lay near Philorth. He fell on that terrible April day when the prince's cause went down. He was just twenty-one years of age, and young David Lascelles, Christian's great-great uncle who ran off to go with him, was fourteen years old. Young Inverallochy was shot when lying wounded after the battle, by General Hawley's orders.
11. Given at Appendix V.
12. Given in full at Appendix IV.

13. Broadsea, often thus rendered.
14. Given in full in Appendix IV.
15. Anne, daughter of 1st Lord Blantyre. She also had by Hamilton a bastard daughter, Margaret, who married 1st Lord Belhaven.
16. Ancrum burned the Fraserburgh Episcopal Church. Saltoun was not a known Jacobite sympathiser or 'out' in the '45, but he was an Episcopalian.
17. He occupied, with distinction, the post of Fraserburgh Parish Schoolmaster for forty-three years. The Parish School was the responsibility of the Kirk, very excellently discharged.

## Chapter Two: Fishing Sales and Highland Clearances (1843–1849)

18. After 1815 to be named 'Grenadier Guards'.
19. At Philorth, the Saltoun home.
20. In 1815.
21. See Chapter I and Appendix I
22. The Congregational Church had been established in Fraserburgh since the turn of the century.
23. See Appendix 1. Christian was referring to her descent from the Frasers of Philorth and thus from the earls of Ross, who became Lords of the Isles.
24. Doric is the version of the Scots language spoken in the eastern parts of the country.
25. The Duffs were earls of Fife – Lords Skene in the peerage of the United Kingdom.

## Chapter Three: Philorth and First Love (1849–1851)

26. See Appendix I.
27. See Chapter IV.
28. Alexander, 17th Lord Saltoun.
29. And even in semi-formal documents 'James Watt Pyper'.
30. Each of Christian's grandmothers was 3rd cousin to Lord Saltoun. See Appendix I.
31. On her coffin plate her age was recorded as 92. Lord Saltoun, with his nephew, looked at this the day before the funeral, and said, 'Ninety-two! But I have reason to know, from some papers I have seen since her death, that my mother was at least five years older than that.' It was suggested that the inscription

might be altered, but he sensibly said, 'No, it doesn't matter, ninety-two is old enough.'

### Chapter Four: Mormond Tam (1852)

32. 'Bents': sand hills with coarse grass – 'dunes' in the south.
33. See Appendix II.
34. Christian was entirely mistaken in these genealogical reflections. By no conceivable logic could Saltoun have been heir to Lovat.

### Chapter Five: A Voyage to America (1854–1857)

35. The Crimean War.
36. The mother of the future Lady Randolph Churchill, Jennie Jerome, Sir Winston Churchill's mother, herself about three years old at this time.
37. The Treaty of Union between England and Scotland was approved by the Scottish Parliament amid scenes of great popular indignation, in 1707, a number of peers being bribed, some for wretchedly small sums.

### Chapter Six: Christian Marries (1858–1861)

38. The Crimean War.
39. Presbytery minutes.
40. See Appendix IV.
41. Mother-in-law.

### Chapter Seven: Return to Broadsea (1860–1869)

42. 1860.
43. 1862.
44. 1866.

### Chapter Eight: A Time of Sorrows (1871–1878)

45. 1876.
46. So Christian wrote: but she was in fact the ninth. Christian always referred to the twins as one birth.
47. In fact, Cairnbulg Castle was 'replenished' – having fallen into ruin it was restored in 1896. It had been the original Philorth, sold by the Frasers when the 'new' Philorth House was built. It was brought into the family again in 1934 by the 19th Lord Saltoun.

48. Lord Zouche.
49. John Forbes of Medwyn.

## Chapter Nine: The Breaking of a Mind (1878–1879)

50. John Noble.
51. Surely less long, in this context. Christian's husband died in August 1877 and she tells of 72 Broadsea being sold in December 1879.
52. Perhaps older: Christian earlier referred to George as being three years younger than Peter (born in 1860): and this was 1879. George was probably sixteen.

## Chapter Ten: Cornhill (1879–1892)

53. Alexander, 12th Lord Saltoun, married Lady Mary Gordon.
54. The Great War of 1914–18.
55. George Baird, 'Squire Abington', son of George Baird who bought Strichen from Lord Lovat, was about twenty-five at this time – a man of great wealth and violent character, whose name was, as Christian said, associated for a while with Mrs Langtry's. He died in 1893 in New Orleans.
56. 18th Lord Saltoun, married Mary Grattan Bellew.
57. In 1886.
58. She did indeed, and would remark, 'My hair turned quite white, all at once, when my dear Lord died!'

## Chapter Eleven: Public Tragedies and Private Reflections (1892–1918)

59. Footdee
60. Daughter-in-law.
61. Skipper Watt's Victoria gross was famous, since he refused to surrender his small ship to a large Austrian–Hungarian fleet commanded at the time by Admiral Horthy, later Regent of Hungary, who treated him with the characteristic chivalry of the sea.
62. Hon. William Fraser, Gordon Highlanders. There was certainly no substance in this tale!
63. Hon. Simon Fraser, Gordon Highlanders, killed 1914.

## Chapter Twelve: Evening (1919–1923)

64. As often, Christian's view was contentious. Mr McLaren, Parish Minister of Fraserburgh, did heroic work in the cholera epidemic. But Christian's opinions derived from her family's treatment by the authorities (Chapter Six).
65. 'The Angels of Mons': a legend which gained currency about an apparition in the sky thought to imply divine intervention for the Allied cause!
66. 16th Lord Lovat, son of Christian's friend 'Shemmy'.

## Appendix IV: Granny Lascelles' account

67. The descent described is complex and, whatever its accuracy a remarkable example of verbal tradition.
68. In fact Sir David Graham's daughter married the earl of Ross, whose daughter married King Robert II.
69. Illegitimate.
70. Robert, Lord of Annandale's first wife, Isabella de Clare, daughter of the earl of Hereford, is generally given as mother of the earl of Carrick, grandmother of King Robert I.
71. By Sir David Graham of Old Montrose. The generations are right in this instance.
72. Presumably, according to the account therefore, descended from a brother of 'Countess Marjorie'.
73. Quoted from the Declaration of Arbroath, the letter from the nobles of Scotland to the Pope, asking for recognition of their independence, and their king, Robert Bruce.
74. See Appendix I.
75. See Appendix I.
76. Sir Alexander Fraser, 8th of Philorth, 1537–1623.
77. Granny Lascelles' grandparents.
78. See Chapter Six.
79. Impossible! The first penal colonies were established in 1788 and William Lascelles died in 1785, and married long before.
80. George, 3rd Earl of Aberdeen, died 1791.
81. Christian's mother.
82. Ann, elder daughter of the 12th Lord Saltoun.
83. Fourth son of 14th Lord Saltoun. Captain in 59th Regiment.
84. A Gordon of Kinnellar, sister of the wife of the 14th Lord Saltoun.

## Appendix V: James Lascelles' Will

85. Christian's paternal grandfather.

# Glossary

| | |
|---|---|
| Arles: | earnest money of engagement to work |
| Ase: | ash and rubbish |
| Ashet: | large dish |
| Bauchle: | old shoe |
| Bawbee: | halfpenny |
| Ben: | inner room, kitchen |
| Birn: | burden |
| Blauding: | injuring |
| Brook: | soot |
| Brose: | food made from oatmeal on which boiling water is poured |
| But: | outer room, parlour |
| But and Ben: | two-roomed (ground floor) house |
| Butt-hoose: | kitchen, outer room |
| Capon: | dried haddock |
| Cassie, Cassa: | a brae, hillside |
| Chaumer: | separate building for farm or house servants |
| Chave: | hard, slogging work |
| Cheer: | chair |
| Chiel: | fellow |
| Clake: | news, gossip |
| Coggie: | small wooden vessel for milk, ale etc. |
| Cranny: | finger |
| Creel: | basket |
| Cut: | a term of reproach |
| Deece: | a long settle |
| Deeve: | deafen |
| Dide, Didy: | grandfather |
| Dirl: | make shake |

| | |
|---|---|
| Dookit: | dovecot |
| Dowp: | buttocks |
| Flechie: | flea-ridden |
| Frachting boat: | cargo boat |
| Fraits: | trouble |
| Goodmother: | mother-in-law |
| Greet: | weep |
| Hairst: | harvest |
| Howdie wife: | midwife |
| Hunkersleed: | to act in an underhand way |
| Hurl: | wheel |
| Jeuk: | avoid, dodge |
| Kersehad: | birthmark or cleft palate |
| Kist: | chest, also a verb to place the dead in coffin |
| Kwite: | coat, petticoat |
| Lave: | rest, remainder |
| Lie: | shelter |
| Loon: | lad |
| Lozen: | window |
| Lug: | car |
| Lum: | chimney |
| Mark: | murky |
| Minneer: | hullabaloo |
| Moss: | a place where peats may be dug |
| Mutch: | cap, bonnet |
| Neeper: | neighbour |
| Neuk: | corner |
| Nowt, Nought: | cattle |
| Panjotral: | dish made of various kinds of meat. Sometimes gingerbread. |
| Park: | grazed land round a house |
| Peening mannie: | bum bailiff |
| Preen: | pin |
| Quine, Quinie: | lass |
| Redd: | prepare |
| Reek: | smoke |
| Riggen: | roof |
| Riggs: | potato drills |
| Ring down: | overpower |
| Rinking: | rattling |
| Roozer: | hot-water can |

| | |
|---|---|
| Roup: | auction |
| Rummel root: | noise heard preceding a gale |
| Sark: | shirt |
| Scaup: | oyster or mussel bed |
| Siccar: | safe, secure |
| Skeelie: | skilful |
| Skowth: | freedom |
| Skurry: | gull |
| Spiletree: | fishermen's pole for hanging nets |
| Stank: | cesspit |
| Stoup: | jug |
| Stroup: | spout |
| Swack: | supple |
| Sweirt: | lazy |
| Swick: | cheat, swindle |
| Tacket: | nail |
| Teem: | empty |
| Teename: | nickname |
| Thole: | endure |
| Tinker, Tinkie: | travelling folk of the road, living a life similar to gypsies. |
| Tippings: | horsehair for tying hook to line |
| Trance: | passage |
| Wagat: | 'wag at the wa' – a clock hanging with pendulum exposed |
| Weer: | knitting needle |
| Wupping: | binding |